Monarchy and Religious Institution
in Israel under Jeroboam I

*THE SOCIETY OF BIBLICAL LITERATURE*
**MONOGRAPH SERIES**

E.F. Campbell, Editor
Jouette M. Bassler, Associate Editor

Number 47
MONARCHY AND RELIGIOUS INSTITUTION
IN ISRAEL UNDER JEROBOAM I

by
Wesley I. Toews

Wesley I. Toews

# MONARCHY AND RELIGIOUS INSTITUTION IN ISRAEL UNDER JEROBOAM I

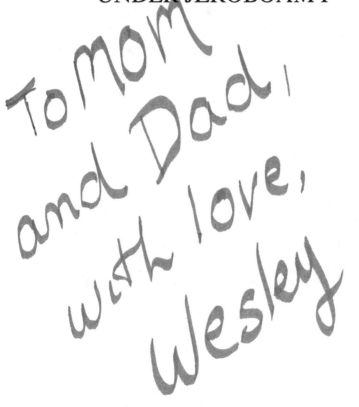

Scholars Press
Atlanta, Georgia

# MONARCHY AND RELIGIOUS INSTITUTION
## IN ISRAEL UNDER JEROBOAM I

by
Wesley I. Toews

**Library of Congress Cataloging in Publication Data**
Toews, Wesley I.
    Monarchy and religious institution in Israel under Jeroboam I/
Wesley I. Toews.
        p. cm. — (Monograph series/ The Society of Biblical
Literature; no. 47)
    Includes bibliographical references and index.
    ISBN 1–55540–876–1 (alk. paper). — ISBN 1–55540–877–X (pbk.)
    1. Jeroboam I, King of Israel. 2. Bible. O.T. Kings, 1st, XI,
26–XIV, 20—Criticism, interpretation, etc. 3. Idols and images—
Biblical teaching. 4. Bible. O.T.—Theology. 5. Jews—History—
953–586 B.C.        I. Title.    II. Series: Monograph series (Society
of Biblical Literature, no. 47)
BS580.J44T64        1993
222'.5306—dc20
                                                    93–13508
                                                    CIP

Printed in the United States of America
on acid-free paper

# Contents

# Acknowledgements

As this work has evolved over the course of the last five years through the dissertation stages at Princeton Theological Seminary and finally into this form as monograph, I have become indebted to many friends, teachers, and colleagues. I owe acknowledgment and thanks first of all to Katharine Doob Sakenfeld who directed my dissertation project, and then to C. Leong Seow and Patrick D. Miller who together with her formed the committee that steered the project to a successful conclusion. The students in Dr. Seow's Northwest Semitic Epigraphy and the History of Israelite Religion seminar and the participants in the Winnipeg Biblical and Cognate Literature Colloquium have given valuable criticism toward the formation of the argument in section III. A. Waldemar Janzen contributed at various points but especially in reading and responding to the final chapter. Larry Hurtado, in numerous conversations, guided me in the strategies and procedures of getting a document published. Jacqueline Klassen provided valuable service in proofreading the manuscript. The University of Manitoba gave most welcome support in providing a Post-Doctoral Fellowship for the 1991-1992 academic year.

Finally, I dedicate this volume to my wife Sherry who has shared with me the labors and joys of bringing this project to completion.

*Wesley I. Toews*
*Winnipeg, Fall 1992*

# Abbreviations

Most of the abbreviations used are standard for SBL as listed in "Instructions for Contributors," *JBL* 107/3 (1988) 579-96, and in subsequent editions of the *Membership Directory and Handbook*. Abbreviations not included there:

*AIR*   *Ancient Israelite Religion*. Ed. P. D. Miller, Jr., P. D. Hanson, and S. D. McBride. Philadelphia: Fortress, 1987.

KHAT   Kurzer Hand-Commentar zum Alten Testament

*KTU*   Dietrich, M., Loretz, O., and Sanmartin, J. *Die keilalphabetischen Texte aus Ugarit*. Teil I: *Transkription*. Neukirchen-Vluyn, 1976.

NCBC   The New Century Bible Commentary

# Introduction

This monograph undertakes an historical inquiry into the religion of the Israelite State, i.e., the political entity that emerged under Jeroboam I after the dissolution of the Davidic-Solomonic Empire. Ambiguity may arise from the usage of the term "Israel" because the biblical texts themselves use this term for somewhat varying referents. In some places the term "Israel" designates a twelve-tribe association whose constitutive members, though they may vary, always include Judah (e.g., Num 1, 2, 26; Deut 33); or the term signifies the kingdom as established by David and Solomon (e.g., 2 Sam 8:15, 1 Kgs 4:1). In other places the term is used more narrowly to designate the northern "tribes" in the Davidic Kingdom (e.g., 2 Sam 19:41, 21:1), or to signify the Israelite State as a political entity distinct from Judah as it emerged after the collapse of the Davidic-Solomonic Kingdom (e.g., 1 Kgs 12:16-20 and repeatedly thereafter).

In the course of the following investigation, the term "Israel" will often refer to the political entity that emerged under Jeroboam after the dissolution of the Davidic-Solomonic empire. In these cases the context of the discussion will make the referent of the terminology clear, as, for instance, in those contexts where both Israel and Judah are named in the discussion as distinct political entities. Where the context would leave matters ambiguous the term "Israelite State" shall designate the political entity that emerged under Jeroboam.

At times it will be necessary to use the term "Israel" in a more general sense in which case its referent may also include what pertained to Judah. For instance, such usage occurs in reference to the antecedents of the Israelite State, particularly in the discussion in chapter one of aspects of Israelite religion antecedent to the religion of the Israelite State as established under Jeroboam. Again, the context will clarify the reference. However, where the Davidic or Solomonic Kingdom is the specific referent, it will be named as such, or it will be referred to as "the United Monarchy". The term "Israel" will not be used to designate that specific entity.

As intimated above, this investigation will focus on religion as officially sponsored in the Israelite State. Royal administration in national states of the ancient Near East integrated religious and political institutions. For a national state to exist independently, it required religious institutions under its sovereign control. It follows, then, that after its secession from the Davidic-Solomonic kingdom, the Israelite State will have developed independent religious institutions. Consequently, the religion of the Israelite State, in some measure, will have constituted a unique phenomenon. That phenomenon warrants an independent investigation that avoids simply subsuming it under Israelite/Judahite religion.[1] The present inquiry offers the first stage of such an investigation by focusing on the officially sponsored religion in the Israelite State during the period of Jeroboam I, leaving for future consideration two more periods for which sufficient data is available to justify investigation, namely, the periods of the Omride dynasty and of the Jehuite dynasty.

The biblical authors report very little about the religious initiatives or policies of Jeroboam I. The pertinent material may be found essentially in 1 Kgs 12:26-33, 13:33, and in 2 Chr 11:13-15 and 13:8-9. However, the biblical evaluation of the impact of Jeroboam's initiatives for religion

---

[1] Israelite/Judahite religion" denotes that which characterizes the religions of both Israel and Judah in their similarities. One may legitimately refer to that overarching commonality in such a manner precisely because the similarities are so substantive. As an analogy one might suggest the term "Christianity" which must encompass more and more sub-groups the further one moves from the New Testament period. However, at issue here is that scholars have tended to gloss over the differences between the religion of Judah and the religion of Israel, and have failed to distinguish between the two, thus arriving at a kind of hybrid Israelite/Judahite religion. To use the analogy of Church history again, it is as if one were to present that history without distinguishing between the Roman and the Byzantine Churches, or without distinguishing between the Roman Catholic and the Protestant Churches.

as offered by the DtrH[2] (1 Kgs 15:26, 30; 16:2, 7, 19, 26, 31; 22:52; 2 Kgs 3:3; 10:31; 13:2, 11; 14:24; 15:9, 18, 24, 28; 17:22) is one of categorical condemnation, suggesting that Jeroboam introduced to the religion of the Israelite State something that was essentially counter to Israelite Yahwism, or something un-Yahwistic, un-Israelite, foreign, and idolatrous.

The goal of the present inquiry is to probe behind the biblical reporting and evaluating to discover what significance Jeroboam's kingship may have had for the course of religion in the Israelite State. One must investigate whether and to what extent Jeroboam introduced innovative features into the religion in Israel that might have been perceived by his contemporaries as un-Yahwistic and un-Israelite, or whether the reality of the situation in Jeroboam's time has actually been obscured by prejudiced reporting and evaluating by the Judahite authors who edited and shaped the traditions into their present form. Thus, an important task for the following pages will be to search out evidence of when and why various perceptions of Jeroboam arose. Did Jeroboam's contemporaries perceive him as one who pushed aside their ancient and revered traditions in favor of new religious practices, or did they perceive him as one who supported those ancient traditions? When and on what grounds did the unequivocal denunciation of Jeroboam arise?

The following inquiry is organized into six chapters. The first chapter enters into a preliminary inquiry concerning one central aspect of the religion in Israel before the time of Jeroboam. It inquires about the identity of the deities revered in earliest Israel. This preparatory step is essential if, at a later point, one wishes to inquire whether Jeroboam maintained or abandoned the ancient traditions. In particular, it will prepare for the question regarding the identity of the god(s) represented by the calf images which Jeroboam reportedly established (1 Kgs 12:28-

---

[2] In this monograph DtrH signifies the Deuteronomistic Historian(s) responsible for pre-exilic composition of the Deuteronomistic History. This definition indicates a preference for those explanations that construe the formation of the Deuteronomistic History in terms of pre-exilic composition with subsequent editing during the exilic period, but it does not commit itself to any one of the particular, competing construals such as one may find, for example in R. D. Nelson, *The Double Redaction of the Deuteronomistic History* (JSOTSup 18; Sheffield, 1981); I. Provan, *Hezekiah and the Book of Kings* (BZAW 172; Berlin/New York: Walter de Gruyter, 1988); M. A. O'Brien, *The Deuteronomistic History Hypothesis: A Reassessment* (OBO 92; Göttingen: Vandenhoeck & Ruprecht, 1989); or S. L. McKenzie, *The Trouble with Kings: The Composition of the Book of Kings in the Deuteronomistic History* (VTSup 42; Leiden: E. J. Brill, 1991). For the purposes of this investigation an attempt at greater precision would serve little purpose and would only run the risk of cluttering the discussion.

30, 2 Chr 13:8) and the question of whether and to what extent these so-called "other gods" that he had made (1 Kgs 14:9) fell into continuity or discontinuity with ancient Israelite traditions.

The second chapter will seek, on a text-critical, form-critical, and traditio-historical basis, to analyze the primary texts which pertain to Jeroboam as a preparatory step for the use of these materials as evidence.

The main tasks of this monograph will be taken up in the third and fourth chapters. Chapter three will inquire regarding the purpose and significance of Jeroboam's various initiatives, always keeping in view the question of whether and to what extent Jeroboam introduced innovative policies that marked significant departures from Israelite religious traditions. Proceeding on the assumption that significant departures from tradition would have provoked opposition among Jeroboam's contemporaries, the fourth chapter will investigate those biblical texts that might be interpreted to show evidence of such. In this way it can offer somewhat of a check on the conclusions of the chapter that precedes it. The fifth chapter will draw together conclusions on the basis of the investigation presented in the third and fourth chapters.

The sixth and final chapter will carry forward with an inquiry into why Jeroboam's cult and, specifically, the calf images which he installed, finally met with such categorical rejection by biblical authors such as Hosea and the DtrH.

# CHAPTER I

# Aspects of Israelite Religion
# Before Jeroboam I

At the outset it is necessary to set forward the basic presupposition that underlies both this preparatory sketch of early Israelite religion and the entire work that follows, namely, that a substantial cultural unity existed between earliest Israel and its Canaanite environment, and thus between the religion of the Israelites and the religion of their Canaanite neighbors. The adoption of this as a working presupposition finds ample justification in the results obtained in modern scholarship.

Contributing to and following upon the abandonment of the perspective advanced by scholars of the so-called Biblical Theology Movement, who emphasized the uniqueness of Israel over against its religious environment,[1] an ever growing body of research has underlined the commonality between Israelite culture and that of its Canaanite environment. This has been achieved in recent decades through the application of various disciplines—archaeological, epigraphical, anthropological, and sociological—to the study of early Israelite culture and religion. Thus, in recent decades archaeologists who have evaluated and interpreted the material remains have remarked on the similarities rather than the dissimilarities between the Israelite and the pre-Israelite

---

[1] As, for instance, in G. E. Wright, *The Old Testament Against its Environment* (London: SCM, 1950).

cultures. W. G. Dever has recently written, "It must be stressed that in the light of archaeology today, it is the LB-Iron I *continuity*—not the discontinuity—that is striking, and the more so as research progresses."[2] Also, the discovery of Canaanite inscriptions, especially of the Ugaritic mythological texts, has opened vast new possibilities for understanding Canaanite religion and for investigating the relationships between Canaanite religion and that attested in the Hebrew Bible. For instance, the work done by F. M. Cross has served to show very significant lines of continuity between the mythic patterns and motifs associated with El and Baal-Haddu at Ugarit, on the one hand, and Yahweh in the Hebrew Bible, on the other.[3] Moreover, G. E. Mendenhall's model for the emergence of Israel in Canaan by process of internal revolt[4] and N. K. Gottwald's massive exposition and development of this thesis[5] have introduced to modern scholarship an Israel that was ethnically of Canaanite origin. Though this model has not by any means found universal acceptance, it has had a decisive impact on modern perspectives concerning the relationship of the emergent Israel to its Canaanite environment. The perspective on early Israel as drawn by much of the work in recent scholarship finds apt expression in B. Halpern's comments, though they are focused specifically on the religion of Israel:

> Scholars sometimes speak of the "introduction" of the cult of Baal into Israel in the 9th century B.C.E., of Canaanite influence on Israel's religion . . . . . But Israelite religion did not import Canaanite. Israel's religion was a Canaanite religion.[6]

Thus, with regard to the ethnic identity of Israel, modern research has in a surprising way borne out the rather literal genealogical truth of Ezekiel's words (though he directed them as an indictment specifically against Jerusalem) that, in terms of its origin and birth, Israel was progeny of Canaanite culture (16:3).

---

[2] "The Contribution of Archaeology to the Study of Canaanite and Early Israelite Religion," in *AIR*, 236. Cf. M. D. Coogan's concluding remarks in his essay in the same volume, "Canaanite Origins and Lineage: Reflections on the Religion of Ancient Israel," in *AIR*, 120.

[3] See especially the essays in *Canaanite Myth and Hebrew Epic: Essays in the History of the Religion of Israel* (Cambridge: Harvard University Press, 1973).

[4] "The Hebrew Conquest of Palestine," *BA* 25 (1962) 66-87.

[5] *The Tribes of Yahweh* (Maryknoll, New York: Orbis, 1979).

[6] *The Emergence of Israel in Canaan* (SBLMS 29; Chico: Scholars Press, 1983) 246.

If the substantial cultural unity of Israel with its Canaanite neighbors is adopted as a given for the purposes of the following investigation, then Canaanite epigraphic, iconographic, and material evidence may be fully utilized for the illumination that they may shed on the unknown or unclear aspects of religion in Israel under Jeroboam. Nevertheless, this approach must always be balanced by the readiness to recognize that which is unique in the religion of the Israelite State.

The question concerning the identity of the deities served by the ancestors of Israel and by the early Israelites has received, and continues in modern times to receive, intriguing illumination from comparative studies between biblical texts and the Canaanite epigraphic and iconographic materials. The mythic texts from Ugarit, especially, have afforded welcome insight into the characters of deities such as El, Baal-Haddu, Asherah, and Ashtarte. These divine names correspond with those of several deities whom, according to various biblical texts, the ancestors of Israel and the early Israelites revered. Of these deities, El seems to have secured an especially prominent place, and the worship of El appears to have always been accepted as legitimate among Israelites. Evidence for the relative standings of the deities Baal-Haddu,[7] Asherah, and Ashtarte alongside El in the worship of earliest Israelites is very scanty and indecisive. Nevertheless, one should reckon with the probability that these deities and possibly others as well did have a place in the Israelite cult.

In approaching the question of the religion practised antecedent to Jeroboam among the ancestors of Israel and among early Israelites, one may begin with the thesis argued by A. Alt that the gods of the ancestors were designated by the names of the ancestors with whom they stood in

---

7 Both the biblical texts and the Ugaritic mythological texts often use the common noun *ba'al* (meaning "lord" or "master") in reference to a god. In Canaanite epigraphic materials the term appears as a title for various gods. However, in the Ugaritic mythological texts the literary context indicates unambiguously that the divine referent of the title is Baal-Haddu (e.g., the pairing of the terms Baal and Haddu in parallel lines as at *KTU* I.5.i.22-23). By way of contrast, the biblical texts never indicate clearly the divine referent (except in one case where it refers to Yahweh, Hos 2:18=Eng 2:16). Nevertheless, scholars have usually understood the referent in at least some biblical texts to be Baal-Haddu. Given the prominence of Baal-Haddu in Late Bronze Age and Early Iron Age Canaan, this would appear to be a reasonable identification. However, in view of the lack of specificity in the biblical texts, this cannot simply be assumed. This subject will receive further consideration below. It should be evident that within the context of this inquiry, it will be necessary to consistently qualify the term in order to make clear the intended meaning.

special relationship.[8] These designations were of the type "the Shield of Abraham," "the Fear of Isaac," and the "Mighty One of Jacob," or of the type "the god of Abraham" (the god of PN). These deities, according to Alt, were not the local Canaanite ʾēlîm of which one reads in the ancestral narratives, but they were patron deities of the clan who entered covenant relationship with that clan.

F. M. Cross advanced beyond Alt's understanding of ancestral religion by his argument that these deities were not in fact nameless tutelary deities, but that they were high gods whom the immigrant ancestors quickly identified with corresponding gods of the Canaanite pantheon.[9] Cross underlined, particularly, that the Israelite ancestors identified their god with the Canaanite high god El.[10] Since El appears as a proper divine name in most Semitic contexts, as is evident, for instance, in Akkadian names from the Sargonic period (2340-2150 BCE), in Amorite names from the eighteenth century BCE, in Old South Arabic onomastica, and especially in the Ugaritic myths,[11] the possibility would exist for persons of various Semitic origins to identify their deity El with the Canaanite El.

Evidence for the worship of El among Israel's ancestors or in early Israelite cult derives in large part from what appear to be archaic expressions concerning El embedded in the ancestral traditions. The element ʾēl in the expression ʾēl ʾĕlōhê yiśrāʾēl (Gen 33:20) unambiguously denotes the divine proper name El,[12] and thus the epithet explicitly identifies El as the god of Israel. Similarly, ʾēl[13] ʾĕlōhê ʾăbîkā (Gen 46:3) invites the interpretation, "El, the god of your father."

---

[8] "The God of the Fathers," in *Essays on Old Testament History and Religion* (Oxford: Basil Blackwell, 1966) 3-77.

[9] *Canaanite Myth and Hebrew Epic*, 3-12.

[10] *Ibid.*, 13-75; and *idem*, "ʾēl," *TDOT* I: 253-61.

[11] J. J. M. Roberts, "El," *IDBSup*, 255; and M. H. Pope, *El in the Ugaritic Texts* (VTSup, 2; Leiden: E. J. Brill, 1955) 1-24.

[12] So Cross, *Canaanite Myth and Hebrew Epic*, 49; Roberts, "El," *IDBSup*, 257; C. Westermann, *Genesis 12-36* (Minneapolis: Augsburg, 1985) 529. But see also O. Loretz ("Die Epitheta ʾl ʾlyj jśrʾl [Gn 33,20] und ʾl ʾlhj ʾbjk [Gn 46,3]," *UF* 7 [1975] 583) for a contrary argument, that ʾēl should be interpreted as the appellative "god".

[13] Deleting the definite article as the pentateuchal author's attempt to render the divine name as an appellative. In any case, if one accepts the formula as an archaic survival from ancestral times, the article must be omitted on the grounds that it only came into use at the beginning of the Iron Age. So Cross, *Canaanite Myth and Hebrew Epic*, p. 46, n. 13.

That the Israelite ancestors and early Israelites, whatever their geographical and ethnic origins, perceived their deity El as identifiable with
the Canaanite El is evidenced by numerous apparently archaic divine
titles or epithets in the Hebrew Bible which closely resemble or parallel
epithets applied to the Canaanite El. The formula *ʾēl ʿelyôn qōnēh šāmayim
wāʾāreṣ* ("El Elyon, creator of heaven and earth," Gen 14:19, 22) parallels
the bilingual inscription from Karatepe, *ʾl qn ʾrṣ* (El, creator of earth).[14]
Since in the Karatepe inscription *ʾēl* is clearly a proper divine name in a
list of divine names, one may conclude that *ʾēl* in the biblical formulation
is also proper and that the formula designates El as the creator of the
heavens and the earth.[15] To the biblical title *ʾēl ʿôlām* (Gen 21:33) one may
compare the Sinai epithet *ʾl d ʿlm* (El, the eternal one),[16] and the Ugaritic
description of El as *drd<r>* (ageless one)[17] and as *mlk ʾab šnm* (the king,
father of years).[18] To these El epithets one may probably add *ʾēl bêt-ʾēl*
(Gen 35:7, cf. 31:13)[19] and possibly *ʾēl šadday*.[20]

---

[14] *KAI* 26.A.iii.18. Cf. the divine name Ilkunirsa in the Hittite adaptation of a
West Semitic myth. For a more complete listing of inscriptional parallels and for
bibliography see C. L. Seow, *Myth, Drama, and the Politics of David's Dance* (HSM 46;
Scholars Press, 1989) 20-21.

[15] The biblical formula differs from that at Karatepe in two points: 1) it adds the
term *ʿelyôn* after *ʾēl*, and 2) it ascribes the creation of the heavens as well as the earth
to the deity. The term *ʿelyôn* should probably be understood as an epithet of El as
may also be the case in *ʾl wʿlyn* (El, that is, the Most High) of the Sefire I inscription
(*KAI* 222.A.11; on the interpretation see Cross, *Canaanite Myth and Hebrew Epic*, 51;
and Seow, *Myth, Drama*, p. 52, n. 146). Thus, *ʾēl ʿelyôn* in Gen 14:18-22 would mean
"El, Most High," or the like.

[16] Cross, *Canaanite Myth and Hebrew Epic*, 50.

[17] *KTU* I.10.iii.6.

[18] *KTU* I.1.iii.24; I.2.iii.5; I.3.v.8; I.4.iv.24; I.5.vi.2; I.6.i.36; I.17.vi.49. Cf. *KTU*
I.3.v.31 and I.4.iv.42 where El's wisdom is said to be *ʿm ʿlm* (everlasting).

[19] On the grounds that in the pre-Israelite and early Israelite times the name
*bêt-ʾēl* probably meant "Temple of El." Then the expression *ʾēl bêt-ʾēl* (the god of
Bethel) would refer to El. See Cross, *Canaanite Myth and Hebrew Epic*, p. 47 n. 14, and
p. 60. It was only at a later time, perhaps by the seventh century BCE, that Bethel
gained independent status as a West Semitic deity. See W. F. Albright, *Archaeology
and the Religion of Israel*, 5th ed. (Baltimore: John Hopkins, 1968) 168-74; J. P. Hyatt,
"Bethel (Deity)," in *IDB* I: 390-91; and M. S. Smith, *The Early History of God: Yahweh
and the Other Deities in Ancient Israel* (San Francisco: Harper & Row, 1990) 25, 145-56.

[20] In Genesis the epithet appears mostly in P material (17:1, 28:3, 35:11, 43:14,
48:3), but its attestation in the old poem at Gen 49:25 (correcting the Hebrew according to the Greek, Samaritan, and Syriac versions) suggests that P probably drew on
ancient tradition. On the age of the poetry in Genesis 49 see F. M. Cross and D. N.
Freedman, "The Blessing of Moses" *JBL* 67 (1948) 192; W. F. Albright, *Yahweh and the*

Several other expressions formulated with ʾēl in the Hebrew Bible appear to have their origin in Canaanite myth about El, and thus they add to the evidence that Israel originally identified its god with the Canaanite El. F. M. Cross[21] cites (1) ʿădat ʾēl ("council of El" in Ps 82:1) which may be compared with the Ugaritic ʿdt ʾlm (KTU 1.15.ii.7, 11); (2) kôkĕbê ʾēl ("stars of El" in Isa 14:13) which may be compared with hkkbm ʾl in the Pyrgi inscription;[22] (3) bĕnê ʾēlîm (Ps 29:1, 89:7) which, by comparison with Ugaritic bn ʾil and bn ʾilm, may be understood as "sons of El";[23] (4) ʾēl raḥûm wĕḥannûn (Exod 34:6), perhaps a pre-Yahwistic formula meaning "El the compassionate and merciful," reflective of the Ugaritic ltpn ʾil dpʾid; and (5) ʾēl gibbōr "El the Warrior" (Isa 9:5, 10:21; cf. Exod 15:3 Samaritan and Syriac).

The biblical materials offer considerable evidence to suggest that certain Israelite cities were important cult centers for the worship of El. Moreover, exactly these particular cities played significant roles in the establishment of the new Israelite state under Jeroboam. This applies above all to Shiloh which was the home of Ahijah who designated Jeroboam as king. Similarly, it applies to Shechem, Jeroboam's royal residence city. There is also good evidence for an early El cult at Bethel, a town whose sanctuary received special attention from Jeroboam.

At Shiloh the early Israelites apparently adopted as their own a sanctuary that already had an ancient venerable standing. According to the reports on excavations conducted during 1981-84, Shiloh was an important religious center as early as Middle Bronze IIC.[24] Even during most of the Late Bronze age, cultic activity continued at the site though it was otherwise unoccupied. For the Iron I level several rather elaborately planned and architecturally sophisticated buildings were found which Finkelstein, one of the excavators, dates to the mid-twelfth

---

Gods of Canaan (London: Athlone, 1968) 17; and Cross, Canaanite Myth and Hebrew Epic, 123. On šadday as a possible epithet of either the Canaanite El or the Amorite El see Cross, Canaanite Myth and Hebrew Epic, 52-60; and T. N. D. Mettinger, In Search of God: The Meaning and Message of the Everlasting Names (Philadelphia: Fortress, 1988) 69-72.

[21] Canaanite Myth and Hebrew Epic, 44-46; and "ʾēl," TDOT I: 257-58.

[22] See J. A. Fitzmeyer, "The Phoenician Inscription from Pyrgi," JAOS 86 (1966) 285-97.

[23] The mêm in ʾl-m of Ps 29:1 and 89:7 is understood as an enclitic.

[24] The evidence of cultic activity at Shiloh for this period includes two cultic stands, votive bowls, a bull-shaped zoomorphic vessel, and metal objects of a cultic nature. See I. Finkelstein, S. Bunimovitz, and Z. Lederman, "Excavations at Shiloh 1981-1984: Preliminary Report," Tel Aviv 12 (1985) 163.

century. He interprets that Israelites built these buildings as store-rooms
and as other annexes for the sanctuary which must have stood towards
the east on the summit. Unfortunately the summit itself could not be
excavated. That the buildings functioned as store-rooms or annexes in a
cultic complex is evidenced by the approximately twenty pithoi they
contained, fragments of a cultic stand, and a large quantity of animal
bones.[25] In view of the fact that these public buildings appear to have
occupied most of the Iron age town, Finkelstein suggests that Israelite
Shiloh may not have been an ordinary village but, rather, totally a
sacred enclosure. Furthermore, judging that the buildings would have
required more resources than Shiloh's small population or the
population of its outlying villages could have provided, Finkelstein
interprets that the sanctuary must have served as an inter-regional cultic
center for the Israelite hill country, in fact the first of its kind, in the late
twelfth and early eleventh centuries.[26]

Though substantive evidence for the deity worshiped at the pre-
Israelite cult of Shiloh is lacking, several lines of evidence indicate that
the deity El received worship in the early Israelite cult at that place. The
evidence has recently been presented in some detail by C. L. Seow and
T. N. D. Mettinger, and consequently it requires only a summary
presentation here.[27] First, several personal names which appear in
connection with the cult at Shiloh in 1 Samuel 1 contain ʾēl as the
theophorous element. The name ʾelqānâ recalls the designation of El as
creator or progenitor (qny) in various Canaanite texts;[28] the name
yĕrāḥām, probably a shortened form of yrḥmʾl[29] (El gives compassion),

---

25 *Ibid.*, 167-69; and also I. Finkelstein, *The Archaeology of the Israelite Settlement*
(Jerusalem: Israel Exploration Society, 1988) 220-27, especially 226.

26 Finkelstein, Bunimovitz, and Lederman, "Excavations at Shiloh 1981-84,"
168-69; and Finkelstein, *The Archaeology of the Israelite Settlement*, 228-34. Even at the
earlier MB IIC level excavators found little evidence of domestic dwellings, and they
judged from the small size of the town that its small population could hardly have
built the large MB IIC fortifications. Finkelstein suggests that Shiloh may have
already served as a sacred *temenos* for a larger geographical area at that time
("Excavations at Shiloh 1981-84," 164).

27 Seow, *Myth, Drama*, 11-54; Mettinger, "YHWH SABAOTH—The Heavenly King
on the Cherubim Throne," in *Studies in the Period of David and Solomon and Other
Essays*, ed. T. Ishida (Winona Lake: Eisenbrauns, 1982) 130-31.

28 *KTU* 1.10.iii.5-6; *KAI* 26.A.iii.18. Cf. the divine name Ilkunirsa in Hittite adaptation of West Semitic myth, and the divine title ʾēl ʿelyôn qōnēh šāmayim waʾāreṣ in
Gen 14:19, and 22. On El as creator and progenitor see section III.A.3.b below

29 This reconstruction of the name is presupposed by the Greek of 1 Sam 1:1
which reads *ieremeēl*. To this one may compare the Hebrew name yĕraḥmĕʾēl in 1 Chr

expresses the same characteristic of El as the Ugaritic epithet *lṭpn ʾil dpʾid*; and the name *šĕmûʾēl* probably derives from *\*šimuhu-ʾilu* (His name is El).[30]

Second, several features of the depiction of El in the Ugaritic literature also characterize Yahweh in the narrative of 1 Sam 1:1-7:2 which is set geographically at Shiloh. 1) As El acts on behalf of Kirta and Danel to grant them progeny in the Ugaritic myth, so in 1 Samuel 1 Yahweh grants Hannah and Elkanah a son.[31] Though, according to the biblical narrative, Hannah had received this favor from Yahweh, she named her son *šĕmûʾēl* (His name is El) rather than *šmyh*[32] (His name is Yah). This suggests either that the story originally involved a deity named El, but that the divine name Yahweh has displaced the divine name El, or that the story teller could treat the two names as pertaining to one and the same deity because Yahweh originated as an El figure. 2) As El typically reveals himself to humans by way of a dream or audition at Ugarit, so the deity appears to Samuel in 1 Sam 3:1-21.[33] 3) El at Ugarit is king of all the gods and, according to Sanchuniathon, the Canaanite El was commander of the divine armies.[34] Yahweh at Shiloh appears to have held these same honors. Probably the title *yhwh ṣĕbāʾôt* (1 Sam 1:3, 11; 4:4) designated Yahweh as king in the heavenly council and as commander of the heavenly armies.[35] Such an interpretation of this title finds support in the datum that this title is also found in association with the iconography of the cherubim and ark in the expanded title *yhwh ṣĕbāʾôth yōšēb hakkĕrūbîm* (Yahweh Sebaoth, enthroned on the cherubim), again in the context of a narrative set geographically at Shiloh (1 Sam 4:4). The iconography of cherubim and the ark represented Yahweh's throne and

---

2:25-26. Also, one may compare the Hebrew name in the inscription on a bulla, *lyrḥmʾl bn hmlk* ("[Belonging] to Yerahmeel son of the king"), published by N. Avigad, "The Contribution of Hebrew Seals to an Understanding of Israelite Religion and Society," in *AIR*, 199. Avigad dates this bulla to the period of Jeremiah.

[30] See Seow, *Myth, Drama*, 30.

[31] See the discussion of the parallels in Seow, *Myth, Drama*, 25-30.

[32] This name appears on an ostracon from Arad published by A. F. Rainey, "Three Additional Ostraca from Tel Arad," *Tel Aviv* 4 (1977), p. 97, #110:1.

[33] Mettinger, "YHWH SABAOTH," 131.

[34] Sanchuniathon as recounted by Philo of Byblos according to Eusebius, *Praeparatio Evangelica* I: 10, para 17-21 in H. W. Attridge and R. A. Oden, Jr., *Philo of Byblos: The Phoenician History* (CBQMS 9; Washington: Catholic Biblical Association of America, 1981) 47-51.

[35] Cross, *Canaanite Myth and Hebrew Epic*, 60-71; and Mettinger, "YHWH SABAOTH." Both Cross and Mettinger identify *ṣĕbāʾôt* as originally a part of an El epithet.

footstool,[36] and thus it undoubtedly symbolized Yahweh as king at the Shiloh sanctuary. This iconographic representation of Yahweh corresponds closely with the depiction of El the king with throne and footstool in the Ugaritic texts (*KTU* 1.4.iv.23-30, 1.5.vi.11-14, and 1.6.iii.14-16) and also with the portrayal on a stele from Ugarit of El seated on a throne with his feet on a footstool.[37] The iconography of cherubim and ark is, in fact, that of the deity El,[38] and it would appear either that Yahweh absorbed El and inherited features associated with El or that Yahweh originated from the figure El.

As mentioned above, Finkelstein interprets from the material remains of Iron Age Shiloh that Shiloh served as a central sanctuary for an Israelite federation of the twelfth-eleventh centuries. The biblical traditions give evidence pointing in the same direction. It is indicative of the importance of that sanctuary that David and Solomon adopted its cultic apparatus, namely, the cherubim, the ark, and perhaps the tent,[39]

---

36 For this interpretation see Eissfeldt, "Silo und Jerusalem," in *Volume du Congress: Strasbourg 1956* (VTSup 4; Leiden: E. J. Brill, 1957) 138-47; Mettinger, "YHWH SABAOTH," 128-34; and also O. Keel, *Jahwe-Visionen und Siegelkunst: Eine neue Deutung der Majestätsschilderungen in Jes 6, Ez 1 und 10 und Sach 4* (SBS 84/85; Stuttgart: Verlag Katholisches Bibelwerk, 1977) 15-35. For a contrary position and bibliography see G. Fohrer, *History of Israelite Religion* (Nashville: Abingdon, 1972) 108-110.

37 See the stele in *ANEP*, # 493. The correspondence between the description of El in the Ugaritic texts listed above and the depiction on the stele invites the identification of the god as El. On this point see also K. Jaroš, *Die Stellung des Elohisten zur kanaanäischen Religion* (OBO 4; Göttingen: Vandenhoeck & Ruprecht, 1974) 353; and O. Keel, *Die Welt der altorientalischen Bildsymbolik und das Alte Testament*, rev. ed. (Zürich and Neukirchen-Vluyn: Benziger and Neukirchener, 1977) 186.

38 So Cross, *Canaanite Myth and Hebrew Epic*, 69; and *idem*, "The Priestly Tabernacle in the Light of Recent Research," in *Temples and High Places in Biblical Times* (Jerusalem: Hebrew Union College/Jewish Institute of Religion, 1981) 173. The association of the ark and cherubim throne with El also finds support in Psalm 132. Though that psalm does not explicitly mention El, in connection with the procession of the ark to the sanctuary it refers to the deity as *ʾăbîr yaʿăqōb* (Bull of Jacob) (vv. 2 and 5); and that title originally referred to El, as one may confirm from the ancient verse in Gen 49:25 where it occurs in parallel with *ʾēl ʾăbîkā* (El your father). For fuller discussion of these titles and their correspondence with the Ugaritic *tr ʾil ʾabk* see section III.A.3.b below.

39 For the argument that the cherubim and ark iconography originally belonged to the sanctuary at Shiloh, see Eissfeldt, "Silo und Jerusalem," 138-47 and Mettinger, "YHWH SABAOTH," 128-34. Regarding the existence of the tent at Shiloh, see Seow, *Myth, Drama*, 31-41. Probably only the ark survived the destruction of Shiloh, on the supposition that the Philistines preserved it by capturing it as booty. David re-established the ark when he brought it to Jerusalem where he kept it in a tent (2 Sam 6:17 and 7:2), probably in deference to the Shilonite tradition of the tent (Ps 78:60, 67).

for their sanctuary at Jerusalem. As has generally been recognized, David and Solomon signalled thereby that Jerusalem had become heir to Shilonite traditions and should now be considered the central sanctuary of the Kingdom. Thus they implicitly recognized the formerly prominent status of Shiloh. Furthermore, several biblical texts refer to Shiloh's antecedent position with respect to Jerusalem, presupposing that Shiloh had ranked as the most important sanctuary in its time (Ps 78:60, 67-69; Jer 7:12-14; 26:6; cf. Judg 18:31). One may conclude that the cult practised at Shiloh had held great prestige in early Israel. If, as argued above, the cult at Shiloh centered around the worship of El, then one may also conclude that the worship of El held a central place in early Israelite religion. To anticipate the discussion below, the key function and influence of Shiloh as a religious center for Israel apparently continued even after the destruction of Shiloh (mid-eleventh century) in the very consequential direction given by Ahijah the Shilonite prophet in designating Jeroboam as king.

The sanctuary at Shechem also had had a long history reaching back to the Middle Bronze Age.[40] The biblical texts may preserve two divine titles associated with the cult of that sanctuary from pre-Israelite times, namely ba$^c$al bĕrît (Judg 9:4) and ʾēl bĕrît (Judg 9:46). If so, the evidence these titles provide regarding the pre-Israelite deity worshiped at this site must be regarded as altogether ambiguous since both ba$^c$al and ʾēl may be interpreted either as appellatives or as divine names. It could be either that El was revered as "lord of covenant" or that Baal-(Haddu?) was honored as "god of covenant." However, at Ugarit ʾil brt (El of the covenant) appears as an epithet of El.[41] Then El may also have been revered as god or lord of the covenant at Shechem, and perhaps one might reconstruct from Judg 9:4 and 9:46 an original divine title ʾēl ba$^c$al bĕrît (El, lord of the covenant).[42]

---

Possibly Solomon carried that tent with the ark and other sacred vessels into the new temple (1 Kgs 8:4—regarding the reliability of this note concerning the tent see the comments by Seow, *Myth, Drama*, 38-39; but cf. J. Gray, *I & II Kings*, 2d revised ed. [OTL; Philadelphia: Westminster, 1970] 209). Finally, when Solomon built the temple he re-established the Shilonite tradition of the cherubim throne in the holiest place.

[40] G. E. Wright, *Shechem: The Biography of a Biblical City* (New York: McGraw-Hill, 1965) 80-102; and L. E. Toombs, "Shechem, Addendum" *IDB* IV: 315.

[41] *KTU* I.128.14-15. See Smith, *Early History of God*, 11, and bibliographical references cited there.

[42] Cross, *Canaanite Myth and Hebrew Epic*, pp. 39, 49 n. 23 and p. 60. Note also Halpern's (*The Emergence of Israel*, p. 28 n. 35) arguments for viewing the title ba$^c$al bĕrît as a secondary literary development in the context of Judges 8-9.

As to the name of the deity early Israel worshiped at Shechem, the title of Jacob's altar near Shechem testifies unambiguously, ʾēl ʾĕlōhê yiśrāʾēl ("El is the god of Israel," Gen 33:20). Since the combination ʾĕlōhê yiśrāʾēl elsewhere always refers to the god of the people Israel, and since the identification of Jacob by the name Israel appears to be a secondary feature in the Israelite genealogical structure, one may conclude that the altar name in Gen 33:20 means that El is the god of the people Israel rather than of the patriarch Israel.[43] Furthermore, since the Hebrew Bible gives no evidence of the existence of a clan or tribe named Israel, but only applies the term to an association of tribes, one may conclude that the altar's name attests to the El worship of a tribal confederation called Israel.

Thus the title ʾēl ʾĕlōhê yiśrāʾēl designates Israel as a federation in covenant under El at Shechem. But, whereas this title only implies the existence of a federated Israel at Shechem, two other biblical texts (Deut 27 and Josh 24) explicitly refer to the formation and existence of a federated Israel at Shechem. In these latter two texts, however, the federation makes its covenant under Yahweh. In view of the fact that the name yiśrāʾēl is composed with the theophoric element ʾēl, one may venture the conclusion that the Israelite worship of its deity under the name El at Shechem must have preceded the time when the divine name Yahweh became dominant in the Israelite cult.[44] Evidently, then, Shechem functioned as a confederate center for earliest Israel.[45] In spite of what may have been serious reversals for Shechem as reflected in the Abimelech narrative (Judg 9), its prestige as a political and cultic center continued even into the time of Rehoboam since it was to Shechem that he went to be installed as king over Israel (1 Kgs 12:1). To anticipate the discussion below, one might expect that the cultic traditions of El worship at Shechem would have formed part of the heritage taken over by the new Israelite State when Jeroboam established his royal residence at Shechem.

Bethel could also boast a long and venerable history as a sacred place reaching back at least to the Middle Bronze I period when the first

---

43 With Gottwald, *The Tribes of Yahweh*, p. 770 n. 420; and Westermann, *Genesis 12-36*, 529. Contrast Cross, *Canaanite Myth and Hebrew Epic*, p. 46 n. 13.

44 Cf. Gottwald, *The Tribes of Yahweh*, 494; Ahlström, "Where did the Israelites Live?" *JNES* 41 (1982) 134; and Smith, *Early History of God*, 7.

45 Cf. M. Noth, *The History of Israel*, 2d ed. (New York: Harper & Row, 1960) 91-92; Gottwald, *The Tribes of Yahweh*, 494; and Halpern, *The Emergence of Israel*, 92-93.

archaeologically attested temple was built on the site.[46] The biblical traditions carry the memory that the place had once been called Luz (Gen
28:19, 35:6), and they make the further claim that Jacob had named the
place Bethel (Gen 28:19). However, probably Gen 28:11-12, 16-19 preserves an old pre-Israelite etiological story that told of the discovery of
the holy place and of its naming. The story was transmitted in the sanctuary of Bethel until the Israelites took up the story and introduced
Jacob into it as the one who discovered the holy place.[47] Thus the
Israelites adopted the sanctuary and its tradition as their own.

For the identification of the deity worshiped at Bethel, the place
name itself suggests that the place was originally known as the temple
of El, and if the foregoing assessment of Gen 28:11-12, 16-19 as a pre-
Israelite etiological narrative is correct, then the worship of El was
already practised there before the Israelite period. Beyond the evidence
given by the place name one may add that the etiological story exhibits
El's typical mode of self-revelation through a dream.

In the preceding pages, evidence for the existence of an ancient cult
to El at Shiloh, Shechem, and Bethel has been adduced from onomastica,
from apparently frozen divine titles, and from literary traditions pertaining to each of these particular locations. It may be added that in its
broad development the biblical narrative from Genesis 12 to Exodus 6
makes a most compelling claim. Both the E and P traditions (especially
Exod 3 and 6) explicitly acknowledge a pre-Yahwistic stage in Israelite
religion. P specifically names the deity of this stage El Shaddai. But the
name El Shaddai, in its earliest attestation in biblical literature, appears
in the old poem in Gen 49:25.[48] There its use as an epithet of El is confirmed by the formulation ʾēl ʾābîkā (El your father) in the parallel line.
Thus, the E and P traditions give witness to a pre-Yahwistic, pre-Mosaic
stage of Israelite religion when Israel revered its chief deity under the
name El.

The overall cumulative evidence derived from the traditions of
Jacob's encounter with God in Genesis, the traditions of Moses'

---

[46] According to J. L. Kelso in W. F. Albright and J. L. Kelso, *The Excavation of
Bethel (1934-1960)* (AASOR, 39; Cambridge: American Schools of Oriental Research,
1968) 22.

[47] Westermann, *Genesis 12-36*, 452-54.

[48] Emending ʾet to ʾēl with some Hebrew manuscripts, and with the Samaritan
and Peshitta texts. Compare also the Greek which reads *ho theos ho emos*. So also F.
M. Cross and D. N. Freedman, *Studies in Ancient Yahwistic Poetry* (SBLDS 21;
Missoula: Scholars Press, 1975) p. 91, n. 79.

encounter with Yahweh in Exodus 3-6, and the traditions of the sanctuary at Shiloh in 1 Sam 1:1-7:2 indicates a certain unity in the worship of El in the hill country of Israel at the sanctuaries of Shechem, Shiloh, and Bethel.[49]

The discussion of ancestral and early Israelite religion has, to this point, centered around the deity El. It has drawn evidence mostly from biblical texts where the authors apparently judged that the Israelite ancestors or the Israelites themselves were engaged in legitimate worship. However, according to some biblical texts, particularly in the editorial framework provided by DtrH for the book of Judges, the early Israelites revered gods other than El or Yahweh. These gods are designated by the terms *habbaʿal*, *habbĕʿalîm*, *hāʿaštārôt*, and *hāʾăšērôt* (Judg 2:11-13; 3:7; 10:6, 10; 1 Sam 7:3; and 12:10). In Canaanite epigraphic sources these same terms function, in singular and undetermined forms, as proper or quasi-proper[50] names to denote particular deities. The biblical forms in the texts listed above have a different significance. The presence of the definite article with each of these forms and the use of the plural in three of the forms indicates that these terms have a generic significance, that they denote male and female deities in general rather than specific deities named Baal, Asherah, or Ashtarte.

Unambiguous evidence for an actual cult to Asherah, to Ashtarte, to some particular Baal (e.g., Haddu), or to any deity other than El or Yahweh in pre-monarchic Israel is almost totally lacking in the biblical texts. Recently, M. S. Smith has appraised the evidence and concluded that ". . .[d]uring the Judges period, the major deities in the territory of Israel included Yahweh, El, Baal, and perhaps Asherah."[51] However, the evidence for a particular Baal or for Asherah as deities revered in early Israel is often allusive and ambiguous, as Smith himself recognizes at several points. The evidence can hardly provide a secure basis on which to determine how significant a place either deity held in early Israel. Even so, one should make allowance for the probability that the biblical texts omit and obscure much pertinent evidence because the biblical

---

[49] Cf. the argument by O. Eissfeldt, "Jakobs Begegnung mit El und Moses Begegnung mit Jahwe," *OLZ* 58 (1963) 325-331.

[50] *baʿal*, of course, is a common noun often used as a title. However, in the mythological texts from Ugarit it functions as if a quasi-proper noun. Though it often parallels the name Haddu in balancing lines, sometimes it stands alone as a designation for Haddu as if it were a proper noun.

[51] *The Early History of God*, 6. His presentation and discussion of the evidence appears on pp. 1-40.

authors wished to portray the worship of deities other than Yahweh only as an aberration, as a vestige of purportedly foreign, Canaanite practice. Consequently, it may be safest to simply assume that some deities such as Baal-Haddu and Asherah received worship in early Israel.

The evidence for a pre-monarchic Israelite cult to a deity identified by the term *ba'al* warrants particular consideration because biblical authors so persistently make the claim that the early Israelites revered *habba'al*. DtrH repeatedly mentions Israel's devotion to *habbĕ'ālîm* (Judg 2:11, 13; 3:7; 8:33; 10:6, 10; 1 Sam 7:4; 12:10). In evaluating this datum one should recognize that at these places DtrH offers a theological scheme rather than historical data. In this scheme the precise identification of the deities designated by *habbĕ'ālîm* appears to hold little significance for DtrH. Rather DtrH wishes to emphasize the broad theological claim that Israel's misfortunes have come about as divine judgment for Israel's apostasy to other gods. For this purpose DtrH has no need to identify *habbĕ'ālîm*. Nevertheless, there is no good reason to doubt the claim by DtrH that various *bĕ'ālîm* received worship in pre-monarchic Israel, but these claims cannot constitute evidence for Israelite worship of Baal-Haddu or of any other particular Canaanite deity in the pre-monarchic period.

Direct worship to a deity entitled Baal in the pre-monarchic period is attested in only two biblical texts. (1) Num 25:1-5[52] recounts that while at Shittim the Israelites entered into the worship of the Moabite god(s) (v. 2) and that in this way "Israel yoked himself to *ba'al pĕ'ôr*" (v. 3). Considering the Moabite claims to the territory in this vicinity one may speculate that the Moabite god here identified as *ba'al pĕ'ôr* (i.e., Lord of Peor) was in fact Chemosh.[53] But in this vicinity, in the valley opposite Beth-peor, there was apparently also an important Reubenite sanctuary to Yahweh which tradition later remembered as the place where Moses promulgated the law (Deut 4:46) and as the location of Moses' grave (Deut 34:6).[54] Possibly the Yahweh cult at Beth-peor held a dominant place there, but alongside this the cult of *ba'al pĕ'ôr*, i.e., Chemosh, also found at least a temporary place. (2) According to Judg 6:25-32 Jerubbaal (i.e., Gideon) destroyed the altar of *habba'al* and the asherah belonging to

---

[52] The narrative of the events at Baal Peor lacks unity. An old source (J[E]?) appears in Num 25:1-5 while vv. 6-15 are attributable to P. See G. B. Gray, *A Critical and Exegetical Commentary on Numbers* (ICC; Edinburgh: T. &. T. Clark, 1903) 380.

[53] So Gray, *Numbers*, 382-83.

[54] F. M. Cross, "Reuben, First-Born of Jacob," *ZAW* 100, Sup (1988) 50-52.

his father, Joash, and put in their place an altar to Yahweh. The datum that a father with a Yahwistic name (Joash) gave his son a name formed with the theophoric element *ba⁽al* (Jerubbaal) may signify that in this family Yahweh and a deity entitled Baal were worshiped side by side and that their cults were considered compatible or that the two deities had been identified. On the other hand, in the name Jerubbaal one could also interpret the element *ba⁽al* as an appellative intended as a reference to Yahweh. Leaving aside whatever these personal names might signify, the narrative of Judg 6:25-32, as it stands, concerns a local religious conflict between the cult of Yahweh and that of *habba⁽al* at Ophrah. It remains an open question whether the story accurately reflects an actual religious conflict in the pre-monarchic period or whether it merely reflects the particular ideological interpretation of history attributable to the editors of the larger Gideon story. Considering the latter possibility, the editors may have placed Judg 6:25-32 in its present context in order to demonstrate that Israel had indeed fallen away to the worship of other gods, thus bringing punishment upon themselves, and that in order for the Midianite scourge to be lifted this idolatrous cult had to be removed. In favor of this possibility, one may note that the story concerning Gideon's destruction of the sanctuary of *habba⁽al* has only a redactional connection to the preceding narrative of Gideon's call and to the following narratives of his victory over the Midianites.

From these biblical accounts one may gather that at Beth-peor and possibly also at Ophrah (if the story reflects an actual religious conflict from the pre-monarchic period) the cult of a Canaanite god existed alongside the cult of Yahweh. However, the identification of the Canaanite deity at either place remains uncertain. At Beth-peor the deity was probably Chemosh. At Ophrah the deity may well have been Baal-Haddu although other candidates could be suggested as well.

The Hebrew Bible preserves many place names within the boundaries of Israel and Judah which are formed with the theophoric element *ba⁽al*: *ba⁽al* (1 Chr 4:33), *ba⁽al-gād* (Josh 11:17; 12:7; 13:5), *ba⁽al hāmôn* (Cant 8:11), *ba⁽al ḥāṣôr* (2 Sam 13:23), *ba⁽al ḥermôn* (Judg 3:3, 1 Chr 5:23), *ba⁽al mĕ⁽ôn* (Num 32:38, 1 Chr 5:8, Ezek 25:9), *ba⁽al-pĕrāṣîm* (2 Sam 5:20, 1 Chr 14:11), *ba⁽al šāliša* (2 Kgs 4:42), *ba⁽al tāmār* (Judg 20:33), *ba⁽ălâ* (Josh 15:11, 29), *ba⁽ălāt* (Josh 19:44), *ba⁽ălat-bĕ⁾ēr* (Josh 19:8); *bāmôt ba⁽al* (Josh 13:17), *bĕ⁽ālôt* (Josh 15:24), and finally *qiryat-ba⁽al*=*qiryat yĕ⁽ārîm* (Josh 15:60; 18:14)=*ba⁽ălâ* (Josh 15:9, 1 Chr 13:6)=*ba⁽ălê-yĕhûdâ* (2 Sam 6:2). Recent toponymic studies suggest that the appearance of places with *ba⁽al* names coincided with the emergence of the Israelites/Judahites in

Canaan.[55] Undoubtedly these toponyms refer to the deity of the place concerned, but ambiguity exists as to the particular divine referent of the element *ba‘al*. In this connection A. F. Rainey writes:

> That such names occur only in Iron Age documents, viz., the Bible, may possibly be taken as evidence for some early, non-Yahwistic elements in the tribal groups that came to make up Israel. It is also possible that *Ba‘al*, or the name *Ba‘al* at least, may have achieved widespread popularity at local shrines only toward the end of the Late Bronze Age or the beginning of the Iron Age. Such a development cannot be traced since the local documentation is inadequate.[56]

On the basis of the available toponymic evidence, it cannot be excluded that Baal-(Haddu?) may have received cult at these places from Israelites, but positive evidence to confirm this is lacking.

From the early monarchical period several names formed with the element *ba‘al* are attested. In some cases these occur in apparently Yahwistic families. Thus Saul, whose devotion to Yahweh is never questioned in the biblical traditions, gave the Yahwistic name *yĕhônātān* to one of his sons, but he named another son *ʾešbā‘al* (1 Chr 8:33; cf. 2 Sam 2:8).[57] Saul's son Jonathan, in turn, named his son *mĕrîbbā‘al* (1 Chr 8:34; cf. 2 Sam 4:4). Similarly, David named two of his sons *ʾădōniyyâ* and *šĕpaṭyâ* (2 Sam 3:4) in honor of Yahweh, but another son he named *bĕʿelyādāʿ* (1 Chr 14:7; cf. *ʾelyādāʿ* of 2 Sam 5:16 and 1 Chr 3:8). From these personal names one could infer (i) that people identified Yahweh and Baal-(Haddu?), or (ii) that they worshiped both Yahweh and Baal-(Haddu?), or (iii) that the appellative *ba‘al* served as an epithet for Yah-

---

55 For discussion and bibliography see B. Rosen, "Early Israelite Cultic Centres in the Hill Country," *VT* 38 (1988) 114-117; and cf. B. Mazar, "The Early Israelite Settlement in the Hill Country," *BASOR* 241 (1981) 81.

56 "The Toponymics of Eretz-Israel," *BASOR* 231 (1978) 4. Also see the discussion of toponyms by J. C. de Moor, *The Rise of Yahwism: The Roots of Israelite Monotheism* (BETL 91; Leuven: Leuven University Press, 1990) 34-40; and especially his judgment concerning the significance of *ba‘al* toponyms on 38-39.

57 The discrepancy between equivalent names preserved with the element *bʿl* by the Chronicler but with the element *bōšet* in 2 Samuel is best resolved if one takes the *bʿl* names as original and the *bōšet* names as mutilation of those names by tradents who understood them as a references to an illegitimate deity entitled Baal and therefore found them offensive.

weh. Names such as *beʿălyâ* ("Yahweh is lord," 1 Chr 12:5) and *yhwbʿl* (from an eighth-sixth century seal)[58] suggest the third interpretation.[59]

The influence of Baal-Haddu in pre-monarchic and early monarchic Israelite religion is most clearly evident in the absorption of the mythology, attributes, epithets, and functions characteristic of Baal-Haddu into Yahweh.[60] This occurs already in the most ancient poetry such as Exodus 15, Judges 5, Deuteronomy 33, Psalm 18 (=2 Samuel 22), and Psalm 29 where the patterns and motifs characteristic of the theophany of Baal-Haddu as warrior god and weather god are clearly apparent.[61] One may also perceive patterning after the myth of Baʿal-Haddu in the story of the journeys of the ark (1 Sam 4-6) and in the ritual drama of David's transfer of the ark from Kiriath-jearim to Jerusalem (2 Sam 6).[62] These accounts model Yahweh after Baʿal Haddu. But what does the absorption of these patterns and motifs into Yahweh presuppose with regard to the actual worship at early Israelite sanctuaries? Such an integration or convergence of Baal-Haddu into Yahweh could probably have arisen in a polytheistic context in which both deities received worship. It is also conceivable that sufficient phenomenological and functional similarities were perceived between the immigrant deity Yahweh and the Canaanite Baal-Haddu that a certain amount of identification could occur and Baal-Haddu characteristics could be absorbed into Yahweh.

In summary, the biblical texts do attest to early Israelite worship of gods referred to generically as *habbĕʿālîm* or, in a few places, entitled

---

[58] N. Avigad, "Hebrew Seals and Sealings and their Significance for Biblical Research," in *Congress Volume: Jerusalem 1986*, ed. J. A. Emerton (vtsup 40; Leiden: E. J. Brill, 1988) 8. Avigad dates the seal between the 8th and 6th centuries BCE.

[59] Similarly P. K. McCarter, *II Samuel* (AB 9; Garden City: Doubleday, 1984) 87. But contrast M. Noth, *Die israelitischen Personennamen im Rahmen der gemeinsemitischen Namengebung* (Hildesheim: Georg Olms, 1966) 120-22.

[60] For bibliography and for a brief discussion see Smith, *The Early History of God*, 49-55.

[61] For discussion of mythic language pertinent to Baal-Haddu in these poems see Cross, *Canaanite Myth and Hebrew Epic*, 99-101, 112-44; and also P. D. Miller, *The Divine Warrior in Early Israel* (HSM 5; Cambridge: Harvard University Press, 1973), especially pp. 29-30, 36-7, and 60. Regarding the early date of these poems see in addition, D. A. Robertson, *Linguistic Evidence in the Dating of Early Hebrew Poetry* (SBLDS 3; Missoula: SBL, 1972); Albright, *Yahweh and the Gods of Canaan*; Freedman, "Divine Names and Titles in Early Hebrew Poetry," in *Magnalia Dei: The Mighty Acts of God*, ed. F. M. Cross, W. E. Lemke, and P. D. Miller (Garden City: Doubleday, 1976) 56-107.

[62] For the full development of this perspective see Seow, *Myth, Drama*, 55-144.

ba‘al. All pertinent texts lack the specificity required for an identification of the god(s) concerned. Often the texts appear intent on simply making a general accusation regarding apostasy in Israel. Various toponyms that probably first appeared in early Iron Age Palestine give further evidence for the reverence of god(s) entitled ba‘al in early Israel. The onomastica in early monarchic Israel also evidence that some deity received reverence as ba‘al. However, it appears that Israelites applied the title to various gods, including Chemosh (ba‘al pĕ‘ôr), Yahweh (be‘ălyāh, cf. Hos 2:18=Eng 2:16), and probably Haddu. Given the prominence of Baal-Haddu in late Bronze Age and early Iron Age Canaan, and given the evident impact that the mythology and epithets of Baal-Haddu has had on the biblical representation of Yahweh, one can only conclude that Baal-Haddu must have been an easily recognizable divine figure in early Israel. In all probability Baal-Haddu also received cult, though unambiguous evidence is lacking. In conclusion, it may be said regarding the deities of the Israelite ancestors and of earliest Israel that the archaic divine titles and epithets preserved in the biblical traditions attest to the prominence of the worship of El at the sanctuaries in the Ephraimite hill country during this period.[63] Various lines of evidence indicate that the worship of El was practised at Shechem, Shiloh, and Bethel, all of which figure prominently in the account concerning the establishment of the Israelite kingdom under Jeroboam. In particular the title ’ēl ’ĕlōhê yiśrā’ēl makes the most impressive claim that El was the god of Israel, implying that El held the most prominent place in the Israelite cult. This claim, nevertheless, allows for the possibility and even for the likelihood that other deities, perhaps Baal-Haddu, Chemosh, Asherah, Ashtarte, and others also received honor in the Israelite cult, though in a rank secondary to that of El.[64]

---

[63] Similarly, de Moor (The Rise of Yahwism, 10-41), arguing on the basis of biblical onomastic and toponymic evidence, concludes that El must have been the most important god in pre-monarchic Israelite religion. De Moor also finds that in this early context the name Yahweh had long existed as an identification for El.

[64] On hierarchy in the Canaanite and Israelite pantheons, see L. K. Handy, "Dissenting Deities or Obedient Angels: Divine Hierarchies in Ugarit and the Bible," BR 35 (1990) 18-35. In early Israelite religion one of the goddesses probably held a position in the top level of the hierarchy as consort to El=Yahweh. S. M. Olyan, for instance, rather tentatively assigns this function to Asherah (Asherah and the Cult of Yahweh in Israel [SBLMS 34; Atlanta: Scholars Press, 1988] 33-35), but B. Halpern argues that Ashtarte held the honor as Yahweh's asherah ("The Baal [and the Asherah?] in Seventh-Century Judah," an unpublished essay, 1991, archived on the IOUDAIOS electronic discussion group's listserver, LISTSERV@YORKVM1.BIT NET).

## CHAPTER II

# *A Critical Analysis of the Biblical Texts Concerning Jeroboam I*

### A. A General Evaluation of the Texts and Versions

There are two text complexes in the Hebrew Bible in which Jeroboam I figures prominently, namely, 1 Kgs 11:26-14:20 and 2 Chr 10:1-11:4; 11:13-17; 13:3-20. Alongside these texts one may consider LXX 3 Reigns 11:26-13:34 as a third text complex because it diverges too significantly from MT 1 Kgs 11:26-14:20 to be considered simply a translation of it.[1] From these texts one may isolate the relatively small section 1 Kgs 12:26-33, its corresponding section in the LXX 3 Reigns 12:26-33, and 2 Chr 11:13-17; 13:8-9 as material that reports about or pertains most specifically to Jeroboam's activity with respect to religious affairs in the emergent Israelite State. Also, one may separate out the two larger pericopes, 1 Kgs 13:1-32 and 14:1-18 which

---

[1] At this point one may also mention the work of Flavius Josephus in *The Jewish Antiquities* 8.212-45 as another text pertaining to Jeroboam. However, this material is relatively late, deriving from the first century CE, and essentially it overlaps with that of the biblical texts isolated above. From a comparison with the biblical texts, it is evident that Josephus depended fundamentally on them, only offering his own retelling and interpretation. Hence Josephus does not constitute an independent source of evidence. Cf. the general comments concerning Josephus as a historical source in J. M. Miller and J. H. Hayes, *A History of Ancient Israel and Judah* (Philadelphia: Westminster, 1989) 316.

correspond to 3 Reigns 13:1-32 and 12:24$^{g-n}$, respectively, as texts directly pertinent to Jeroboam's religious policies because they appear to give evidence of some opposition to those policies.[2]

The intention of this chapter is to engage in an analysis and evaluation of these text complexes in as far as that is required to prepare the groundwork for the following inquiry. Since, to a great extent, the three text complexes ultimately reflect a common textual tradition,[3] the first task will be to offer some account of the unique features of each and to decide in a general way whether one of the texts is to be preferred for historical reconstruction or whether each of them merits equal consideration on its own terms.

2 Chr 10:1-11:4 reproduces its source in 1 Kgs 12:1-24 practically verbatim. On the other hand, the material in 2 Chr 11:13-17 and 13:3-20 does not directly parallel anything in 1 Kgs 11:26-14:20. Yet the materials in 2 Chr 11:13-17 and particularly in vv. 8-12 from the text in 2 Chronicles 13 do correspond essentially with 1 Kgs 12:26-32, adding several details of their own: 1) that the priests, i.e., the sons of Aaron, and the Levites left their homes in Israel and went to Rehoboam in Judah because Jeroboam and his sons had expelled them from serving in the cult (11:13-14 and 13:9); 2) that persons from all the tribes of Israel who wished to worship Yahweh went to Jerusalem to sacrifice there (11:16); and 3) that satyrs had a place in Jeroboam's cult alongside the calves he had made (11:15).

For the evaluation of 2 Chr 11:13-17 and 13:8-12 as evidence for historical reconstruction, one may judge, as many modern scholars have, that in most cases where the Chronicler offers unique material (in com-

---

[2] In connection with the discussion of opposition to Jeroboam's religious policies (chapter IV below), Exodus 32 and Judges 17-18 will also require consideration. Since Exodus 32 issues a strong invective against the bull iconography in the cult, it should be asked whether Exodus 32 is not intended as a criticism levelled specifically against the cult as established by Jeroboam. Similarly, since Judges 17-18 reproaches the cult at the sanctuary of Dan, one may inquire whether that text in some way intended to register opposition to the cult as Jeroboam established it there. However, since neither Exodus 32 nor Judges 17-18 explicitly mention Jeroboam, and since these texts have no redactional connection with the text complexes listed above, it is appropriate to delay the analysis of these texts to the point at which they are taken up into the discussion.

[3] This is evident from the datum that 2 Chr 10:1-11:4 corresponds to 1 Kgs 12:1-24 practically verbatim and that 3 Reigns 11:26-13:34 essentially translates 1 Kgs 11:26-13:34 aside from the section 3 Reigns 12:24$^{a-z}$ which has nothing to correspond to it at the same location in 1 Kings 12.

parison with the Chronicler's biblical sources) that material probably derives from late, post-exilic traditions or from the Chronicler's own reworking of biblical materials rather than from ancient sources independent of those preserved in the Hebrew Bible.[4] Such an assessment holds true for the sections 2 Chr 11:13-17 and 13:8-12. At these points the Chronicler appears to have drawn on 1 Kgs 12:26-32,[5] making inferences from it,[7] making explicit its implicit judgments,[6] and supplementing its information.[8] Through this means the Chronicler has achieved a portrayal of Israel under Jeroboam as an apostate people worshiping in an illegitimate cult in contrast to Judah which continued in faithful worship of Yahweh. Given this analysis of 2 Chr 11:13-17 and 13:8-12, it is extremely doubtful that these passages offer anything independently of

---

4 Cf. R. H. Pfeiffer, "Chronicles, I and II," *IBD*, I:578-79; P. Ackroyd, "Chronicles, I and II," *IDBSup*, 157; P. Welten, *Geschichte und Geschichtsdarstellung in den Chronikbüchern* (WMANT 42; Neukirchen: Neukirchener Verlag, 1973); and R. Braun, *1 Chronicles* (WBC 14; Waco: Word Books, 1986) 23. The particular sections under discussion above (2 Chr 11:13-17 and 13:8-12) fall within the larger section Welten chose for his analysis in 2 Chronicles 10-36. Regarding the Chronicler's unique material in 2 Chronicles 10-36 Welten concludes that only a few pericopes or fragments could depend on ancient and perhaps official sources, namely, the notes in 2 Chr 11:5b, 6a-10ab, 22f; 21:1-4; and 26:6a, 10. But other material such as the stories that concern military expeditions which came to a fortunate resolution for Judah (2 Chr 13:3-20; 14:8-14; 20:1-30; 26:6-8) is the Chronicler's own creation written for the Chronicler's own theological purposes.

5 Cf. H. G. M. Williamson, *1 and 2 Chronicles* (NCBC; Grand Rapids: Eerdmans 1982) 243; and M. Noth, *Überlieferungsgeschichtliche Studien I: Die sammelnden und bearbeitenden Geschichtswerke im Alten Testament* (Schriften der Königsberger Gelehrten Gessellschaft 18, 2; Halle: Max Niemeyer, 1943) 219.

7 From the statement in 1 Kgs 12:31b that Jeroboam appointed priests who were not from among the Levites, the Chronicler apparently inferred that Jeroboam dismissed the Levites or the existing priests from their cultic responsibilities (2 Chr 11:13-14; 13:9). From the comments in 1 Kgs 12:26-27 which attribute to Jeroboam the fear that his subjects will return to the temple in Jerusalem for worship, the Chronicler apparently inferred that the priests and laity in Israel who were faithful to Yahweh relocated or at least made pilgrimage to Jerusalem to worship there (2 Chr 11:16).

6 Whereas 1 Kgs 12:26-32 only *implies* negative judgments concerning Jeroboam's initiatives for religion (aside from the secondary note at v. 30a), the Chronicler in the context of King Abijah's speech to Jeroboam and all Israel makes the explicit judgment that the calves Jeroboam has made are not gods (13:10) and that Israel has abandoned all legitimate worship and thus forsaken Yahweh (13:11).

8 For instance, by mentioning satyrs alongside the golden calves as part of Jeroboam's cult.

their source in 1 Kgs 12:26-32 that could be of value for a reconstruction of the history of Jeroboam's period.

The texts in 3 Reigns 11:26-13:34 essentially offer a translation of the Hebrew of 1 Kgs 11:26-13:34 except for two significant divergences. First, according to 1 Kgs 12:1-20 Jeroboam returned from Egypt in order to participate in the negotiations with Rehoboam at Shechem (vv. 3, 12a), but according to 3 Reigns 12:1-20 Jeroboam played no part in the assembly of the tribes against Rehoboam at Shechem (cf. vv. 3, 12a).[9] Second, in a section to which 1 Kings has no direct counterpart, 3 Reigns 12:24$^{a-z}$ offers an alternate account of the events leading to Jeroboam's emergence as king. Within this section at vv. 24g-n a version of the story corresponding to 1 Kgs 14:1-18 finds its place.

Since the problem of the discrepancy concerning Jeroboam's absence or presence at the negotiations with Rehoboam at Shechem has no direct bearing on the subject of Jeroboam's initiatives for religion, it does not require resolution here. On the other hand, the material at 3 Reigns 12:24$^{a-z}$ may be of significance, particularly because it contains a variant account of Ahijah's denunciatory oracle concerning Jeroboam and his son. Therefore it is necessary to evaluate 3 Reigns 12:24$^{a-z}$ by inquiring whether it depends on a textual tradition independent of, and equally ancient as, the proto-MT tradition for the divergent and unique material it presents.

For the section 12:24$^{a-z}$ and particularly for 24g-n this question should probably be answered in the negative for at least two reasons. 1) At the completion of its presentation concerning Jeroboam at 13:34 the text of 3 Reigns departs from the otherwise consistently maintained pattern in 3 and 4 Reigns of marking the end of a king's reign with a formula concerning the rest of his acts, his death, his burial, and the accession of his successor. Oddly, for Jeroboam these formulae are completely lacking in 3 Reigns though they are present in 1 Kgs 14:19-20. The simplest explanation for this datum is that someone inserted the material translated by 3 Reigns 12:24$^{a-z}$ into a text that already con-

---

9 According to 1 Kgs 12:2 the reason for Jeroboam's return to Israel was that he had heard that Rehoboam had gone to Shechem to be made king, and according to v. 3a and v. 12a Jeroboam went with Israel to that assembly. In 3 Reigns, on the other hand, material that corresponds to 1 Kgs 12:2-3a is located after the formula announcing Solomon's death and burial but before the formula announcing Rehoboam's accession in 11:43. Thus, according to 3 Reigns 11:43 the occasion for Jeroboam's return to Israel was that he had heard that Solomon had died. 3 Reigns 12:3 and 12 do not include Jeroboam among the participants at Shechem.

tained the story of the prophet Ahijah at 14:1-18, and then, because 14:1-18 was repetitive of 12:24g-n, it was deleted. With this deletion the concluding regnal formula in 14:19-20 was accidentally lost. The loss of the customary regnal formula for Jeroboam suggests that the text of 3 Reigns is the product of the re-organization of a text similar to the MT. 2) Some of the differences between 3 Reigns 12:24g-n and 1 Kgs 14:1-18 give the appearance that a text which was essentially equivalent to MT 1 Kgs 14:1-18 has been adapted to make it fit a new setting at 3 Reigns 12:24g-n: a) Whereas 1 Kgs 14:1-18 mentions the blindness of the prophet Ahijah in order to accentuate Ahijah's clairvoyance, the corresponding note in 3 Reigns 12:24g-n serves no function at all. At 1 Kgs 14:5b-6 Ahijah, in spite of his blindness, perceives the identity of the woman who has entered his house and stands at a place where a sighted man might recognize her. On the other hand, according to 3 Reigns 12:24k the woman has not yet entered the range of normal vision when Ahijah perceives that she is coming and sends out his servant to meet her. b) 3 Reigns 12:24m contains a truncated form of a judgment oracle. It preserves only an announcement of punishment for Jeroboam without the indictment that must originally have preceded it. By way of contrast, 1 Kgs 14:10-12 has an announcement of punishment which corresponds to 3 Reigns 12:24m, but preceding it in 7b-9 there stands an indictment of Jeroboam as one would expect in the judgment oracle form. Of course, because 1 Kgs 14:7b-9 indicts Jeroboam for his failure as king to follow the example of David, it would be a very inappropriate indictment in the setting of 3 Reigns 12:24g-n, in which context Jeroboam has not yet become king. From the presence of the truncated judgment oracle in 3 Reigns it appears that the person responsible for the material at 3 Reigns 12:24g-n has adapted the judgment oracle from 1 Kgs 14:7b-11 in a rather clumsy fashion in as far as it could be used in the new setting.

In addition to these considerations one should note that 3 Reigns 12:24a-z represents but one of several instances where 3-4 Reigns presents its own peculiar material or its own version of material existing at another spot in the MT (cf. also 3 Reigns 2:35a-o, 46a-l; 16:28a-h; 4 Reigns 1:18a-d). D. W. Gooding has argued cogently that all of these sections peculiar to 3 and 4 Reigns together with many other smaller re-arrangements within various texts (e.g., the transfer of 1 Kgs 12:2-3a to 1 Reigns 11:43) are part of a "deliberate thoroughgoing interpretative reorganization of the original."[10] Thus 3 Reigns in most of its peculiarities over against 1 Kings does not give witness to an independent textual tradition. Rather, 3 Reigns represents an interpretive development of a Hebrew text that was probably closely akin to the MT.

Since both 2 Chr 11:13-17 with 13:8-12 and 3 Reigns 12:24$^{a-z}$ in their peculiarities over against 1 Kgs appear to be interpretive reworkings of texts closely akin to MT 1 Kings, preference must be given to the texts in MT 1 Kings in the investigation that follows. But the texts in 1 Kings also require critical analysis in preparation for their use as evidence. That task must be undertaken in the remainder of this chapter.

## B. An Analysis of the Compositional Units
### in 1 Kgs 11:26-14:20

The intention in this context is not to offer a detailed literary-critical or text-critical analysis of all the individual pericopes in 1 Kgs 11:26-14:20 that may be pertinent to the present investigation. That task may be accomplished, in as far as it is required, in context as each of the texts comes up for discussion in the chapters that follow. Rather, the goal at this point is to comprehend the larger compositional relationships within 1 Kgs 11:26-14:20. Since that text complex is comprised of smaller individual texts, it will be necessary to isolate the individual literary units in order to distinguish between various units that may constitute independent sources of evidence. Toward this end a form-critical analysis of these texts will serve to facilitate the recognition of literary units. Furthermore, consideration of the form of these units will indicate the extent to which they may be expected to bear historical evidence. Finally, in order to approach nearer to the historical realities of which the texts relate, it is necessary to understand the perspectives under which they were written and to perceive the prejudices that may have shaped them. A consideration of provenance and tradition history will serve this purpose.

Though 1 Kgs 11:26-14:20 exhibits a degree of literary unity in that Jeroboam plays a central role from its beginning to its end, yet that unity

---

[10] "Problems of Text and Midrash in the Third Book of Reigns," *Textus* 7 (1969) 20; *idem*, "The Septuagint's Rival Versions," *VT* 17 (1967) 173-89. On 3 Reigns 12.24$^{a-z}$ in particular, see J. A. Montgomery, *A Critical and Exegetical Commentary on the Books of Kings* (ICC; New York: Scribners, 1951) 252-54; more comprehensively and most recently, McKenzie, *The Trouble with Kings*, 21-40.

is a secondary unity given to it by the redactor(s) who brought its several originally-independent components together, reworking or rewriting some of them substantially but taking up others practically in the condition in which they were found and arranging them into one coherent account. The fairly recognizable seams in the account permit a somewhat provisional isolation of the following independent units: Ahijah's designation of Jeroboam as king over Israel in 11:26-40, the account of the non-renewal of the United Monarchy in 12:1-20, an explanation of why Rehoboam did not reunite the Kingdom by force in 12:21-24, an account pertaining to Jeroboam's capital and initiatives for religion in 12:25-32, a prophetic story about a man of God from Judah and a prophet at Bethel in 13:1-32, and a prophetic story about Ahijah's response to Jeroboam's inquiry regarding the health of his son in 14:1-18. Besides these units there are notes cast in the usual Deuteronomistic formulaic style to mark the conclusion of the reign of Solomon in 11:41-43 and the conclusion of the reign of Jeroboam in 14:19-20, and two redactional bridge passages at 12:33 and 13:33-34.

By way of substantiation of this provisional outline of the literary units in 12:26-14:20, one may begin with a discussion of 1 Kgs 13:1-32 and 14:1-18 since there the delimitation of the literary units and the identification of their literary forms is relatively clear.

1 Kgs 13:1 introduces a new character in the man of God from Judah and a new plot about his denunciation of the altar at Bethel and the subsequent testing of that prophetic word for its authenticity by the prophet from Bethel. Hence, at 13:1 a new narrative begins. This narrative is connected to the material that precedes it by a redactional bridge passage in 12:33 which takes up phrases and concepts from 12:32 and repeats them with slightly new emphases in order to prepare for the story in 13:1-32.[11] At the end of this story the section 13:33-34 functions as another redactional bridge in that it first of all refers back to the story of vv. 1-32 with the words ʾaḥar haddābār hazzeh lōʾ šāb yārobʿām middarkô hārāʿâ ("After this Jeroboam did not turn from his evil way"), then it picks up from 12:31 the theme of the priests whom Jeroboam conse-

---

[11] On 12:33 as bridge passage see McKenzie, *The Trouble with Kings*, 51-52. Contrast Provan (*Hezekiah and the Books of Kings*, 78-81) who argues that the redactional bridge begins at 12:31 on the grounds that 13:34 resumes the narrative from 12:30, thus indicating that all the intervening material has been inserted secondarily. This argument fails to consider seriously enough the implications of the extensive repetition that 12:33 makes of 12:32. The repetition indicates that the real discontinuity occurs between 12:32 and 12:33. For further comment see sections III.D and IV.A.

crated for the high places (a theme that has no continuity with the intervening story in vv. 1-32), and finally it creates a link with the following
story in 14:1-18 by anticipating the motif of the destruction of
Jeroboam's dynasty. However, the reason offered by 13:33-34 for that
destruction differs from the one given by DtrH at 14:8-9.[12] This suggests
that 13:1-32 with its redactional connections at 12:33 and 13:33-34 is a
secondary insertion that does not owe its present placement to DtrH.[13]

At 1 Kgs 14:1 one finds a new slate of characters and a new plot
about an inquiry made to the prophet Ahijah concerning the health of
Jeroboam's son Abijah. This story ends at 14:18 after which the typical
Deuteronomistic concluding regnal formulae appear.

By way of form, the two narratives 13:1-32 and 14:1-18 may be
categorized as prophetic legends because they center primarily on the
prophet and the prophetic word. The prophetic legend in 14:1-18, apart
from its Deuteronomistic expansions, exhibits the interest of tradents
from the Israelite State in its focus on the Shilonite prophet Ahijah and
his prophetic word for the son of Jeroboam, king of Israel. One may assume its transmission in prophetic circles of the Israelite State.[14] The
provenance of 1 Kgs 13:1-32 is less certain. Because the story concerns
the denunciation of an Israelite sanctuary by a man of God from Judah,
one might consider it a Judahite polemic and conjecture its transmission
in Judah. However, in its use of the particular designation "man of God"
and in its portrayal of the miraculous it best parallels Israelite prophetic
stories such as those about Elijah and Elisha.[15] Furthermore, because it
explains the existence of a particular tomb at Bethel and concerns the
altar at Bethel, it locates itself most securely at that sanctuary. One
should probably place its tradents among prophets from the Israelite
State who shared reservations about the cult at Bethel (cf. Hosea 10:5,

---

[12] On the DtrH's authorship of 14:8-9 see section IV.D.

[13] For more detailed arguments see McKenzie, *The Trouble with Kings*, 51-52; but
also O'Brien, *The Deuteronomistic History Hypothesis*, 186-87; and Provan, *Hezekiah and
the Books of Kings*, 78-81, and references cited there. Contrast M. Noth, *The
Deuteronomistic History* (JSOTSup 15; Sheffield, 1981) 69-70; and Nelson, *The Double
Redaction*, 82.

[14] So M. Noth, *Könige* (BKAT IX/1; Neukirchen-Vluyn: Neukirchener, 1968) 312;
Gray, *Kings*, 333.

[15] So W. E. Lemke, "The Way of Obedience: I Kings 13 and the Structure of the
Deuteronomistic History," in *Magnalia Dei: The Mighty Acts of God*, ed. F. M. Cross,
W. E. Lemke, and P. D. Miller (Garden City: Doubleday, 1976) 314-15; and
McKenzie, *The Trouble with Kings*, 55.

8).[16] Thus 1 Kgs 13:1-32 and 14:1-18 are two prophetic legends, probably both of Israelite provenance, that are tradition-historically independent of each other.

For the analysis of the remaining literary units in 1 Kgs 11:26-12:32 one may isolate first of all a section in 11:26-40. This material clearly does not comprise an original literary unity because vv. 26-28 function to introduce an account about Jeroboam's rising against Solomon and v. 40 reports Solomon's reaction to that uprising, but the intervening material in vv. 29-39 does not actually report Jeroboam's rebellious activity.[17] Probably one should conclude that such a report followed vv. 26-28 but that it has been replaced by the account of the designation of Jeroboam as king by Ahijah.[18]

Though in its present condition the account of the designation of Jeroboam by Ahijah evidences a thoroughgoing Deuteronomistic perspective, one may possibly detect a pre-Deuteronomistic source behind this material.[19] For the purposes of this investigation it is not necessary to attempt the difficult task of isolating pre-Deuteronomistic material. It is sufficient to note the evidence of its Northern origin in its focus on the two Israelite characters Jeroboam the Ephraimite and Ahijah the Shilonite, in its interest in the prophetic designation of a king for the Israelite State, and in its perspective that the separation of Israel from Judah is a divinely legitimated secession rather than a rebellion against Judah. Since the Shilonite prophet Ahijah figures centrally in this material, and since material such as this is presupposed by the prophetic legend in 1 Kgs 14:1-18 at v. 2b, one may conclude that it also derived

---

[16] See Noth, *Könige*, 294-95, for a different argument to the same conclusion.

[17] However, the repetition between 26b and 27a of the statement that Jeroboam raised his hand against the king suggests that even vv. 26-28 may be composite. Though the present state of the context renders any positive determination difficult, possibly one may find in vv. 27b-28 a fragment of a report about Jeroboam's uprising.

[18] So also Nelson, *The Double Redaction*, 110; and W. Dietrich, *Prophetie und Geschichte* (FRLANT 108; Göttingen: Vandenhoeck & Ruprecht, 1972) 54-55.

[19] See Nelson (*The Double Redaction*, 110-114) for a convincing demonstration that DtrH did in fact use an older written source, and more specifically, an Israelite prophetic source. Similarly Gray, *Kings*, 288; S. J. DeVries, *1 Kings* (WBC 12; Waco, Texas: Word Books, 1985) 149-50; and I. Plein, "Erwägungen zur Überlieferung von I Reg. 11:26-14:20" *ZAW* 78 (1966) 9-10. Contrast Noth (*Könige*, 245-46, 58ff); McKenzie (*The Trouble with Kings*, 41-47); and Provan (*Hezekiah and the Books of Kings*, 100-105), all of whom argue that 11.29-39 derives from DtrH (apart from a few later glosses).

from prophetic legend that was transmitted among prophetic circles of the Israelite State.

The fragmentary material that presently envelops 1 Kgs 11:29-39, namely, vv. 26-28+40, together with the full report of Jeroboam's rebellion which it must originally have contained, may possibly have been part of the narrative of the non-renewal of the United Monarchy which follows in 12:1-20. However, closer determination of the relationships that might have existed is not required for the present context.

For the rather tightly structured narrative in 1 Kings 12 the problem is to determine its ending. Arguments will be adduced below to show that vv. 25-32 do not offer a continuation of the narrative begun at 12.1. Certainly vv. 21-24 stand independently of vv. 1-20 as a brief prophetic narrative to explain why Rehoboam did not reunite the kingdom by military force. With regard to vv. 1-20, then, one may observe that though v. 16 forms a suitable climax for the preceding story, it requires further resolution to explain what happened after "Israel departed to their tents."[20] This conclusion must occur in vv. 18-20.[21] V. 17, on the other hand, interrupts the continuity between v. 16 and v. 18, and it raises the question of Israelites under Rehoboam's jurisdiction in a way for which the narrative hardly prepares. It must therefore be secondary to the narrative. Within the narrative of vv. 1-20, one should recognize at least one further editorial addition at v. 15. In contrast to v. 15 the rest of the narrative exhibits no interest in prophets in general nor in Ahijah in

---

[20] Contrast B. O. Long (*I Kings with an Introduction to Historical Literature* [The Forms of the Old Testament Literature 9; Grand Rapids: Eerdmans, 1984] 134) who points to the "appendix-like character" of vv. 17-20 and finds in v. 16 a satisfactory conclusion to the story that precedes. Other commentators have diverged widely in their opinions about what in vv. 17-20 is original, and each one of the verses is excluded by one or another of the commentators. Noth (*Könige*, 269) reckons vv. 18-20 with the basic narrative but excludes v. 17; E. Würthwein (*Das Erste Buch der Könige Kapitel 1-16* [ATD 11/1; Göttingen: Vandenhoeck & Ruprecht, 1977] 150-51) judges that v. 20 does not belong with the basic narrative because together with vv. 2 and 25 it belongs to a short annalistic report of Judahite provenance, and that v. 19 is a later addition to vv. 1, 3b-19, a narrative of Israelite provenance; Gray (*Kings*, 300) considers v. 18 an addition originating probably from a near-contemporary source and thinks the narrative ended at v. 19.

[21] It may be noted that 2 Chronicles 10 omits the note found in 1 Kgs 12:20. However, this hardly constitutes evidence that v. 20 is secondary in 1 Kings 12. The Chronicler will have omitted v. 20 because it told of the installation of a king in the Israelite State. The Chronicler characteristically does not report on the affairs of the Israelite State unless they impinge very directly on Judah.

particular. Furthermore, v. 15 has no integral place within the story.[22] The addition probably stems from the hand of DtrH who could thereby enhance the prophecy-fulfillment pattern in the Deuteronomistic History.

With respect to its form, 12:1-20*[23] is most suitably designated a story.[24] It has a fairly fully portrayed central character in Rehoboam and a well developed plot around the question of whether or not the Northern tribes will acknowledge the kingship of Rehoboam. With regard to the place of composition of the story and its transmission history, the negative depiction of Rehoboam should not be taken as a decisive criterion for its provenance in the Israelite State.[25] As the succession narrative in 2 Samuel 9-20, 1 Kings 1-2 indicates, a Jerusalemite historian would not necessarily shy away from a negative depiction of even so honored a king as David. In this way one can quite readily explain how the negative depiction of Rehoboam could stem from spheres in Jerusalem that basically assented to the Davidic dynasty but objected to the way Rehoboam, in particular, had failed in carrying out his responsibilities.[26] The narrative in 12:1-20* actually does exhibit the perspective of a Judahite who knew and said a great deal about the deliberations of Rehoboam and his advisors but had very little to say, if anything, about matters of specifically Israelite concern.[27] Furthermore, a very clear Judahite bias marks 12:1-20* at v. 19 because it makes the claim that the secession of Israel actually constituted rebellion against the house of David. As I. Plein has argued, both the noun and the verb of the root $pš^c$ in their biblical usage consistently bear a negative moral judgment against the perpetrator(s) of the action signified by $pš^c$,[28] and this kind of

---

[22] So also Würthwein, *Könige*, 150, 155-56, and Noth, *Könige*, 269. Then the form of the narrative cannot be designated prophetic legend.

[23] The asterisk character (*) denotes the material delimited by the references given, less the secondary accretions as isolated in the foregoing discussion.

[24] So also Noth, *Könige*, 270; Gray, *Kings*, 299; Würthwein, *Könige*, 150; Long, *I Kings*, 136. Since the narrative exhibits a folkloristic or popular character rather than a primary interest in the report of some historical circumstance, one can hardly call it a historical work. Contrast Plein ("Erwägungen zur Überlieferung," 14-15). Yet the story may furnish historically reliable information regarding the breakup of the kingdom.

[25] Contrast Würthwein, *Könige*, 150.

[26] See Noth, *Könige*, 271, and Plein, "Erwägungen zur Überlieferung," 11ff.

[27] Cf. DeVries, *I Kings*, 156.

[28] "Erwägungen zur Überlieferung," 10.

judgment on Israel's secession would most likely have originated in Judah.[29]

The foregoing argument serves to demonstrate that 1 Kgs 12:1-20* is of Judahite provenance and hence of independent origin from the Israelite traditions in 11:29-39, 13:1-32 and 14:1-18. However, the matter regarding the relationship of 12:25-32 to 12:1-20* still requires resolution.

The material in 12:25-32 coheres in that outside of v. 25 it all pertains to the initiatives of Jeroboam for religion in Israel. V. 25 could be separated from vv. 26-32 and considered separately, but it exhibits a certain coherence with what follows in that it shares an annal-like form with it. Critical opinion regarding the form of 12:25-32 varies widely. Noth finds in this section a continuation of the story found in 12:1-20*.[30] I. Plein and H. Donner recognize in it extracts from annalistic sources which have been heavily reworked by the DtrH.[31] McKenzie and Würthwein regard it as a composition by DtrH.[32] B. Long concludes that the section is a "literary miscellany" comprised of a fragment of a story in vv. 26-30 and reports of building cities in v. 25 and of building cultic establishments in vv. 31-32.[33]

In some of its parts vv. 25-32 does appear annal-like. It preserves information which would have been of interest to the court of the Israelite State in a notice pertaining to Jeroboam's measures in city building (v. 25) and in several notices about his initiatives for the cult, namely, "he made two golden calves" (v. 28ab), "he set one in Bethel, and the other he put in Dan" (v. 29), and "Jeroboam appointed a feast on the fifteenth day of the eighth month" (v. 32a). In fact the whole of vv. 25-32 has an annalistic characteristic in that it offers no explicit evaluation or interpretation of Jeroboam's initiatives, aside from v. 30a. The attitude of its writer(s) can only be discerned by inference.

Nevertheless, vv. 26-29 viewed in its entirety does not fit the form of official annals because it has several features of a story. It develops a little plot, and it presents the inner thoughts, fears, and motivations of a

---

[29] *Ibid.*; also Noth, *Könige*, 271; Würthwein, *Könige*, 158.

[30] *Könige*, 269-70; cf. Gray, *Kings*, 300.

[31] Plein ("Erwägungen zur überlieferung," 21) thinks vv. 23ab, 29, 30b, 32aa and ba belong to the annalistic source. H. Donner ("The Separate States of Israel and Judah," in *Israelite and Judaean History*, ed. J. H. Hayes and J. M. Miller [OTL; Philadelphia: Westminster, 1977] 383) simply refers to vv. 25-31 as extracts from annals.

[32] McKenzie, *The Trouble with Kings*, 52 and 99; and Würthwein, *Könige*, 162ff.

[33] *I Kings*, 142.

central character, Jeroboam, who faces and resolves a problem concerning his own political security. So vv. 26-29 should be read as a story fragment composed to offer an explanation of how it came about that Jeroboam made two golden calves which he then set up in the sanctuaries at Bethel and Dan.

The form designation of vv. 25-32 as annals is also unsuitable because, though the annal-like material preserved in this section would be of interest for the Israelite, the perspective under which it is presented is pervasively Jerusalemite.

This Jerusalemite perspective is evident first of all in vv. 26-27 where the author presents as Jeroboam's fear that "the heart of this people will turn again to *their lord*, to Rehoboam king of Judah, and they will kill me . . . ." The implication of such a formulation of Jeroboam's thought is that Jeroboam himself acknowledges Rehoboam as the legitimate ruler of his own Israelite subjects. But this is the perspective of a Davidic loyalist. Surely Jeroboam himself would not have thought in this way, and no patriotic author from the Israelite State would have presented him in this way.

Furthermore, the author sets up Jeroboam's dilemma as one of determining how to prevent his Israelite subjects from making pilgrimage to the temple at Jerusalem on such a large scale that it results in all Israel returning to and accepting the overlordship of the Davidic dynasty. In this formulation of the dilemma the author writes as if there had been a deeply grounded and persistent unity between Israel and Judah that could not be undone even by a rupture such as occurred at Shechem, and as if it became an urgent matter for Jeroboam to adopt policies and to develop institutions that would foster further the breakdown of relations between Israel and Judah. However, this way of perceiving the basic fabric of the United Monarchy betrays a Jerusalemite author who refused to acknowledge that the rupture at Shechem actually resulted from the long developing rift which was rooted in the fundamental duality of Israel and Judah.[34] Furthermore, this author's

---

34 That a certain political dualism had existed between Judah and Israel since the time of David or even before is frequently recognized. See A. Alt, "The Monarchy in the Kingdoms of Israel and Judah," in *Essays on Old Testament History and Religion* (Oxford: Basil Blackwell, 1966), especially p. 242; M. Noth, *The History of Israel*, 187; Donner, "The Separate States of Israel and Judah," 383-35; Miller and Hayes, *A History of Ancient Israel and Judah*, 178; and see also the summary of evidence for dualism between Israel and Judah in T. N. D. Mettinger, *King and Messiah: The Civil and Sacral Legitimation of the Israelite Kings* (ConBOT 8; C.W.K.

formulation of Jeroboam's dilemma presupposes that the impetus towards centralization of the cult at Jerusalem had progressed so far in Solomon's time that Jerusalem had become the focal point of an all-Israelite cult to which all Israel in Jeroboam's day would have been accustomed and even anxious to make regular pilgrimages. This notion hardly corresponds to the historical circumstances at the time of Solomon or of Jeroboam, and it betrays the much later setting of an author who knows of a more securely established and centralized religio-political status for Jerusalem than would have pertained in Solomon's time.

The story fragment in vv. 26-29 reports that Jeroboam resolved his security problem by fashioning two golden calves and by installing them in the sanctuaries at Bethel and at Dan. Thus the story offers an aetiology for the establishment of the royal sanctuaries, the motivation for which arose out of Jeroboam's considerations for political and personal security. However, this is not the way an Israelite author would have described the establishment of the royal sanctuaries of the Israelite State. The sympathetic Israelite author would have highlighted their legitimacy, perhaps by appealing to the ancient and venerable traditions of those two sacred sites, rather than portraying their selection by Jeroboam merely as a measure calculated to maintain his political security and the independence of his state.

The Jerusalemite perspective is also evident in vv. 31-32. The note in v. 31 that Jeroboam established priests for his sanctuaries would have a quite neutral significance except that the formulation turns negative in saying that he appointed priests from among people who were *not* Levites. The official court annals of the Israelite State would not have recorded criticism against royal policy, so perhaps this also stems from the Jerusalemite author or editor. The perspective of the note in v. 32 that compares Jeroboam's festival to the one in Judah must also be Jerusalemite because an author from the Israelite State would hardly

---

Gleerup, 1976) 298-301; but contrast G. Buccellati, *Cities and Nations of Ancient Syria* (Studi Semitici 26; Rome: Istituto di Studi del Vicino Oriente, 1967) 137-93.

To whatever historical time one traces the roots of Israelite-Judahite dualism, the clear datum remains that under David and Solomon the unity between Israel and Judah was tenuous. Jeroboam probably needed to do little to foster a complete break between the two. Nevertheless, it should be admitted that Jeroboam possibly had some Davidic loyalists among his subjects, and it will have been in his interests to win their loyalty. But certainly 1 Kgs 12:26-28 exaggerates greatly when it suggests that Jeroboam had to take active measures to prevent the reunion of Israel and Judah.

point out that this Israelite festival had its precedent in a Judahite festival.

The foregoing analysis indicates that 1 Kgs 12:25-32 contains a miscellany of forms, edited or composed with a very pervasive Jerusalemite bias. Vv. 26-29 appears to contain a story fragment constructed to explain from a sarcastic Jerusalemite point of view why Jeroboam fashioned the calf images and established the royal sanctuaries at Bethel and Dan. V. 25 is annalistic in form, and vv. 26-32 may also include annalistic notes or build on annalistic material from the court of the Israelite State. However, outside of v. 25 insufficient points of reference exist to allow one to isolate the annalistic material with confidence.

The story fragment in vv. 26-29 could hardly have been an original continuation of the story in vv. 1-20*. Whereas vv. 1-20* focuses on Rehoboam and his misguided politics, vv. 26-29 focuses on Jeroboam and his misguided religious initiatives. But what is true of vv. 26-29 is also true of the entire section in vv. 25-32. Given its mixture of formal features, none of which connects up with vv. 1-20*, one may conclude that vv. 25-32 originated independently from vv. 1-20*.

With regard to the identity of the editor or composer of vv. 25-32, the case is not altogether clear. From the foregoing discussion of the implied criticisms in vv. 26-32, one may gather that the issues at stake are those of DtrH. The discrediting of the cult of the Israelite State at Bethel and Dan may have its motivation in DtrH's conviction that all worship of Yahweh should occur in Jerusalem; the complaint about the installation of non-levitical priests may have its in DtrH's conviction that only Levites should be priests. Indeed, several commentators recognize vv. 26-32 as the work of the DtrH.[35] However, the section offers no obvious reference points in terms of DtrH's phraseology, and given the very direct nature of DtrH's usual criticisms, especially with respect to the very central theme of the sin of Jeroboam (e.g., 1 Kgs 15:26, 30, 34; 16:2-4, 7; 2 Kgs 10:29), it would be rather astonishing if DtrH should here present a basic report of Jeroboam's activities pertinent to religion but offer only veiled and implicit criticisms. Possibly, then, vv. 25-32 existed in the sources used by DtrH.

The conclusions reached above regarding the form and tradition history of 1 Kgs 12:26-32 have significant consequences for judgments

---

35 McKenzie, *The Trouble with Kings*, 52 and 99; Würthwein, *Könige*, 102-103; and H. Donner, "Hier sind deine Götter, Israel!" in *Wort und Geschichte: Fest. K. Elliger* (AOAT 18; Neukirchen-Vluyn, 1973) 49.

about the historical reliability of its various claims. One must beware of
the distortion arising from the Jerusalemite polemical stance toward the
cult in the Israelite State. Also, one may anticipate that only those of
Jeroboam's initiatives that were of interest for the Jerusalemite author's
polemical purposes will have been highlighted whereas many other
details that would have been of interest to the historian of religion did
not serve the author's purpose and were consequently omitted. In the
available material, though it may depend in part on annals, it is impossible to isolate those annalistic components with confidence. By all
appearances the Jerusalemite author exercised considerable freedom in
using available sources and in composing the section vv. 25-32.
Nevertheless, the judgment that the author simply fabricated vv. 25-32
in its entirety out of polemical intentions would be far too severe.
Certainly there is a significant basis in historical fact behind the various
initiatives attributed to Jeroboam.

These various religious initiatives undertaken by Jeroboam will
provide the subject for the next chapter. They may be investigated suitably under four headings: 1) the manufacture of the golden calf images,
2) the establishment of royal sanctuaries at Bethel and Dan, 3) the
appointment of a priesthood for the new state, and 4) the institution of a
festival. Each of these points requires an investigation of its own which
takes into account the pertinent information from various sources, both
from other biblical texts and from archaeology, to clarify more fully the
nature of the actions Jeroboam took.

## C. A SUMMARY OF RESULTS

The interest in this chapter has been to analyze the biblical texts
pertaining to Jeroboam in preparation for their use as evidence in the
following inquiry. It has been concluded with respect to materials concerning Jeroboam that neither LXX 3 Reigns nor 2 Chronicles offer a
witness independent of the MT 1 Kgs 11:26-14:20. Rather, both 3 Reigns
12:24$^{a-z}$ and 2 Chr 11:13-17; 13:8-12 in their peculiarities over against
corresponding materials in MT 1 Kgs 11:26-14:20 appear to be nothing
more than interpretive reworkings of older texts closely akin or identical
to what has been preserved in the MT. Therefore the MT 1 Kgs 11:26-14:20
must be regarded as the basic biblical textual source for this
investigation.

In the foregoing analysis of 1 Kgs 11:26-14:20, particular attention has been given to the isolation of the various individual literary units and to the determination of their provenance in order that the independent witnesses with their various perspectives within that text complex might be recognized. Attention has also been devoted to the formal analysis of these units in recognition of the fact that the quest for historical information must pay due regard to the capacities of the different forms to carry historical information. Since among the several units in 1 Kg 12:26-14:20 the section 12:25-32 speaks most explicitly concerning Jeoroboam's policies for religion, it has received a proportionate amount of attention above. The prophetic legends in 1 Kings 13 and 14 will receive more detailed attention below in sections IV.A and D.

One may isolate the following tradition units in 1 Kgs 11:26-14:20: 1) three prophetic legends of Israelite origin in 11:29-39, 13:1-32, 14:1-18; 2) one prophetic legend of Judahite origin in 12:21-24; 3) one story of Jerusalemite origin in 12:1-20*; and 4) one miscellany of forms of Jerusalemite origin in 12:25-32.

These diverse traditions have been brought into a redactional unity so that they now offer a coherent account concerning Jeroboam. If one inquires concerning the identity of the persons responsible for this collection and editing of materials one may note that DtrH has left imprints at many points. As has been noted above, DtrH has substantially reworked 11:29-39. Furthermore, to anticipate the results of the analysis in section IV.D below, DtrH has also edited and reshaped 14:1-18. In the editorial addition at 12:15 one may also note DtrH's interest in the theme of prophecy and its fulfillment. Aside from one rather significant, secondary interpolation at 12:33-13:34, it appears that DtrH collected and edited all of the various materials to form the account concerning Jeroboam in 1 Kgs 11:26-14:20.

# CHAPTER III

# *Jeroboam's Initiatives for Religion*

## A. The Manufacture of the Golden Calf Images

This inquiry into the significance of Jeroboam's installation of the golden calves will take up three related questions: 1) What god(s) were the images intended to represent? 2) What was the origin of this cult image from a history of religions perspective? 3) What was the significance of the calf image in its association with the deity?

### 1. The Identity of the God(s) Represented by the Calf Image

DtrH condemns Jeroboam's manufacture and installation of the calf images as an act of apostasy from Yahweh and as an act of idolatry (1 Kgs 14:9;[1] cf. the formulae in which successive kings are condemned for following in the sin of Jeroboam, e.g., 1 Kgs 15:30, 34; 16:2, 7, 19, 26, etc.). In Mesopotamian and Canaanite iconography the bull (calf) symbol often has close association with the storm-/warrior-gods.[2] Given such data (among others), it follows rather naturally that some scholars have recognized a "Baalistic" derivation for Jeroboam's calf images[3] and that they have discerned in popular Israelite perception some linkage of the

---

[1] Regarding DtrH's authorship of this material, see section IV.D.

[2] See the data presented in III.A.2.

[3] E.g., Smith, *The Early History of God*, 51; and H. Th. Obbink, "Jahwebilder," *ZAW* 47 (1929) 268.

calf image with the Canaanite fertility deities or with Baal-Haddu.[4] The extent to which these opinions are accurate will require further consideration below.

However, at this point one may appropriately note that according to biblical sources covering a fairly long period of the history of the Israelite State, Yahwist circles did not oppose Jeroboam's golden calves, and certainly they did not attack these cult images for supposed connections with the Canaanite fertility religion or as representations of Baal-Haddu.[5] One looks in vain for any such opposition to the calf images in the prophetic story of the unnamed man of God who prophesies against the altar at Bethel (1 Kgs 13) or in the prophetic story which tells about Ahijah's negative oracle regarding Jeroboam's son (1 Kgs 14:1-18).[6] Similarly, the accounts about Elijah's and Elisha's conflict with *habbaʿal* offer no hint that either of these prophets opposed the calf images, nor can one find evidence of such opposition in the prophetic oracles of Amos. Even the ardent Jehu who destroyed the temple of *habbaʿal* at Samaria in his zeal for Yahweh (2 Kgs 10:18-28) apparently took no measures against the golden calves, presumably because for him and his contemporaries they did not represent *habbaʿal*. In fact, DtrH commends Jehu for eradicating the worship of *habbaʿal* from the Israelite State with the words, "Thus Jehu wiped out *habbaʿal* from Israel" (2 Kgs 10:28), but then goes on immediately to condemn Jehu for his failure to "turn aside from the sins of Jeroboam the son of Nebat, which he made Israel to sin, the golden calves that were in Bethel and in Dan" (2 Kgs 10:29). From these evaluative comments it would appear that even DtrH, who otherwise expresses strong disapproval for the golden calves, did not consider the calf images as representations of *habbaʿal*.

---

[4] E.g., Provan, *Hezekiah and the Books of Kings*, 64-65; and E. W. Nicholson, *Deuteronomy and Tradition* (Oxford: Basil Blackwell, 1967) 72.

[5] Cf. De Vaux, *The Bible and the Ancient Near East* (Garden City: Doubleday, 1971) 100; Hahn, *Das "Goldene Kalb"*, 350-51; Cross, *Canaanite Myth and Hebrew Epic*, 75; and T. Mettinger, "The Veto on Images and the Aniconic God in Ancient Israel," in *Religious Symbols and their Functions*, ed. H. Biezas (Stockholm: Almqvist and Wiksell International, 1979) 22-23. Even Hosea (13:1-3) does not explicitly identify the calf image with *habbaʿal*, but seems rather to say that the cult of the calf constituted a further step on the way of guilt than even the devotion to *habbaʿal*. Tobit 1:5, however, identifies the calf as Baal.

[6] The claim regarding 1 Kgs 14:1-18 anticipates conclusions argued below in section IV.D that the material which condemns Jeroboam for making molten images (v. 9) derives from DtrH.

This conclusion finds support in other comments by DtrH as well. When DtrH evaluates Ahab as the worst of all the kings of the Israelite State, the grounds for this evaluation are that Ahab went beyond the sin of Jeroboam by marrying Jezebel, by serving *habba⁽al*, and by erecting an altar to *habba⁽al* (1 Kgs 16:30-32). Again, at 2 Kgs 3:2-3 DtrH writes that though Jehoram removed the pillar of *habba⁽al* he did not forsake Jeroboam's sin. These texts imply that the worship of *habba⁽al* by Israelite kings began with Ahab and that for DtrH the sin of Jeroboam had nothing to do with worship of *habba⁽al*.

Judging from the perspective of political expediency one must judge it most likely that Jeroboam intended the golden calves not as the introduction of the worship of a new deity nor of a deity that to this point had held a peripheral place in Israel's worship. Rather, he must have intended to represent precisely that deity that to this time had held the most prominent place in Israelite worship.[7] For Jeroboam to have introduced some new worship to replace or compete with ancient religious traditions at a time so insecure as the time during the establishment of the new kingdom and the establishment of his own new kingship would have been self-destructive politically.

For evidence towards the identification of the god(s) represented by the golden calves one may look to the formula *hinnēh ʾĕlōhêkā yiśrāʾēl ʾăšer heʿĕlûkā mēʾereṣ miṣrāyim* ("Look, your god[s], oh Israel, who brought you out of the land of Egypt") which, according to 1 Kgs 12:28, Jeroboam proclaimed before his Israelite subjects in reference to the calves. From its representation in this context as well as in the context of Exod 32:4, 8 one may judge that this formula or a formula essentially like it must have constituted a central affirmation of the cult of the Israelite State. This judgment may be maintained even though the formula of 1 Kgs 12:28d appears in the context of material written from a Jerusalemite perspective, and even though one might legitimately suspect the Jerusalemite author of having editorially introduced an implicit charge of polytheism into the original formula in order to slander the cult of the Israelite State. Of course, the perception of such an implicit charge depends solely upon whether or not one interprets that the plural number of the noun and the verb in *ʾĕlōhêkā . . . ʾăšer heʿĕlûkā* requires a plural

---

7 Cf. Cross, *Canaanite Myth and Hebrew Epic*, 74; De Vaux, *The Bible and the Ancient Near East*, 100; Würthwein, *Könige*, 169; and Noth, *Könige*, 284.

divine referent.[8] But regardless of how one decides the issue concerning the interpretation of the number of the divine referent in this formula, and regardless of whether or not the Jerusalemite author actually intended to introduce a connotation of polytheism, the formula itself makes a claim that the Jerusalemite author would hardly have invented. One can hardly suppose that the Jerusalemite author would have fabricated the connection between Jeroboam's despised calves and the Exodus tradition if that connection had not in fact existed in the religion of the Israelite State. Hence that connection and the formula itself must be authentic to the cult of the Israelite State.

If this formula belongs to the authentic traditions of the Israelite State, it gives decisive though also ambiguous evidence for the identification of the deity represented by the golden calves. On the one hand, it shows clearly that the golden calves represent the *ʾĕlōhîm* who brought Israel up from the land of Egypt. In almost every place where this for-

---

[8] The issue of whether the formula should be interpreted as a reference to one deity or to more than one cannot find its resolution on purely grammatical or syntactical grounds. Though the plural noun and verb appear to imply a plural interpretation, one may note various Hebrew constructions where the subject *ʾĕlōhîm*, though clearly referring to a singular god, is modified by a plural predicate noun (1 Sam 28:13, 1 Sam 4:8, and Ps 58:12), or appears with a plural verb (Gen 20:13, 35:7; 2 Chr 32:15; and 2 Sam 7:23). (In each of the latter four cases where *ʾĕlōhîm* appears with a plural verb, *BHS* holds out the possibility of emendation to a singular verb on the basis of the versions. The versions are most probably "correcting" these points in the Hebrew text to make them consistent with usage elsewhere in the Hebrew Bible where *ʾĕlōhîm* in its singular sense is construed with a singular verb or a singular predicate adjective. Consequently the plural verb forms in these texts should be accepted as original on text-critical bases.) For further grammatical and syntactical considerations concerning the interpretation of this formula see Donner, "Hier sind deine Götter, Israel!" 45-47.

However, the literary context in which the formula stands at 1 Kgs 12:28 may imply a plural meaning for the formula in this particular setting (cf. Cross, *Canaanite Myth and Hebrew Epic*, 73-74). By bringing the report concerning the making of *two* calves into such close proximity with Jeroboam's recitation of the cultic formula, the Jerusalemite author probably intends to force the reader to understand the formula in a plural sense and thus to understand that Jeroboam had sponsored a kind of polytheism. Thus one may argue that it is only its present literary context, as written by a Jerusalemite author, that gives the formula in 1 Kgs 12:28e a critical connotation. Quite possibly a formula in exactly such a form pre-dates the author of 1 Kgs 12:28 and authentically reflects a central aspect of the cult of the Israelite State.

To this argument contrast the position advanced by Donner, "Hier sind deine Götter, Israel!" 47-49; and for a survey of critical opinion see Hahn, *Das "Goldene Kalb"*, 305. Hahn's survey shows that scholarship has been fairly evenly divided over whether the formula should be interpreted in the plural or in the singular.

mula or a variation of it appears in the Hebrew Bible, the god who brings Israel up from Egypt is identified as Yahweh.[9] From this one may conclude, as Donner does, that the formula signifies conclusively that Jeroboam intended that the golden calves should represent Yahweh in the Yahweh cult.[10]

On the other hand, the ambiguity of the reference of the formula in 1 Kgs 12:28 is underlined by two texts from the oracles by Balaam which attest the Exodus formulation, *ʾēl môṣîʾām mimmiṣrāyim* ("El brought them out of Egypt," Num 23:22; cf. 24:8[11]). Since the Balaam oracles probably belong with the most ancient poetry in the Hebrew Bible,[12] this formulation holds particular significance as a witness to how Israel spoke of the Exodus in the earliest period of its history.[13] The use of several distinct designations for the deity in the larger poetic context within which this formulation appears indicates that *ʾēl* is being used as a proper name and not as a generic appellative.[14] Hence these two texts

---

[9] See Judg 6:13; 1 Sam 12:6; 2 Kgs 17:36; Jer 16:14-15; 23:7-8; Exod 16:6; Deut 1:27; 6:12, 23; 7:8, 19; 1 Kgs 9:9; 2 Chr 7:22.

[10] "Hier sind deine Götter, Israel!" 48.

[11] Num 24:8 differs only in that the object suffix on the verb is 3 m.s. rather than 3 m.p. as in 23:22.

[12] See the evidence presented by W. F. Albright, "The Oracles of Balaam" *JBL* 63 (1944) 208-11 and 216 at n. 54; *idem, Yahweh and the Gods of Canaan*, 1-46; Freedman, "Divine Names and Titles in Early Hebrew Poetry," 66-68; and Cross, *Canaanite Myth and Hebrew Epic*, p. 99 n. 30 and p. 157.

[13] This claim, of course, assumes that Num 23:22 and 24:8 are integral and original in their contexts. Contrast *BHS* which conjectures that Num 23:22 was introduced into its context from 24:8, and O. Loretz ("Die Herausführungsformel in Num 23.22 und 24.8" *UF* 7 [1975] 571-72) who judges that the formula is secondary in both contexts. For convincing arguments showing that the formula at Num 23:22 is integral to its context see A. Tosato, "The Literary Structure of the First Two Poems of Balaam (Num xxiii 7-10, 18-24)" *VT* 29 (1979) 101-4. Corresponding arguments could be formulated with regard to Num 24:8.

Methodologically, if one argues that the formula in Num 23:22 and 24:8 is a secondary insertion, one should be able to explain why the formula was introduced secondarily. It is a unique formula (since it is the only attestation of the Exodus formula using El as a divine name instead of Yahweh in the Hebrew Bible) located in a rather unlikely context (since the Balaam oracles say nothing else about the Exodus, nor do they develop themes likely to attract a statement about the Exodus into this context). This makes it very unlikely that anyone would have introduced the formula at 23:22 and 24:8 secondarily.

[14] The fact that Num 23:8 employs *ʾēl* and Yahweh as corresponding terms in synonymously parallel lines and that 24:16 (cf. v. 4) uses the three divine names *ʾēl*, *ʿelyôn*, and *šadday* in the same way offers a decisive argument towards this conclusion.

indicate that at least some components of earliest Israel could confess that it was El who had brought Israel out of Egypt.

Such a conclusion finds further confirmation in the evidence offered by biblical traditions that originally an Israelite group living in Canaan under the name Israel revered El as their high god.[15] Thus, though there can be no doubt that from very early times the god who brought Israel from Egypt was revered under the name Yahweh (Exod 15:1-18), yet it is evident that some Israelites revered this god under the name El (Num 23:22, and 24:8).[16] The tension between these two traditions may find its resolution either in the thesis that Yahweh originated as an El figure[17] or in the thesis that Yahweh and El became identified after the Yahwist group immigrated into Canaan where El was being revered.[18]

In answer to the question concerning the identity of the god represented by the calf iconography one may conclude that Jeroboam intended to carry on old Israelite traditions in which El, now also identified as Yahweh, received homage as the deliverer in the Exodus experience.

## 2. The Calf Image as Divine Representation in the History of Religions

For the question concerning the origin of Jeroboam's calf iconography, comparative study of religions in the ancient Near East attests to the ubiquitousness of the bull image in the iconography of the entire ancient Near East.[19] Furthermore, the multifarious biblical traditions suggest that components of what eventually made up Israel came from various geographical regions, each with their own historical and religious experiences. Consequently, in the search for the origins of Jeroboam's calf iconography, various options present themselves; and scholars have argued for the provenance of Jeroboam's iconography in

---

[15] See the discussion of this point above in chapter I. Cf. Smith, *The Early History of God*, 7-8; De Moor, *The Rise of Yahwism*, 10-41; Gottwald, *The Tribes of Yahweh*, 494; and Ahlström, "Where did the Israelites Live?" 134.

[16] There is in Deut 32:12 a kind of negative testimony to the tradition of a different god acting on behalf of Israel at the beginning of its history. When it says, "Yahweh alone led him [Israel]; there was no foreign god (*ʾēl*) accompanying," it speaks a clear denial to any tradition that names another god as the one who led Israel through the desert. Thus the verse presupposes the existence of exactly such traditions.

[17] Cross, *Canaanite Myth and Hebrew Epic*, 44-75; and more recently, using a very different argument, De Moor, *The Rise of Yahwism*, especially pp. 223-66.

[18] O. Eissfeldt, "El and Yahweh," *JSS* 1 (1956) 35-37.

[19] Jaroš, *Die Stellung des Elohisten*, 352; and Hahn, *Das "Goldene Kalb"*, 331.

the Egyptian,[20] the Mesopotamian,[21] or the Canaanite[22] religious context.

However, given the ubiquity of the bull symbol as a representation of various deities throughout the ancient Near East, one may question the validity of isolating any one part of that larger religious context as the specific source of the Israelite practice of representing its deity by the calf image. Probably one should rather think of Israel's use of this image as a feature derived from the common iconographic heritage of the ancient Near East.

The Ugaritic texts and various discoveries in the plastic arts have shown that the bull symbol was very much at home in the Syrian and Canaanite religious milieu. The Ugaritic texts place El in a unique association with the bull image by their frequent and exclusive application to him of the epithet *tr* (Bull).[23] In a plastic representation from Ugarit a powerful bull stands to the back of the god El who is attended by two

---

[20] The attempt to find the origins of Israelite calf iconography in the Egyptian religious context has a certain cogency because a very prominent biblical tradition remembers Israel's sojourn in and exodus from Egypt. Some scholars have argued that in this whole experience Israel could not have escaped the influence of Egyptian religion, and furthermore that Jeroboam's stay in Egypt prior to his assumption of kingship in Israel presented a likely conduit of influence that resulted very specifically in the installation of the golden calves by Jeroboam. For a recent statement of such a position see E. Danelius, "The Sins of Jeroboam Ben-Nabat," *JQR* 58 (1967-68) 95-114, 204-23. However, along with the general trend in modern scholarship one should abandon the notion that Jeroboam's calf iconography might have represented one or another of the Egyptian gods. The Israelites would hardly have credited an Egyptian god with delivering them from Egyptian oppression or from the Pharaoh who was himself an Egyptian deity. See Hahn (*Das "Goldene Kalb"*, 313-26) for a summary of arguments both for and against an Egyptian origin for Jeroboam's calf cult. See also L. R. Bailey, "The Golden Calf," *HUCA* 42 (1971) 102-3.

[21] The argument for a Mesopotamian origin of Jeroboam's calf iconography can claim some support from another prominent biblical tradition which preserves the memory that Israel's ancestors came from Ur via Haran. Then Israelite calf iconography could have derived from the religious traditions the ancestors brought with them. Bailey ("The Golden Calf," 97-115) associates Jeroboam's cult specifically with that of the Mesopotamian moon-god Sîn, arguing that the association of the bull with the moon-god was prevalent throughout the ancient Near East and even beyond. However this identification of the god of the fathers as Sîn does not go far beyond conjecture because the biblical traditions offer very slight evidence in this direction. Cf. the comments by Hahn, *Das "Goldene Kalb"*, 336-7.

[22] So the majority of scholars in the modern period. See the survey by Hahn, *Das "Goldene Kalb"*, 326-32.

[23] The epithet *tr* is used of El thirty-one times according to the listing by R. E. Whitaker, *A Concordance of the Ugaritic Literature* (Cambridge, Mass., 1972) 649-50.

armed, young men. Probably the bull in this scene stands as an emblem for El.[24] Similarly, a fourteenth century BCE statue of a bull calf from Tyre may be identified as a symbol of El in consideration of the astral signs which decorate its entire body.[25]

In several other contexts Baal-Haddu or some other storm-god comes into association with the bull symbol. A cylinder seal from Tell Mardikh, ca. 1725 BCE, situates a bull lying on a pedestal in the background of a scene in which Baal-Haddu has prominence.[26] Three reliefs, one from north east of Aleppo dating from the eighth or seventh century BCE, another from Arslan Tash dating back to Tiglath Pileser III, and another from Til-Barsib of the eleventh or twelfth century BCE, all portray bearded storm-gods bearing three pronged thunderbolts and standing on top of bulls.[27]

The datum that the bull symbol could represent or have association with various deities in the Syrian and Canaanite context might lead one to ask which of these deities contributed the bull symbol to the cult of Yahweh in the Israelite State. To reverse the question, one might ask whether the calf symbols in the cult of the Israelite State did not signify some association with the storm-god Baal-Haddu as well as with El. But clearly, this way of formulating questions will mislead. As has been stated above, in a religious context where the bull symbol availed itself as a common representation for various gods one can hardly isolate a specific origin for a particular attestation of the symbol.

The specific question of whether the calf symbol in the cult of the Israelite State signified Baal-Haddu finds its best resolution on evidence provided by the biblical texts. It is certainly true that modern scholarship has drawn significant lines of continuity both between Yahweh and

---

[24] So C. F. A. Schaeffer, "Nouveaux témoignages du culte de El et de Baal a Ras Shamra-Ugarit et ailleurs en Syrie-Palestine," *Syria* 43 (1966) 7-9 and plates I-III. See also the interpretation by P. D. Miller, "El the Warrior," *HTR* 60 (1967) 412.

[25] So Schaeffer, "Témoignages du culte de El et de Baal," 14-16 and pl. IV; and Jaroš, *Die Stellung des Elohisten*, 354 and figure 20 on p. 363. Regarding the astral signs decorating the body of the bull, compare the kôkĕbê ʾēl in Isa 14:13 and the hkkbm ʾl in the Pyrgi inscription (J. A. Fitzmeyer, "The Phoenician Inscription from Pyrgi," 285-97).

[26] Keel, *Die Welt der altorientalischen Bildsymbolik*, 192, figure 290.

[27] *ANEP*, ## 500, 501, and 531. Compare the Babylonian seals collected by W. H. Ward, *Seal Cylinders of Western Asia* (Washington, D.C.: Carnegie Institute, 1910) ## 455-59, 461, and 465, all of which show a god with a trident standing on a bull, and # 468 in which simply the trident appears on the back of the bull. Ward is unable to date the seals but he assigns them to a time following Hammurabi.

El on the one hand and between Yahweh and Baal-Haddu on the other hand. However, in spite of the profound impact ancient conceptualization regarding Baal-Haddu had on the Israelite conceptualization concerning its god Yahweh, the biblical texts offer no evidence that Israelites (or Judahites) perceived Jeroboam's calf images as representations of or as having some association with Baal-Haddu or with any other particular Baal, at least not before the time of Hosea. On the contrary the biblical texts themselves indicate that Jeroboam meant the calf image, in some way, to represent the god who brought Israel out of Egypt. The Hebrew Bible identifies this deity by the name Yahweh or, in two texts, by the name El, but certainly never under the title/name Baal-(Haddu).

One may conclude that Jeroboam employed a symbol readily available in the Canaanite religious context to represent the Israelite deity El=Yahweh, that this iconographic choice was consistent with the customary Canaanite representation of El, and that Jeroboam's cult was Elistic/Yahwistic. In the absence of direct evidence one can hardly conclude that Jeroboam's choice in iconography indicates some kind of "Baalization" of the Yahweh cult.[28]

Several examples of bull iconography which have been found in Palestine serve to illustrate its use in the immediate religious context from which Israel emerged. 1) A ceramic vessel in the shape of a bull, probably a votive object, was recently found at the Middle Bronze level at Shiloh in a storeroom which held other cultic items, including cult stands and votive bowls.[29] 2) During the summer of 1990, excavations of the Middle Bronze IIC level at Ashkelon unearthed a silver plated statuette of a calf lying within its miniature pottery shrine.[30] 3) An elaborate cult stand from Taanach dating to the tenth century BCE exhibits a bull calf in its fourth (top) register.[31] 4) Three bull figures were found at

---

[28] Contrast N. C. Habel (*Yahweh Versus Baal* [New York: Bookmann Associates, 1964] 21) who says in reference to the calf image created by Aaron (Exod 32) that if it represents Yahweh, its most obvious associations are with Baal religion, that Yahweh is being forced into the attire of Baal.

[29] See I. Finkelstein, "Shiloh Yields Some, but Not All of Its Secrets," *BARev* 12 (1986) 29-34.

[30] L. E. Stager, "When Canaanites and Philistines Ruled Ashkelon," *BARev* 17/2 (1991) 25-29.

[31] See R. Hestrin, "The Cult Stand from Taʿanach and its Religious Background," in *Studia Phoenicia V: Phoenicia and the East Mediterranean in the First Millennium B.C.*, ed. E. Lipinski (Orientalia Lovaniensia Analecta 22; Leuven: Uitgeverij Peeters, 1987) 61-77; and *idem*, "Understanding Asherah: Exploring

Megiddo, two from the pre-Israelite period of the 18th-19th dynasty, and one on the surface and hence undated.[32] 5) A broken basalt stela from the Late Bronze II level in Hazor depicts a bull. It matches up with a basalt statue of a god, forming a base for it.[33]

Recently in a remarkable discovery, a small bronze bull figurine was found in Palestine on the top of a high ridge above the ancient road from Dothan to Tirzah. A. Mazar excavated the site and identified it as an open air sanctuary from the early Iron Age.[34] Mazar considers the bull figurine a cultic item of great significance and concludes that Israelites, probably from the tribe of Manasseh, built this cultic site.

Given Mazar's interpretation of this site, the bull figurine offers very significant evidence for the present investigation. As an icon from an early Israelite cultic site it falls into a continuum with the bull icons

Semitic Iconography," *BARev* 17 (1991) 50-59. Hestrin notes the sun-disc above the back of the bull and explains that it symbolized the supreme god in the Mesopotamian, Hittite, and Canaanite pantheons. Hence she concludes that "[t]he young bull represents, or is an attribute of, the chief god of the Canaanite pantheon, Ba'al (who had replaced El, the head of the pantheon in the second millennium BCE)" ("Understanding Asherah," pp. 57-58). Of course, Hestrin's identification depends on her overall interpretation of the relationship between El and Baal-Haddu in second-millennium, West-Semitic religion. C. L'Heureux (*Rank among the Canaanite Gods: El, Ba'al, and the Repha'im* [HSM 21; Missoula: Scholars Press, 1979]) has persuasively argued that El maintained his primacy among the gods of Canaan during the second millennium (cf. Handy, "Dissenting Deities," 19). Then one should interpret that the sun-disc on the cultic stand signifies El and, therefore, that the young bull also represents El (or possibly even Yahweh if the cultic stand was used by Israelites). The presence of attributes of Asherah (tree and lions) on the bottom and on the third registers of the stand would accord with such an identification since from the Ugaritic mythological texts we know of Asherah's frequent and close association with El (but not with Baal-Haddu).

[32] See H. G. May, *Material Remains of the Megiddo Cult* (OIP 26; Chicago: University of Chicago Press, 1935) pl. 34, m 3070, m 2326, m 3032, and comments on pp. 33-34.

[33] See Y. Yadin, "The Fourth Season of Excavations at Hazor," *BA* 32/1 (1959) 5-6. Also, A. Mazar ("Bronze Bull Found in Israelite 'High Place' from the Time of the Judges," *BARev* 9 [1983] 39) offers a photograph of a bronze bull figurine from Late Bronze age Hazor.

[34] A. Mazar, "Bronze Bull," 34-40; and *idem*, "The 'Bull Site'—An Iron Age I Open Cult Place," *BASOR* 247 (1982) 27-42. Mazar's identification of the site as an open air sanctuary has been contested by M. D. Coogan, "Of Cults and Cultures: Reflections on the Interpretation of Archaeological Evidence," *PEQ* 119 (1987) 1-8. Coogan does recognize the bull figurine as a religiously significant artifact, but he thinks it may have had its place in a domestic ritual. For more discussion, see Mazar, "On Cult Places and Early Israelites: A Response to Michael Coogan," *BARev* 15 (1988) 45. The balance of probability seems to lie in Mazar's favor.

found at Shiloh, Megiddo, and Hazor, all of which date to the pre-Israelite era. Moreover, this bull figurine as interpreted by Mazar offers evidence to substantiate that Jeroboam's bull iconography was not an innovation in Israelite religion but that Jeroboam could draw on ancient Israelite precedents dating back to the earliest times of Israel's settlement in the land of Canaan.

Thus it appears likely that Jeroboam, in his installation of the calf images, drew on archaic religious practice known to his subjects from their own religious experience as shaped by their Canaanite religious environment.

### 3. *The Significance of the Calf Image in its Association with the Deity*

This section will inquire regarding the nature of the relationship the calf image bore to El=Yahweh and regarding the meaning of the calf image as a representation of El=Yahweh. This investigation must seek its evidence in the biblical texts, and in addition, in view of the Canaanite context out of which the Israelite cult emerged, the investigation must look for illumination from epigraphic sources or artistic representations pertinent to the calf image in the Canaanite context.

### a. The Relationship between the Signifier and the Signified

In 1929 H. Th. Obbink argued on the basis of the Syrian and Canaanite depictions in which the bull functioned as a base upon which the god Haddu stood that Jeroboam had fashioned the calf images not as Yahweh images but as pedestals above which the invisible Yahweh sat enthroned.[35] W. F. Albright adopted and developed this argument, explaining that the calf images played the same role in the sanctuaries of the Israelite State as the cherubim played in the Jerusalem sanctuary, namely they provided a base for Yahweh's throne, and, furthermore, that both the cherubim and the calf images came to have this significance as the result of the influence of Canaanite iconography. Albright claimed that "[a]mong Canaanites, Aramaeans, and Hittites we find the gods nearly always represented as standing on the back of an animal or as seated on a throne borne by animals—but never as themselves in animal form."[36] Most modern scholars have found the arguments for the

---

[35] "Jahwebilder," 267-68.

[36] *From the Stone Age to Christianity*, 2d ed. (Garden City: Doubleday, 1957) 299.

interpretation of Jeroboam's calf images as pedestals for the invisible Yahweh standing or enthroned on them convincing.[37]

In many Mesopotamian artistic representations animals do function as pedestals upon which the deity stands. Three reliefs already mentioned above (section III.A.2) portray bearded storm-gods bearing three pronged thunderbolts and standing on top of bulls. Often a lion serves the same function especially for the goddess Qudšu (Asherah)[38] but also for Ishtar of Arbela[39] or some other deity.[40] Other animals or composite animals also serve to carry the gods.[41]

Thus the thesis put forward by Obbink and developed by Albright that Jeroboam's calf statues were pedestals for Yahweh carries considerable weight in light of the comparative evidence. Nevertheless, some questions may be raised concerning the precise function of Jeroboam's statues and concerning the suggested analogy with the ark and cherubim.

It is noteworthy that though various gods may be depicted on the backs of various animals, it is usually the storm-god wielding a thunderbolt and often brandishing an axe who stands on top of the bull.[42] But it has been argued above that El=Yahweh and not the storm-god Baal-Haddu is to be associated with the calf image in the cult of the Israelite State. Furthermore, the attested iconography for El consists of

---

[37] E.g., W. Eichrodt, *Theology of the Old Testament*, 2 vols. (OTL; Philadelphia: Westminster, 1961-67) I: 117; Gray, *Kings*, 315; Würthwein, *Könige*, 165; Noth, *Könige*, 284; Cross, *Canaanite Myth and Hebrew Epic*, p. 73, n. 117; and Mettinger, "Veto on Images," 21; but contrast O. Eissfeldt ("Lade und Stierbild," *ZAW* 58 [1940/41] 190-215) who argues that Jeroboam's calf images were actually the crown of a cultic standard which served as a leader symbol. However, his thesis has not gained acceptance.

[38] Thus *ANEP* ## 470-74, all from the second half of the second millennium.

[39] *ANEP* # 522, from Til-Barsib, eighth century.

[40] See *ANEP* # 486, from ʿAmrit in Syria, sixth-fifth century, a god on a lion. See further H. Gressmann, *Altorientalische Bilder zum Alten Testament*, 2d rev. ed. (Berlin and Leipzig: Walter de Gruyter, 1927) ## 331, 338, 345, and 354.

[41] *ANET* # 534, from Asshur in Sennacherib's time, a god on a winged lion with a bull's head. See also # 537, from Maltaya in the time of the Sargonids or Sennacherib, a procession of seven deities on various animals and composite animals.

[42] In addition to the artistic depictions referred to in section III.A.2, see the discussion of the symbols and attributes of the gods in E. D. van Buren, *Symbols of the Gods in Mesopotamian Art* (AnOr 23; Rome: Pontificium Institutum Biblicum, 1945) 67-73 and 159-62; and A. Vanel, *L'iconographie du dieu de l'orage dans le proche-orient ancien jusqu'au VIIe siècle avant J.-C.* (CahRB 3; Paris: J. Gabalda, 1965) especially pp. 31-41.

throne and footstool rather than of the bull as pedestal.[43] Then it may be seriously doubted that the Israelites conceived of the calf images as pedestals upon which El=Yahweh stood. The calf images probably were intended as emblems of El=Yahweh but not specifically as pedestals. Such an interpretation would accord well with the Ugaritic plastic representation in which a powerful bull stands to the back of the god El who is attended by two armed, young men. In this scene the bull evidently constitutes the emblem of El.[44] Similarly, it accords with the fourteenth century statue of a bull calf from Tyre which has been identified as a symbol of El in the discussion above, because this statue also appears to have an emblematic function but not a function as a pedestal.[45]

Some qualification is also required with respect to the analogy suggested by Obbink and Albright between the calf images, on the one hand, and the ark and cherubim, on the other. Unlike the cherubim, the calf images probably did not function as pedestals for the throne of Yahweh. In Mesopotamian iconography, invariably two or four animals together form the pedestal upon which the throne stands.[46] In contrast, according to the biblical text Jeroboam installed the calf images singly at two different shrines. It is doubtful, then, that one should conceive of the calf images in the sanctuaries of the Israelite State specifically in association with El=Yahweh's throne.

However, in at least one very important sense the analogy between the calf image and the cherubim/ark iconography applies. It is evident that both served the function of securing and attesting the active presence of the deity. The biblical texts evidence a presence theology associated with both.[47] Thus, of the ark it was said, "Arise, Oh Yahweh," when it set out, and, "Return, Oh Yahweh," when it rested (Num 10:35-36). And when the Israelites suffered defeat in a war against the Philistines, they decided to take the ark with them for the next engagement in order that Yahweh would go among them (1 Sam 4:3; cf. the Philistine

---

[43] See the discussion of the iconography of El in chapter I above.

[44] See references above in section III.A.2.

[45] Again, see section III.A.2.

[46] Keel, *Jahwe-Visionen und Siegelkunst*, figures 4, 5, 6, 9, 108, 109, 110, 111, 112, 113, and 114.

[47] Cf. W. Zimmerli, "Das Bilderverbot in der Geschichte des alten Israel: Goldenes Kalb, eherne Schlange, Mazzeben und Lade," in *Studien zur alttestamentlichen Theologie und Prophetie: Gesammelte Aufsätze II* (TBÜAT 51; München: Chr. Kaiser, 1974) 249-50.

response, "A god has come into the camp," in 4:7). Similarly when the cultic cry, "Look! your god[s], oh Israel . . . ," is uttered over the calf image, it indicates that that iconography represents the presence of the god. Furthermore, when carried off as booty in war it can be said of both the ark and the calf image that the glory (i.e. the presence of God) has departed from Israel (1 Sam 4:21-22 and Hos 10:5).

A recent essay by T. Jacobsen gives further insight for the question concerning the relationship Israel may have perceived to exist between the calf iconography and the deity represented.[48] Jacobsen demonstrates that the ancient Mesopotamians could, on the one hand, speak of the cultic image as if it were identical with the deity it represented, but, on the other hand, speak of the deity in terms that showed the deity clearly transcended the cultic image. The various depictions in Mesopotamian art also indicate that there was no simple and total identification of the animal symbol with the deity.[49]

These analogies from Mesopotamian art and literature must come into consideration to clarify the significance of the calf images in Israel. Some scholars point to the cultic cry *hinnēh ʾĕlōhêkā yiśrāʾēl ʾăšer heʿĕlûkā mēʾereṣ miṣrayim* (1 Kgs 12:28e) as evidence that Jeroboam's calf image was actually intended or interpreted as a direct representation of God in the shape of a calf. They support their claim using the dubious argument that such a cry would not have been appropriate in reference to a mere pedestal.[50] If one argues this way with regard to the calf images, one should argue similarly that when the Philistines referred to the ark of the covenant with the words *ʾēlleh hēm hāʾĕlōhîm hammakkîm ʾet miṣrayim* ("These are the gods who struck the Egyptians," 1 Sam 4:8) they saw in it a representation of Yahweh in the shape of a box!

Though the formulations in both 1 Kgs 12:28 and 1 Sam 4:8 forbid a rigorous distinction between the cult object and the deity, it is probable that the calf image, like the ark, did not become fully identified with the

---

[48] "The Graven Image," *AIR*, 15-32.

[49] So also Albright, *From Stone Age to Christianity*, 299; Jaroš, *Die Stellung des Elohisten*, 362; and Weippert, "Gott und Stier" *ZDPV* 77 (1961) 106-7.

[50] H. -J. Kraus, *Worship in Israel* (Oxford: Basil Blackwell, 1966) 150; and M. Haran, *Temples and Temple Service in Ancient Israel* (Winona Lake: Eisenbrauns, 1985) p. 29, n. 28.

god it represented. Rather, the images will have "secured and attested to the efficacious presence of the deity at the holy place."[51]

### b. The Divine Attributes Signified

Given that the calf images in the cult of the Israelite State were emblematic of El=Yahweh, one may now inquire what attributes of the deity they represented. In the context of the ancient Near Eastern literature and plastic arts the bull symbol commonly signified two practically inseparable aspects of masculinity, that is, the might of the deity particularly in contexts of battle, and the vigor of the deity in fertility and procreation.[52] It will be argued below that taurine symbolism when applied by Israel to El=Yahweh had this same significance though the biblical texts employ it primarily to depict the strength of the deity.

One could infer from the iconographic representations of storm-gods such as Baal-Haddu standing astride bulls, trident in hand, that taurine imagery in the Syrian and Canaanite context denoted fertility. However, for the purposes of the present investigation, the epithet *tr* ("Bull") as applied to El in the Ugaritic texts holds particular interest. This epithet has a close association with the concept of El as progenitor. Such a connection is apparent in that of the thirty-one times the texts designate El as *tr*, twenty-three of these include the term *'ab* ("father") together with *tr* in an expanded epithet.[53] Moreover, three times the expression "Bull El your father" is paralleled by "Lutpan your sire (*ḥtkk*)."[54] Consistently when *'ab* appears together with *tr* as epithet of El it is determined by a possessive pronominal suffix, the antecedent of which may be either divine or human. Thus the epithet refers to El both as father of the gods and as father of humans. The same is expressed by the epithets *'ab bn 'il* ("father of gods")[55] and *'ab 'adm* ("father of humankind").[56]

In the Ugaritic texts the terminology which signifies El's function as progenitor falls together with that which signifies his function as

---

51 Weippert, "Gott und Stier," 107. Similarly, G. von Rad, *Old Testament Theology*, 2 vols. (Harper & Row, 1962-65) I: 214; and Jaroš, *Die Stellung des Elohisten*, 365, and also n. 4.

52 So Miller, "El the Warrior," 418-19; and Jaroš, *Die Stellung des Elohisten*, 352.

53 Whitaker, *A Concordance of the Ugaritic Literature*, 649-50.

54 *KTU* I.6.iv.10-11; I.1.ii.17-18 in broken text; and I.1.iii.5-6, also in broken text.

55 *KTU* I.40.i.7, 16, 24, 33, 41.

56 *KTU* I.14.i.37, 43; I.14.iii.32, 47; I.14.v.43; I.14.vi.13, 32.

creator.[57] Three times the designation "Bull El his father" has its parallel in the expression "El the king who created him (*dyknnh*),"[58] and twice "Bull El the Kind One" is paralleled by "Creator of Creatures (*bny bnwt*)."[59] Furthermore, in *KTU* I.10.iii.6-7 Baal-Haddu refers to El:

> *kqnym ʿl[m]*
> *kdrd<r> dyknn*
> Indeed our progenitor/creator[60] is eternal
> Indeed everlasting he who formed us.

Thus in the Ugaritic texts El appears as progenitor and creator, and the epithet *tr* associates closely with these concepts. For the present investigation it is of interest that the epithet *tr* always applies to El, never to Baal-Haddu. This corresponds with the distinction between the ways the fertility aspects of these two deities find expression. On the one hand, the texts express the fertility function of Bull El in terms of his fatherhood, i.e., in terms of his progenitive function, and in terms of creation. On the other hand, Baal-Haddu brings fertility primarily through the thunderstorm or through the dew and the mist which render the earth productive.[61]

This perspective on the significance of the *tr* epithet as applied to El at Ugarit may provide a partial background for understanding the significance of the calf symbol as applied to El=Yahweh in the cult of the Israelite State. In fact, at several points the biblical texts show that Israel

---

[57] See J. C. de Moor, "El the Creator," in *The Bible World: Essays in Honor of Cyrus H. Gordon*, ed. G. Rendsburg, R. Adler, M. Arfa, and N. H. Winter (New York: KTAV and the Institute of Hebrew Culture and Education, 1980) 172-77.

[58] *KTU* I.3.v.35-36; I.4.i.4-7; and I.4.iv.47-48.

[59] *KTU* I.4.iii.31-32; I.4.ii.10-11; cf. I.17.i.24-25. Alternatively, one might render this phrase as "Progenitor of the Generations (of the gods)" with de Moor, "El the Creator," 182-83.

[60] De Moor ("El, the Creator," 175-76) has shown that the verb *qny* means both "to have a child" and "to create." The former probably captures its significance in Ashirat's title *qnyt ʾilm* (*KTU* I.4.i.23; I.4.iii.30; I.4.iv.32, etc.) which should be understood in connection with another of her titles *ʾum ʾilm* ("mother of the gods," *KTU* II.31.45) (cf. the same verb used of Eve at childbirth in Gen 4:1). Similarly, in *KTU* I.14.ii.4 the verb *qny* expresses Keret's desire to (be)get sons. The meaning "to create" probably renders *qny* most adequately in the text cited above where it appears in parallel with the intensive stem of *kwn*. However, the Ugaritic texts offer no justification for a sharp distinction between these meanings.

[61] Thus when Keret desires sons it is El who grants him his desire, and when Danel petitions for a son Baal-Haddu can only assist by making intercession on behalf of Danel, but El must grant the petition.

conceptualized its God as progenitor and creator in terms similar to the way in which the Ugaritic texts characterize El.

Several clear points of contact between the characterization of the Israelite deity El=Yahweh and the Ugaritic El appear in the ancient poetry of Gen 49:24-25. In a string of divine epithets this text designates the deity as *ʾăbîr yaʿăqōb* and in a parallel line as *ʾēl ʾăbîkā*. For the interpretation of the former of these epithets one may note that the use of *ʾabbîr* (an equivalent of *ʾăbîr*)[62] in parallel with terminology such as *rĕʾēm*, *ʿēgel*, and *pār* in biblical texts (Isa 34:7, Ps 22:13 and 68:31), and with *rʾum* and *tr* in the Ugaritic texts (*KTU* I.10.iii.20-21, 35-36, and 12.i.31-32) demonstrates clearly the taurine significance of the term. Consequently the combination *ʾăbîr yaʿăqōb* and *ʾēl ʾăbîkā* may be rendered as "Bull of Jacob"[63] and "El your father."[64] This association of epithets parallels the very frequent, though somewhat fluid, Ugaritic formulation *tr ʾabk ʾil* ("The Bull, your father, El") which has been discussed above in connection with El as progenitor and creator.

Thus Gen 49:24-25, like the Ugaritic texts, associates the bull epithet with the concept of divine fatherhood. The assumption that this association of epithets signifies the progenitive or fertility aspect of the deity in the biblical context in the same way as it does in the Ugaritic texts finds confirmation from the context of the epithets in Gen 49:22-26 which goes on to list specifically "the blessings of the breasts and the womb" among the blessings to be conferred on Joseph by the deity.

It bears emphasizing that Gen 49:22-26 pertains to Joseph who, according to the biblical story, is the ancestor of Ephraim and Manasseh, the two most significant tribal groups that later make up the Israelite

---

62 Probably the Massoretes introduced the distinction between *ʾabir* wherever it applies to the god and *ʾabbîr* everywhere else in order to differentiate between the epithet of the god and the common animal term. So B. Vawter, "The Canaanite Background of Genesis 49," *CBQ* 17 (1955) 11.

63 On this interpretation of the epithet see A. Kapelrud, "*ʾabîr*," *TDOT*, I: 42-44; Cross, "*ʾel*," *TDOT*, I: 245; Miller, "El the Warrior," 421; and Jaroš, *Die Stellung des Elohisten*, 366. See also the contrary argument by N. Sarna, "The Divine Title *ʾabhîr yaʿăqôbh*," in *Essays on the Occasion of the Seventieth Anniversary of the Dropsie University*, edited by A. I. Katsch and L. Nemoy (Philadelphia: Dropsie University, 1979) 389-96.

64 The interpretation "El your father" takes into account the evidence of the comparable Ugaritic formulation of the divine name *ʾil* with *ʾab*, in which *ʾab* is usually determined by a possessive personal pronoun. The analogous evidence of these Ugaritic formulae practically excludes the interpretation "God of your father". Cf. Vawter, "The Canaanite Background of Genesis 49," 12-13.

state. Consequently the text with its designation of the deity as ʾābîr and ʾēl quite likely reflects aspects of Israelite religion that stood as direct antecedents to religion as sponsored by Jeroboam. By providing a link between the picture which the Ugaritic texts give of Bull El and the bull symbolism as used in the Israelite context this text offers important illumination regarding the cult sponsored by Jeroboam. It confirms once again the Elistic character of religion at least in the hill country of the Israelite State.

A similar link between El as creator/progenitor at Ugarit and El=Yahweh as creator/progenitor in the Hebrew Bible may be sought in an archaic text at Deut 32:6.[65]

> hălôʾ-hûʾ ʾabîkā qāneka
> hûʾ ʿăśĕkā wayĕkōnĕneka
> Is not he your father, your progenitor?[66]
> He made you, and he created you.

This text offers a remarkable collocation of terms which also appear in the Ugaritic texts in reference to El. In the same way *KTU* I.3.v.35-36 refers to El as ʾab (with a possessive pronominal suffix), and in the parallel colon El becomes the subject of the intensive stem of the verb *kwn* (establish, create):

> ʾany lyṣḥ tr ʾil ʾabh
> ʾil mlk dyknnh
> Loudly he cries out to Bull El his father,
> To El the King who created him.

Moreover, like *KTU* I.10.iii.6-7 (cited above) Deut 32:6 employs the verbs *qnh* (acquire, create, procreate) and *kwn* in reference to the deity as corresponding terms in parallel lines.

---

[65] On the date of this text see O. Eissfeldt, *Das Lied Moses Deuteronomium 32.1-43 und das Lehrgedicht Asaphs Psalm 78; samt einer Analyse der Umgebung des Mose-Liedes* (Berichte über die Behandlungen der Sächsischen Akademie der Wissenschaften zu Leipzig, philologisch-historische Klasse 104, 5; Berlin: Akademie Verlag, 1958); Albright, *Yahweh and the Gods of Canaan*, 15-17; and Robertson, *Linguistic Evidence in Dating Early Hebrew Poetry*, 155.

[66] Since in the second line ʿăśĕkā parallels wayĕkānĕneka synonymously, one may gather on the basis of the structure of the verse that in the first line the term ʾabîka parallels qāneka synonymously. Hence the translation "progenitor" for qāneka is quite fitting. Nevertheless the generative and creative functions, both of which this verb connotes, should be recognized as inextricably connected as the parallelism between the two lines of this verse also suggests.

In a few biblical contexts the root *qnh* appears in direct association specifically with the divine name El. This occurs in the formula *ʾēl ʿelyôn qōnēh šāmayim wāʾāreṣ* ("El Elyon, creator of heavens and earth," Gen 14:19, 22) which closely parallels the divine name *ʾl qn ʾrṣ* ("El, creator of earth")[67] in the bilingual inscription from Karatepe and also the divine name Ilkunirsa ("El, creator of earth") in a Hittite adaptation of a West Semitic myth. The same association occurs in the name of Samuel's father *ʾelqānâ* (1 Sam 1:1). Chapter I above has also noted several details concerning Shiloh and the traditions associated with it that indicate the Elistic nature of its cult. Particularly noteworthy for this context are the Elistic features of the story of Samuel's birth (1 Sam 1). After Hannah makes her petition for a son at the temple of Shiloh, Yahweh acts on her behalf in the same way as El acts on behalf of Kirta and Danel in the Ugaritic myths.[68] In 1 Samuel 1 Yahweh stands as an El figure, and the story itself confirms this in the detail that though Hannah had received this favor from Yahweh she named her son *šĕmûʾēl* ("His name is El"). So the story illustrates the very appropriateness of the name *ʾelqānâ* for Samuel's father. The story suggests that at Shiloh Israel attributed to its deity creative and progenitive functions just as the Ugaritic literature attributes to El.

Now one may add to the foregoing argument that probably the epithet *ʾăbîr yaʿăqōb* originally had a place in the cult at Shiloh alongside the ark and cherubim throne.[69] Furthermore, in consideration of the fact that it was the Shilonite prophet Ahijah that supported Jeroboam's revolt against the Davidic dynasty at Jerusalem, it would appear probable that the Shilonite cult should be viewed as one of the antecedents of and as a significant influence on the Israelite cult as sponsored by

---

[67] *KAI* 26.A.iii.18, and see discussion in chapter I above.

[68] Again, see Seow (*Myth, Drama*, 25-30) for his discussion of the parallels.

[69] So B. C. Ollenburger, *Zion the City of the Great King: A Theological Symbol of the Jerusalem Cult* (JSOTSup 41; Sheffield: JSOT, 1987) 41-2. Ollenburger notes that though the epithet presently has particular connections with the Zion tradition (appearing predominantly in Zion texts: Isa 49:26; 60:16; Ps 132:2, 5; cf. Isa 1:24), it could hardly have its tradition-historical origins there because the name Jacob has no association with Jerusalem from the early period of Israel's emergence in Canaan. Furthermore, he notes the association of the epithet with the ark in Ps 132:2, 5, which is the oldest occurrence of the epithet besides Gen 49:24; and he points out the frequent paralleling of the divine titles "God of Jacob" and "Yahweh of Hosts". Since the ark had an earlier home at Shiloh, and since the title "Yahweh of Hosts" appears to have belonged to the motifs surrounding the ark at Shiloh, one can reasonably posit an earlier use of the epithet *ʾăbîr yaʿăqōb* at Shiloh as well.

Jeroboam. If one draws these connections, it is appropriate that one attempt to understand Jeroboam's calf iconography against the background of the Shilonite cult in which the worshipers referred to their god under the epithet *ʾăbîr yaʿăqōb* and attributed creative and progenitive functions to their god.

The foregoing paragraphs have brought forward evidence that Israel conceptualized its God as progenitor/creator, using terms similar to those used by the Ugaritic texts in reference to Bull El. Moreover, the text in Gen 49:24-25 links this type of conceptualization specifically with the epithet *ʾăbîr yaʿăqōb*, and there is reason to believe that this epithet had a place in the Israelite cult at Shiloh, which, it has been argued, was originally a cult to El. On the strength of this evidence and on the basis of the argument that the cult at Shiloh provided an important antecedent to Israelite religion as sponsored by Jeroboam, one may suggest once again that Jeroboam's calf iconography fell into continuity with symbolization in the earlier Elistic cult of Israel. As such, Jeroboam's calf iconography will have signified fertility functions of the Elistic type.

However, the argument that the Israelites thought of the fertility functions of Yahweh=El in terms of progeniture and creation in continuity with the Ugaritic portrayal of El in no way denies the fact that many biblical texts also depict Yahweh's fertilizing activity using language elsewhere applied to speak of the fertility functions of Baal-Haddu (e.g., Ps 29; 65:10-14=Eng 9-13; 77:17-19=Eng 16-18). It may be that the calf images even suggested to ordinary Israelite worshipers the fertility attributes associated with the various storm-gods, especially with Baal-Haddu in the Canaanite context. However, this inquiry has focused on the official cult of the emergent Israelite State *as sponsored by Jeroboam*. The evidence has indicated a deliberate attempt on the part of Jeroboam to maintain the old Elistic traditions. At the same time, it is probable that in the religion of the Israelite State, epithets and mythic patterns appropriate to Baal-Haddu found their place in the conceptualization concerning El=Yahweh.

In the literature and art of the ancient Near East, taurine symbols also typically signify a second aspect of masculinity, namely strength, especially strength in battle. According to P. D. Miller, "the bull symbol functions as strongly to indicate might and strength as it does to indicate fertility, and may in fact be much more indicative of the former than the latter".[70]

---

[70] "El the Warrior," 425.

With regard to El at Ugarit, though his epithet *tr* has been interpreted above with reference to progenitive functions, it should probably
also be understood as an epithet denoting the might of El. Such an
interpretation finds confirmation in a Ugaritic artistic depiction of El in
which he is accompanied by two identical, fully armed young men, with
a bull following after them.[71] The Ugaritic texts offer a scene which
presents Bull El as a god with such fear inspiring menace and strength
that even Mot cowers before him (*KTU* I.6.vi.26-31):

> *ʾik ʾal yšm[ʿ]k tr ʾil ʾabk*
> *l ysʿ ʾalt tbtk*
> *lyhpk ksʾa mlkk*
> *lytbr ht mtptk*
> *yrʾu bn ʾilm <m>t*
> *ttʿ ydd ʾl gzr*
>
> Yet surely Bull El your father will hear you!
> Indeed he will remove the support of your dwelling!
> Indeed he will overturn the throne of your kingship!
> Indeed he will break the scepter of your rule!
> The Divine Mot was afraid,
> The Beloved of El the hero was in dread.[72]

Another source which may indirectly offer insight into the warrior
might of El is the "Phoenician History" of Sanchuniathon as it has been
preserved by Philo of Byblos according to Eusebius.[73] In this account
Kronos, identifiable with the Canaanite El, enters battle against his
father Uranos to drive him away from his kingship. Kronos=El, with the
support of allies whom the text identifies as Eloim, i.e. the *bn ʾlm* or *běnê*
*ʾělôhîm*, certainly appears as a warrior god in command of an army of
divine beings.

In the Ugaritic myths Baal-Haddu certainly gains much more
prominence than Bull El as a divine warrior, especially in as much as the
texts attribute to him the victories over Yam/Nahar/Leviathan and over
Mot. In describing the contest between Baal-Haddu and Mot, *KTU*
I.6.vi.17-18 employs taurine imagery to signify the might of the
contenders:

---

71 Miller, "El the Warrior," 420; and Schaeffer, "Nouveaux Témoignages du
Culte de El et de Baal," 7-9 and pls. I-III.

72 Compare also *KTU* I.2.iii.15-18 which describes a very similar scene but with
ʿAthtar in place of Mot.

73 *Praeparatio Evangelica* I: 10, para 17-21 in Attridge and Oden, *Philo of Byblos*,
47-51.

*mt ʿz bʿl ʿz*
*ynǵhn krʾumm*

Mot was strong, Baal was strong
They gored each other like wild bulls.

Similar is the depiction of the Devourers who attack Baal-Haddu in the desert (*KTU* I.12.i.30-33):

*bhm qrnm km ṯrm*
*wgbtt km ʾibrm*
*wbhm pn bʿl*

on them are horns like bulls
and humps like buffalo
and against them the face of Baal.

In the outcome of the battle similar terminology describes the vanquished Baal (*KTU* I.12.ii.54-56):

*kn npl bʿl[ ] km ṯr*
*wtkms hd p[ ] km ʾibr*

Thus Baal fell like a bull
and Haddu lay prostrate like a buffalo.

The goddess Anat has a reputation similar to or even greater than Baal-Haddu for her exploits as warrior. The Ugaritic texts credit to her the destruction of Yam/Nahar and of several other divine beings (*KTU* I.3.iii.38-47), the annihilation of Mot (*KTU* I.6.ii.30-37), and an awesome carnage against people at some unspecified location (*KTU* I.3.ii). Her might as warrior can also be described in terms of taurine imagery: *qrn dbʾatk btlt ʿnt qrn dbʾatk*, "the horns of your strength, oh virgin Anat, the horns of your strength" (*KTU* I.10.ii.21-22).

Returning to the Hebrew Bible, it is almost invariable that bull terminology (*ʾabbîr, rěʾēm, šôr, ʿēgel*), when used figuratively, signifies strength whether it is strength in battle or strength to save. Thus Deut 33:17 describes the military prowess of the tribe(s) of Joseph under the metaphor of the bull:

*běkôr šôrô hādār lô*
*wěqarnê rěʾēm qarnāw*
*bāhem ʿammîm yěnaggaḥ*
*yidḥēh[74] ʾapsê měʾereṣ*

---

74 This emendation, suggested by Cross and Freedman ("The Blessing of Moses," 207; cf. *BHS*), requires simply the metathesis of the second and the third

His firstborn bull has majesty,
and his horns are horns of a wild ox.
With them he gores people,
he charges to the ends of the earth.

The idea of a goring horn like that of a wild ox also appears as a symbol of Yahweh's protecting power against the enemy in Ps 92:11, and often the term *qeren* itself functions as a metaphor for might against enemies (1 Sam 2:1, 10; Lam 2:17; Ps 75:11; 89:18, 25) or for saving and protecting strength (2 Sam 22:3=Ps 18:3).

Often in the Hebrew Bible taurine terminology is used as a metaphor for warriors or for powerful, rich nobles.[75] For example Isa 34:6b-7 uses such metaphors in its description of Yahweh's coming slaughter of the armies of Edom:

Indeed Yahweh will hold a sacrifice in Bozrah,
a great slaughter in the land of Edom.
And wild oxen (*rĕʾēmîm*) among them will go down,
And bulls (*pārîm*) among mighty bulls (*ʾabbîrîm*).
Their land will be saturated with blood,
and their soil will grow rich with fat.

The term *ʾabbîr* appears with similar significance in Isa 10:13 as metaphor of the warrior Assyrian king who dethrones kings, and in Ps 22:13 and 68:31 as metaphor of life-threatening enemies.

As stated above, the use of *ʾbr* in parallel with the terms *ʿgl, pr, rʾum*, and *tr* in both the Ugaritic and the biblical texts leaves no doubt as to the primary taurine significance of the term. Comparable to the use of *tr* as an epithet of El at Ugarit, *ʾabîr* occurs several times in the Hebrew Bible as part of the divine title *ʾăbîr yaʿăqōb* (cf. *ʾăbîr yiśrāʾēl*).[76] Each time it serves to emphasize the might of the deity in the context of military conflict. Thus Isa 1:24 reads:

*lākēn nĕʾūm hāʾādôn yhwh ṣĕbāʾôt ʾăbîr yiśrāʾēl*
*hôy ʾennāḥēm miṣṣāray wĕʾinnāqĕmâ mēʾôyĕbāy*

---

letter. The final *hē*, since it is a *mater*, would not have been represented in the original orthography if the poetry indeed dates from the tenth century as Cross and Freedman claim (p. 192).

75 Compare the similar metaphorical use of animal names in Ugaritic literature, especially in *KTU* I.15.iv.6-8, 17-19. See P. D. Miller, "Animal Names as Designations in Ugaritic and Hebrew" *UF* 2 (1970) 178-80.

76 Compare also the personal name *ʾbryhw* attested by one seal of unknown provenance published by N. Avigad, "New Names on Hebrew Seals," *EI* 12 (1975) p. 68, # 7 (in Hebrew).

> Therefore, the oracle of the Lord, of Yahweh Sebaoth,
>      of the Bull of Israel,
> Ah, I will have vengeance on my adversaries,
>      I will be avenged of my enemies.

Isa 49:26 and 60:16 both anticipate the redemption of the exiled Israel when the Bull of Jacob causes reversal on Israel's enemies. Ps 132:2, 5 in its cultic setting belongs with the procession of the ark to Jerusalem after Yahweh, the Bull of Jacob, has had victory over the enemy (e.g., the Philistines as in 2 Sam 5-6).[77] Finally, in Genesis 49:23-25ab the ʾăbîr yaʿăqōb champions Joseph's cause against his enemies:

> wayĕmārărūhû yĕrîbūhû[78]
> wayiśṭĕmūhû baʿălê ṭiṣṣîm
> wattēšeb bĕʾêtān qaštô
> wayyāpōzzû zĕrōʿê yādāw
> mîdê ʾăbîr yaʿăqōb
> miššōmēr benê yiśrāʾēl[79]
> mēʾēl ʾābîka wĕyaʿzĕrekkā
> wĕʾēl[80] šadday wîbērĕkekkē

> They harassed him, they strove against him,
> The archers assailed him fiercely.
> His bow remained firm,
> The arms of his hands were made supple,[81]
> By the Bull of Jacob,[82]
> By the Guardian of the sons of Israel,
> By El your father who strengthens[83] you,
> By El Shaddai who blesses you.

---

[77] See the interpretation of these texts by Seow, *Myth, Drama*, 79-144.

[78] With Samaritan Pentateuch and Greek. So also Cross and Freedman, *Studies in Ancient Yahwistic Poetry*, p. 90, n. 75.

[79] MT does not make sense and it is too long. This reconstruction follows Cross and Freedman (*Studies in Ancient Yahwistic Poetry*, pp. 90-91, n. 77) in recognizing a conflation of two original variants *miššōmēr* and *mērôʿê* in the first two words of the line, *miššām rōʿeh* and in emending ʾeben to bĕnê.

[80] With some Hebrew manuscripts, Samaritan, Peshitta. Greek reads *ho theos ho emos*. So Cross and Freedman, *Studies in Ancient Yahwistic Poetry*, p. 91 n. 79.

[81] This colon and the one preceding are obscure. The Greek here suggests that the hostile archers are discomfited by the Strong One of Jacob.

[82] On the basis of the argument above regarding the meaning of taurine imagery in the Hebrew Bible, the NRSV translation, "the Mighty One of Jacob," must be judged to have correctly captured the sense of the epithet though it does not translate the epithet itself.

[83] Taking ʿzr as root II with Miller, "El the Warrior," p. 421, n. 36, and *idem*, "Ugaritic GZR and Hebrew ʿZR II," *UF* 2 (1970) 159-75.

This survey of the employment of taurine symbols and metaphors in the Hebrew Bible has demonstrated their use to signify might in battle or power to save and to preserve. It bears emphasizing that the Hebrew Bible, when it employs the terms ʾabbîr, šôr, rĕʾēm, ʿegel, and pār in a non-literal sense, employs them predominantly to connote strength.[84]

At this point it should be noted again that the formula at 1 Kgs 12:28e, like the nearly identical formula at Exod 32:4d, connects the calf iconography specifically with the Exodus from Egypt. With regard to the calf image in Exodus 32, J. G. Janzen has argued convincingly that it symbolizes the divine warrior and protector who brought about the Exodus.[85] Janzen draws evidence from various aspects in the literary context of Exodus 32, a few of which may be considered here. A central theme running throughout the book of Exodus has to do with Yahweh's deliverance of Israel from Egypt, a deliverance Yahweh accomplishes through the agency of Moses. This deliverance has a prominent martial character. Yahweh intervenes as "the warrior" (15:3) whose angel serves as commander "going before the Israelite army" (14:19; cf. 13:21; 32:34; 33:2). Within this larger context, the narrative in Exodus 32 opens with a statement about the people's concern over the long absence of Moses, a quasi-military commander "who brought [Israel] up out of the land of Egypt." It is on account of this absence that the people request that Aaron make ʿĕlōhîm "who shall go before" Israel, evidently to carry on the martial leadership Yahweh has fulfilled through the agency of Moses. If this is a correct reading of Exodus 32, then the assumption lies close at hand that Jeroboam intended the calf iconography to re-present El=Yahweh's strength as displayed in the battle against the Egyptians and to symbolize El=Yahweh's continuing power to save Israel. This employment of the symbolism follows altogether consistently with the way the Hebrew Bible generally uses the taurine imagery. In view of

---

[84] This is also true of those few biblical references with taurine figures of speech which did not enter the discussion above. In Job 24:22 ʾabbîr serves as a metaphor for the mighty. Jer 46:21 designates Egypt's mercenary soldiers as kĕʿeglê marbēq, i.e. like well fed bull calves. This is an ironic way of describing the vulnerability of those who should offer defense for the nation. Mal 3:20 holds forward the expectation that those who fear Yahweh will "go forth leaping like bull calves" to "tread down the wicked." Finally, Ps 29:6 celebrates the power of the storm-god's voice by likening its effect on the mountains to the romping of the ʿegel or the rĕʾēm.

[85] "The Character of the Calf and Its Cult in Exodus 32," CBQ 52 (1990) 597-607, but particularly 599-600.

this, one may wonder why Jeroboam's cult images should ever have met with opposition in Israel.

With respect to that opposition against the cult employing the calf iconography, some commentators have claimed that the criticism arose on account of its perceived derivation from idolatrous Canaanite practice. These commentators sense that in Exod 32:6 the words, "the people . . . rose up to play (leṣaḥēq)," are intended to criticize the cult around the calf by ascribing to it a kind of sexual orgy common in Canaanite fertility rites.[86] They base this interpretation of leṣaḥēq on the use of the D-stem of ṣḥq in contexts such as Gen 26:8 and 39:14, 17. However, even if Gen 26:8 and 39:14, 17 allow for such an interpretation of the verb, a more suitable analogy for the use of the D-stem ṣḥq in Exod 32:6 may be found in the use of the D-stem śḥq in 2 Sam 6:5, 21 (cf. 1 Chr 13:8, 15:29).[87]

Exod 32:6 with its context finds an appropriate comparison in 2 Sam 6:5, 21 with its context because both texts describe the celebration of a religious festival. According to Exod 32:5 the celebration occurs at a feast to Yahweh while in 2 Samuel 6 David's transfer of the ark to Jerusalem gives occasion for celebration. Now there is good reason to doubt that the use of the participle mĕśaḥăqîm in 2 Sam 6:5, 21 is meant to imply criticism of the celebration described there, or even that the activity depicted has anything to do with sexual orgies or fertility rites that might have an analogy in Canaanite rites.[88] Rather, the participle

---

[86] Noth, *Exodus*, 248; B. S. Childs, *The Book of Exodus* (otl; Philadelphia: Westminster, 1974) 556 and 566; R. W. L. Moberly, *At the Mountain of God: Story and Theology in Exodus 32-34* (jsotsup 22; Sheffield: jsot Press, 1983) 46; and scholars cited by J. M. Sasson, "The Worship of the Golden Calf," in *Orient and Occident: Essays Presented to Cyrus H. Gordon on the Occasion of his Sixty-Fifth Birthday*, ed. H. A. Hoffner, Jr. (aoat 22; Neukirchen-Vluyn: Neukirchener Verlag, 1973) 152.

[87] Probably these should not be understood as two different roots with similar meanings but as one root with alternative spellings, the first of which occurs only in the Book of Genesis and in Exod 32:6 while the other occurs throughout the rest of the Hebrew Bible. This judgment finds confirmation in Judg 16:25 where ṣḥq and śḥq (both in D-stem) occur with the identical significance, and in the datum that the lxx, in the vast majority of cases, translates these verbs with either *paizō* or *empaizō*.

[88] So McCarter, *II Samuel*, pp. 188-89 and also 180-82. In fact, one should begin by questioning whether such orgiastic rites existed in the Canaanite cult. According to J. Gray ("Social Aspects of Canaanite Religion," in *Volume du Congrès: Genève 1965* [vtsup 15; Leiden: E. J. Brill, 1966] 192) "the licentious rites of imitative magic . . . , incidentally, are not conspicuously in evidence in the Canaanite myths of the fertility cult." Further, see D. R. Hillers, "Analyzing the Abominable: Our Understanding of

*měšaḥăqîm* in 2 Sam 6:5, 21 probably denotes a victory dance, in this case a victory dance on the occasion of the procession of the victorious divine warrior towards the new sanctuary in Jerusalem.[89] By analogy, it is most improbable that the verb *lěṣaḥēq* in Exod 32:6 denotes sexual orgies or fertility rites. On the contrary, as the formula in Exod 32:4b=1 Kgs 12:28e suggests, the celebration around the golden calf focused on the great might of the deity as displayed in the battle against Egypt and in the deliverance of Israel. From the use of the verb *lěṣaḥēq* in Exod 32:6 one should probably conclude that the cult around the golden calf included a victory dance in commemoration of this constitutive event.[90]

Like Exod 32:1-6 and 1 Kgs 12:28, Num 23:22 (cf. 24:8) also associates taurine imagery with the Exodus from Egypt. Thus it gives independent attestation to the theme implied by the former texts that bull-like strength was required to bring Israel up from Egypt. Significantly Num 23:22 identifies the deity as El:

> *ʾēl môṣîʾām mimmiṣrāyim*
> *kětôʿăpōt rěʾēm lô*
> El brought them out of Egypt;
> He has strength like a wild ox.

Grammatically some ambiguity exists as to the one having the strength of a wild ox. However, the 3 m.s. suffix with the preposition *l* (second line, 22b) must refer to El, because in the context of this verse the second line would have no sense unless the strength were El's. Certainly the verse does not celebrate Israel's self-deliverance, and it does not glorify Israel's strength. It is El who brought Israel out of Egypt because El has the strength of a wild ox.[91]

---

Canaanite Religion," *JQR* 75 (1985) 258; and Sasson, "The Worship of the Golden Calf," 152.

[89] See Seow (*Myth, Drama*, 93-97) for a discussion of the evidence for this meaning of *měšaḥăqîm*. He adduces evidence from the use of this root in 1 Sam 18:6-7, Jer 31:4b, Zech 8:5, Ps 2:4-6, and Ps 59:5-9. See also the evidence adduced by Sasson ("The Worship of the Golden Calf") who argues that the activities depicted both by Exod 32:6 and 2 Sam 6:5, 21 consisted of a ritual banquet followed by music, acrobatic feats, and dramatic performances in honor of the deity whose emblems have just been presented.

[90] For additional arguments to similar conclusions see Janzen, "The Character of the Calf and Its Cult in Exodus 32," 600-602.

[91] Thus also Mettinger, "The Veto on Images," 19. For a different argument towards a similar conclusion see H. Rouillard, *La péricope de Balaam* (Études Bibliques, ns 4; Paris: J. Gabalda, 1985) 292-300. For another perspective compare

Num 23:22 (cf. 24:8) holds particular significance for the argument being developed here because it names a deity, El, with whom the bull imagery is brought into association in a context which clearly shows that the imagery signifies the might of the deity. Thus this text offers additional confirmation of the foregoing interpretation that the calf iconography in the cult of the Israelite State was intended to represent the attribute of the warrior might of El=Yahweh, particularly in commemorating the Exodus of Israel from Egypt.

As has often been observed, at several places the presentation of the Reed Sea event in the Hebrew Bible (e.g., Exod 15:1-18; Isa 51:9-10; cf. Ps 74:12-17) corresponds in significant ways with the myths of Anat's and Baal-Haddu's exploits against Yam/Nahar/Leviathan. It appears probable that Jeroboam and his priests readily appropriated aspects of that mythology for El=Yahweh, though one can hardly isolate particular biblical texts as reflective of the cult in the Israelite State to prove that this was the case.

### 4.  Implications and Conclusions

In this context one might raise a question about the appropriateness of the fairly frequent claim (or even value-laden charge) that Jeroboam with his calf iconography moved towards syncretism between Yahweh religion and Canaanite religion (particularly the fertility religion of Baal-Haddu).[92]

In the first place, to speak of syncretism in this connection presupposes that Yahwism as a religion was from the beginning radically distinct from Canaanite religion, a notion that grows naturally enough out of the long-held infiltration or conquest theories according to which Israel with its worship of Yahweh originated and entered from outside Canaan. However, under the impact of criticisms raised by more recent sociological and anthropological models, these views require considerable modification, and the lines of continuity in terms of culture and religion from pre-Israelite Canaan to Israelite Canaan are becoming more and more evident. A reconstruction of the origins of Yahwism along the lines argued by Cross according to whom Yahweh originated as an El figure serves to underline the emergence of Yahweh "out of the

---

Albright ("The Oracles of Balaam," p. 215 n. 47) who claims that the taurine imagery of v. 22b refers to Israel, though he offers no argument to substantiate his claim.

[92] Gray, Kings, 315; Eichrodt, Theology of the Old Testament, I: 117; and by implication, Würthwein, Könige, 165.

gods"[93] of Canaan. Alternatively, one may follow Eissfeldt in seeing an identification between the Yahweh of a late immigrant group and the El already worshiped by Israelite inhabitants of Canaan and see a resulting fusion of distinct but compatible deities, El and Yahweh. If one takes either of these perspectives one must immediately question language that refers to Jeroboam's initiatives with the golden calves as syncretistic.

Furthermore, to charge, as Eichrodt does,[94] that the calf image defined Yahweh's nature one-sidedly as that of a vegetation deity, and that it involved an increasingly materialistic conception of God also runs contrary to both the probable historical development of ideas and the biblical historian's own comments with regard to Jeroboam's calf images. On the one hand, it presupposes that Yahwism had known a less materialistic conception of god. On the other hand it contradicts even the witness of DtrH according to whom the calf represented the deity who brought Israel out of Egypt and by whom the calf image never was opposed for supposedly representing the vegetation deity.

This section has sought to demonstrate 1) the tight association of the calf image with that very prominent god in Israel's experience who brought them out of Egypt, namely El identified with Yahweh; 2) that the calf symbol with its dual connotations for fertility and strength was readily available in the Canaanite context; and 3) that the calf symbol as used by Israel in reference to its deity shows lines of continuity with the manner in which the Ugaritic texts symbolize El in particular. Thus it has been argued that the symbol in reference to Israel's deity signified creative and progenitive functions, but above all that it signified the god's might in battle and power to save. Considering that Jeroboam installed the calf images in old and venerable sanctuaries at Bethel and Dan, the conclusion that lies nearest at hand is that Jeroboam did nothing innovative when he installed the calf images but that he gave official sponsorship to the traditional Israelite worship of El=Yahweh.

---

93 P. D. Miller, "God and the Gods: History of Religion as an Approach and Context for Bible and Theology," *Affirmation* 1/5 (1973) 48.

94 *Theology of the Old Testament*, I: 117. Compare also N. C. Habel, *Yahweh Versus Baal*, 21.

## B. The Establishment of Royal Sanctuaries
### at Bethel and Dan

A note in 1 Kgs 12:29 offers the information that Jeroboam installed his two newly manufactured calf images at the two sanctuaries in Bethel and Dan. Though a few critical questions about the historical reliability of the claim made with respect to Dan will require consideration, the more engaging questions for the historian of religion arise because of what this brief note leaves unsaid. Why did Jeroboam choose these particular places for the installation of his cult images? Did these installations signify that Jeroboam had appointed these two particular sanctuaries to a new and unique status among the various sanctuaries in the Israelite State? Alternatively, did these installations represent particular measures taken on behalf of these two sanctuaries while other measures of equal importance were taken for other sanctuaries in the Israelite State? Finally, if Jeroboam's newly fashioned cult images actually had so significant a role in the cult sponsored by Jeroboam as 1 Kgs 12:26-28 implies, why did Jeroboam not reserve the prestige of such an installation for a central royal sanctuary in his capital city? These questions will provide the basic focus for the investigation below.

### 1. *An Historical-Critical Evaluation of 1 Kgs 12:29*

Regarding the historical reliability of 1 Kgs 12:29, on the one hand E. Nielsen has questioned whether the reference to Dan actually belonged to the original text,[95] and on the other hand H. Motzki followed by E. Würthwein suspects that the mention of Dan alongside Bethel is simply a fiction intended to disparage Jeroboam's cult as idolatrous.[96] These kinds of doubts regarding 1 Kgs 12:29 arise in part from the datum that while various biblical texts give ample confirmation that Bethel existed as an important sanctuary, even as a royal sanctuary during the period of the Israelite State (Amos 7:13, 4:4, 5:5; Hos 10:5), no comparable biblical evidence attests to the existence of an important sanctuary at Dan during this same period, aside from the note under question in 1 Kgs 12:29 (cf. 2 Kgs 10:29).

---

[95] *Shechem: A Traditio-Historical Investigation* (Copenhagen: G. E. C. Gad, 1955) 195-96.

[96] H. Motzki, "Ein Beitrag zum Problem des Stierkultes in der Religionsgeschichte Israels," *VT* 25 (1975) 475-76; Würthwein, *Könige*, 164; cf. Montgomery, *Kings*, 255.

From the story fragment in 1 Kgs 12:26-28 Nielsen notes that Jeroboam feared he would lose the loyalty of his Israelite subjects if they continued to make pilgrimage to Jerusalem, and that in order to resolve his problem Jeroboam established attractive sanctuaries at both Bethel and Dan to replace the Jerusalem sanctuary for his subjects. Nielsen thinks that this explanation fits logically for Bethel since Bethel lay near to the highway leading to Jerusalem, but the explanation does not suit for the establishment of a sanctuary at Dan because of its location far from Jerusalem. Consequently Nielsen doubts that the reference to Dan actually belonged to the original text. He argues that the text originally spoke only of the installation of a single calf at Bethel and of a ritual procession as far as Dan to present the image to the population. Later someone misinterpreted the text to mean that Jeroboam had installed a golden calf at Dan as well as at Bethel.

One may respond to Nielsen's argument by asking what in vv. 26-29 suggests that proximity to Jerusalem was the only important criterion in Jeroboam's selection of sanctuaries. One need not assume that Jeroboam's whole intent was to intercept pilgrims on their way to Jerusalem. Rather, Jeroboam may have considered other criteria such as the venerability of a sanctuary or the convenience of a location more accessible to subjects living in the Galilean region.[97]

Even so, one might still question whether in historical fact Jeroboam took any measures for the sanctuary at Dan. Perhaps, as Motzki and Würthwein have suggested, Jeroboam's action pertained only to Bethel, but the author of 1 Kgs 12:29 mentioned Dan alongside Bethel in order to disparage Jeroboam's cult as poly-Yahwistic in that it fragmented the cult of Yahweh through the multiplicity of shrines. In response to such a claim one may ask why the author should resort to fabrication. Other biblical sources confirm the multiplicity of Yahwistic cult centers in the Israelite State (Amos 4:4, 5:5; cf. Hos 4:15). Hence the author of 1 Kgs 12:29 could just as well have named an existent cult center such as Gilgal alongside Bethel to make the insinuation that Jeroboam had fragmented the Yahwistic cult.

---

97 The text of v. 30b appears to be damaged in that the *hāʾeḥād* requires a balancing *hāʾeḥād*. Nielsen (*Shechem*, 196) overcomes this difficulty by reconstructing as the original reading of vv. 29-30, "And he placed the calf (*hᵉgl* [instead of *hāʾeḥād*]) at Bethel, and the people went in procession before it even unto Dan." Such a reading is appropriate for Nielsen's historical reconstruction, but it is highly conjectural and without support from the ancient manuscripts and versions.

Material evidence from Tel Dan enhances the credibility of the biblical report concerning Jeroboam's activity at the sanctuary of Dan.[98]
Excavations carried out under the direction of A. Biran have unearthed a
monumental platform structure which Biran identified as a *bāmâ* (an
open air sanctuary) set within a larger sacred area.[99] Biran dated the
construction of the platform to the tenth or early ninth centuries on the
basis of pottery, and he surmised that Jeroboam I may have built it.[100]
Admittedly nothing in the material record firmly links this building
activity with Jeroboam. Nevertheless, the size of the structure indicates
that the sanctuary was one of considerable importance. Possibly the
sanctuary at Dan had already been built up in this way and had already
achieved prominence before the time of Jeroboam. Then it would have
been reasonable for Jeroboam to incorporate it into his religious program because of its significance. On the other hand, it is also conceivable
that Jeroboam may have sponsored a building program at the sanctuary
of Dan to render it suitable for his needs, and the material remains may
give silent record of that activity.

----

[98] For preliminary reports on excavations at Tel Dan see A. Biran, "Twenty
Years of Digging at Tel Dan," *BAR* 13 (1987) 12-25; *idem*, "Dan," in *Archaeology and
Biblical Interpretation: Essays in Memory of D. Glenn Rose*, ed. L. G. Perdue, L. E.
Toombs, G. L. Johnson (Atlanta: John Knox, 1987) 101-111; and annual issues of *BA*
and *IEJ* since 1974.

[99] For the identification of this site as a sanctuary one may mention a horned
altar found at the site. Since clear stratigraphic evidence was lacking, Biran dated it
to the 9th century or earlier on typological bases, comparing it to an altar from Tell
Beit Mirsim dated by Albright to the 11th-10th centuries (Biran, "An Israelite
Horned Altar at Dan," *BA* 37 [1974] 107). A rectangular building to the west of the
"high place" yielded several stone altars, two iron shovels, and ashes from bones.
This building was probably built in the 8th century and attests to the ongoing cultic
activity at the site (Biran, "Notes and News: Tel Dan, 1984," *IEJ* 35 [1985] 187-88; and
"The Dancer from Dan, the Empty Tomb and the Altar Room," *IEJ* 36 [1986] 179-87).

[100] For Biran's discussion of the *bāmâ* see "Tel Dan," *BA* 37 (1974) 40-43; "Tell
Dan Five Years Later," *BA* 43 (1981) 175-76; and "Dan," in *Archaeology and Biblical
Interpretation*, 108-9. Biran determined that building on the platform structure had
taken place in three stages. The first of these stages had been destroyed by fire. For
the dating of this stage Biran drew on the evidence of tenth century pottery which
had been found in the layer of ash from the destruction of the first stage and pottery
of the mid-ninth century which was found under the masonry of the second stage.
Dating the end of the first stage at latest to the mid-ninth century also found confirmation in the datum that the masonry of the second stage was of the same style as
that of the monumental buildings at Samaria and Megiddo, attributable to the
Omrides. Hence Biran thinks that the most likely period for the construction of the
first stage would be the reign of Jeroboam I.

The material evidence of a significant cultic structure at Dan dating to approximately the time of Jeroboam lends plausibility (but does not prove) the biblical claim that Jeroboam took action on behalf of the sanctuary at Dan by installing a calf image there. To further underline this plausibility, one may note that the importance of the Danite shrine is also underlined by the fact that traditions concerning its establishment have been preserved in the Hebrew Bible at Judges 17-18.[101] Also, from Amos 8:14 one may gather that the cult at Dan enjoyed some prominence in the Israelite State. That text refers to the presumably popular Israelite practice of swearing by the deities of well known sacred places such as Dan, Beersheba, or Samaria.

The arguments against the historical reliability of the information offered in 1 Kgs 12:29 are not persuasive. The balance of probability favors the conclusion that Jeroboam did pay some attention to the sanctuary at Dan. /

## 2. *The Status of Bethel and Dan as Royal Sanctuaries*

In the time of Amos, Amaziah the priest could designate Bethel as *miqdaš melek* ("a royal sanctuary") and *bêt mamlākâ* ("a temple of <the> kingdom") (Amos 7:13). Considering the claims of 1 Kgs 12:29, it is reasonable to think that Jeroboam as the first king of the Israelite State gave Bethel this status and that his installation of the calf image may have been a step taken in preparing the sanctuary to make it suitable for its new role. Jeroboam reportedly did the same for the sanctuary at Dan. Then Jeroboam elevated both Bethel and Dan to a new status as royal sanctuaries.

Perhaps 1 Kgs 12:31a with its note about Jeroboam's temple (*bêt bāmôt*) building program also alludes to Jeroboam's initiatives at Bethel or at both Bethel and Dan. Though the meaning of this note is somewhat obscure[102] it is possible that the temple building of which it speaks

---

[101] See the discussion of this text in section IV.B below.

[102] As de Vaux (*The Bible and the Ancient Near East*, 105) explains, since the phrase *wayyaʿaś ʾet-bêt bāmôt* has the sign of the direct object, it could mean that *bêt bāmôt* is a proper noun, possibly the name of Jeroboam's temple at Bethel (cf. the place name *btbmt* in Mesha's inscription, *ANET*, 320, after line 25). However, de Vaux's solution is not altogether compelling when one considers the total lack of evidence elsewhere for the naming of a temple at Bethel and the frequency with which undetermined accusatives occur with the sign of the direct object. (Twenty-one examples are listed in *GKC*, section 117.d.) Then perhaps one should rather consider *bêt bāmôt* as two common nouns in construct and compare the formulation *bêt habbāmôt* in 2 Kgs 17:29, 32. As for the problematic singular *bêt* before the plural

constituted part of Jeroboam's overall program in refurbishing Bethel or in refurbishing both Bethel and Dan to suit them as royal religious centers.

On the other hand, 1 Kgs 12:31a allows for another interpretation because it does not specify that the temple building took place at Bethel or at Dan. Possibly the temple building occurred at several other sanctuaries in which case Bethel and Dan may have been only a part of a network of royal religious centers established by Jeroboam. Certainly texts such as 1 Kgs 13:32; 2 Kgs 17:29, 32; 23:19 support such an interpretation because they suggest that temples stood in various cities of the Israelite State. However, these texts belong to the editorial work of DtrH, and their intention may simply be to reproach the Israelite State for its multiple sanctuaries. Consequently one cannot rely on their evidence very heavily.

In seeking to explain why Jeroboam chose Bethel and Dan as royal sanctuaries, a partial answer may be that Jeroboam sought old and respected sanctuaries that had long associations with Israelite worship, and that Bethel and Dan presented themselves as suitable options.

In the case of Bethel, biblical tradition gives it a double claim to legitimacy as a cultic site by attributing the establishment of its sanctuary both to Abram (Gen 12:8; 13:3-4) and to Jacob (Gen 28:10-22 and 35:1-7). Furthermore, in the early Israelite period the sanctuary at Bethel housed the ark for a time (Judg 20:27). Also, Samuel's circuit included Bethel along with three other cult sites at Gilgal, Mizpah, and Ramah. But long before Israelite times Bethel was already a holy place (at which time its name was Luz [Judg 1:23]). The very long history of Bethel as a holy place appears to have been confirmed archaeologically. Excavators have found a building in what they labelled a Middle Bronze I stratum, and this building they have identified as a temple. Moreover, this building was built immediately above a bedrock high place.[103] Thus, in choosing Bethel as a sanctuary of the state, Jeroboam aligned himself with ancient and honored sacral traditions that reached back into Israel's earliest history and, beyond that, into the pre-Israelite history of the city.

---

*bāmôt*, it could perhaps be corrected to *battê habbāmôt* (apparently presupposed by the Greek and Vulgate). This agrees with the construction used in 1 Kgs 13:32 and 2 Kgs 23:19. If this is the correct understanding of the phrase in 1 Kgs 12:31, then the reference could be to several temples that Jeroboam built.

[103] So Kelso, *The Excavation of Bethel*, 22. The evidence that the bedrock had served as a high place consists of animal blood stains on the surface of the rock, some animal bones, and some rock surface and stones that appeared to have been subjected to very hot fire (p. 20).

For the sanctuary at Dan the story in Judges 17-18 makes the claim that the Danites established it at the time they took the city by conquest from its former inhabitants (at which time its name was Laish [Judg 18:29]). Excavations of this city confirm that it was already a city state of considerable importance in the third millennium BCE, so presumably it will also have had its own sanctuary before Israelite times even though it has not yet been found.[104] Hence, for Dan the biblical text in Judges 17-18 alone gives clear testimony to its long history as a holy place. Evidently, in his choice of Dan, Jeroboam again selected a recognized sanctuary to serve an official function for the state.

Thus there is good reason to think that Jeroboam chose Bethel and Dan in part because of the venerable cultic traditions associated with them. Another reason for Jeroboam's choice of Bethel in particular might be sought in 1 Kgs 12:26-28 if one understands the implication of v. 27 to be that Jeroboam sought to make Bethel attractive in order to lure aside pilgrims who might otherwise journey on to the temple at Jerusalem via the north-south highway running just east of Bethel.[105] Though there may be an element of truth in this explanation, one should recognize that vv. 26-28 certainly makes an overstatement, and it does so from a Jerusalemite point of view as has been argued above.[106] Possibly Jeroboam did wish to foster a more distinct break between Israel and Judah, though that break already existed. However, Jeroboam's more urgent concern will have been to identify royal sanctuaries marking the jurisdiction of the Israelite State and to establish an official cult that would serve to give identity and unity to the new state. For these purposes the sanctuaries of Bethel and Dan probably presented themselves as very suitable because of their ancient and revered cultic traditions.

Though the foregoing considerations give plausible explanations for Jeroboam's selection of Bethel and Dan as royal sanctuaries, another question still requires resolution. In elevating Bethel and Dan as royal sanctuaries, did Jeroboam give them a unique status among all the sanctuaries in the Israelite State? If so, Jeroboam's actions would contrast rather sharply (at least by all appearances) with the Davidic and

---

[104] Biran ("Twenty Years of Digging at Tel Dan," 18) explains that excavations have not proceeded below the remains of the Israelite sanctuary. That would be the likely spot to look for an older pre-Israelite sanctuary.

[105] So Hahn, Das "Goldene Kalb", 345; Nielsen, Shechem, 195; and A. Šanda, Die Bücher der Könige (EHAT 9; Münster: Aschendorffsche Verlagsbuchhandlung, 1911) 343.

[106] See chapter II.

Solomonic strategy of establishing the royal sanctuary in the political capital. Neither Bethel nor Dan became Jeroboam's capital.

By appointing Jerusalem as both the political and the religious center of the Kingdom, David and Solomon launched a powerful impetus towards centralization of power in Jerusalem and in the King. Such a collocation of the central religious and central political institutions as essential aspects of the administration in the capital city was typical in the ancient Near East. Of its ideological grounding and practical significance G. W. Ahlström writes:

> The cosmological aspect of the city has its roots in the idea of the city as the abode of the god, the ruler of cosmos and nation. Because the temple as the visible expression of his domain, was, at the same time, the king's property, the capital was the ruling center of both the god and his vice regent (Akkad. *sakkanakku*), the king. *Therefore, temple and palace should be seen as two aspects of the same phenomenon; together they constituted the essence of the state.*[107]

One would expect that Jeroboam, as God's vice-regent over the Israelite State, would also wish to locate his own palace and royal court in a city where Yahweh was known to dwell. Jeroboam's apparent pursuit of a policy different from this calls for explanation.

The explanation has been advanced that in selecting two sanctuaries at Bethel and Dan as royal sanctuaries Jeroboam showed that he aligned himself with a popular impetus against the policy of centralizing power in the king and in his capital.[108] According to this explanation, Jeroboam and Israel had rebelled on ideological grounds against the absolutism of the administration developed by David and Solomon. That administration had imposed an onerous burden in taxation, corvée labor, and conscription in order to erect the monumental buildings in the capital, to support its administration, and to support the military machinery required for imperial expansion and defense. In contrast, the new Israelite State under Jeroboam had a less centralized administration that would not require a central sanctuary in the capital city, nor even a capital city but only a royal residence city.[109]

---

[107] *Royal Administration and National Religion in Ancient Palestine* (Leiden: E. J. Brill, 1982) 3-4 (emphasis mine). See also F. S. Frick, *The City in Ancient Israel* (SBLDS 36; Missoula: Scholars Press, 1977) 86 and context.

[108] So Hahn, *Das "Goldene Kalb"*, 345; and J. P. J. Olivier, "In search of a Capital for the Northern Kingdom," *JNSL* 11 (1983) 131.

[109] Olivier, "In Search of a Capital," 117-32.

The foregoing explanation has its foundations in the presupposition of an ideological conflict between Israel and Judah regarding kingship and statehood. More specifically, since the selection of a capital and the policies concerning it would most likely be determined at the royal court, this explanation presupposes that even the Israelite king and his royal court based their administrative policies on a political ideology fundamentally different from that of the Judahite king and his royal court.

For such a distinction between Israelite and Judahite ideologies one might appeal to various studies in modern scholarship. Olivier, for instance, notes Alt's distinctions between the ideology of dynastic kingship in Jerusalem and that of charismatic kingship in Israel.[110] Also, he points to the distinction argued by Cross between the ideology of kingship by eternal decree in Jerusalem and the ideology of conditional kingship in Israel.[111] Furthermore, Olivier appeals to Buccellati's distinction between the national state and the territorial state.[112] According to Buccellati the associative bonding of the population in the territorial state arises from the common territory it inhabits around the city-state which is its capital, and from their common allegiance to one king. Unlike the territorial state, in the national state the associative bonding depends on factors such as kinship, national history, common heritage, and common religion; and because the national state is determined in this way it does not depend on a central capital or on kingship for its unity to the same degree as does the territorial state. Olivier concludes, then, that the Israelite state with its ideology of a charismatically and conditionally appointed king fits the model of the more decentralized national state whereas the absolutist, imperial government of David and Solomon at Jerusalem resembled the expanded territorial model.

This argument that Judah and Israel followed fundamentally different ideologies is open to several criticisms. First, Buccellati himself does not characterize the Davidic-Solomonic kingdom as an expanded territorial state. To the contrary, he considers it a national state. Indeed, if national history, common heritage, and kinship are key determining factors for the identity of the national state, then one must recognize the

---

[110] Olivier, "In Search of a Capital," 130, referring to Alt, "The Monarchy in the Kingdoms of Israel and Judah," 239-59.

[111] *Canaanite Myth and Hebrew Epic*, 219-73.

[112] Buccellati, *Cities and Nations*, 11-135.

role these factors played in grounding the Davidic-Solomonic kingdom, as for example, in the undergirding role the Yahwistic narrative plays in telling the common history that binds together various patriarchs in kinship relationship as ancestors to the people of that kingdom. Thus Buccellati does not distinguish typologically between the Davidic-Solomonic kingdom and the Israelite kingdom, nor between the Judahite kingdom and the Israelite kingdom. In Buccellati's opinion, they were all national states. Second, Alt's distinction between dynastic kingship in Jerusalem and charismatic kingship in Israel has proven untenable in light of various more recent analyses.[113] Finally one must question to what extent the two different kingship ideologies as described by Cross actually found concrete expression in the independent political histories of Israel and Judah.

---

[113] See Buccellati, *Cities and Nations*, 195-212 and the literature cited there. To this one may add T. Ishida, *The Royal Dynasties in Ancient Israel* (BZAW 142; Berlin/New York: Walter de Gruyter, 1977).

In this context one may only summarize some of the most telling arguments against Alt's thesis:

i) According to Alt, a charismatic royal appointment in Israel was characterized by two distinct features, namely, designation by Yahweh (through a prophet) and acclamation by the people. However, in the succession of kings of the Israelite State preceding the relatively enduring dynasty of the Omrides, the biblical texts evidence a royal appointment with these two features only in the case of Jeroboam I (1 Kgs 11:29-39; 12:20). These features are not evident in the emergence of the kingships of Baasha, Zimri, or Omri. In the period following the Omrides only Jehu's rise to kingship fits Alt's thesis.

ii) According to the biblical texts (in as far as they give evidence), the kingships of Saul and of the kings the Israelite State were always perceived to be dynastic, both by the kings themselves and by their subjects. Saul, Jeroboam, and Baasha were each succeeded by their sons, and in no case do the texts give evidence that these successions were contested by the populace wishing to put forward a charismatically appointed king instead. Rather, the biblical sources implicitly acknowledge the legitimacy of these successions when they explain that the failure of each of these succeeding kings came about as a result of the evil they did rather than as a consequence of their illegitimacy.

iii) Israel is reported to have requested a king "like all the nations" (1 Sam 8:5). But kingship in neighboring nations was always dynastic (Ishida, *Royal Dynasties*, 6-25, and 51-54). Evidently Israel desired a stable dynastic pattern of government from the start.

iv) David implicitly recognized the legitimacy of the Saulide dynasty when a) he avenged the death of Saul's successor Ishbaal (2 Sam 4:5-12); b) he reclaimed Michal the daughter of Saul as wife (2 Sam 3:12-16) evidently to establish for himself a claim to a legitimate place in the Saulide dynasty; and c) he took over King Saul's harem (2 Sam 12:8).

Cross argued that the Israelite State subscribed to a conditional kingship ideal according to which the king held office subject to the conditions that he obey the legal traditions of Israel and that the spirit of Yahweh remain with him. In Judah, on the other hand, royal theology held that Yahweh had established the Davidic kings in Zion by eternal decree. Therefore the rule of the Davidic kings was subject to no conditions.

It may be agreed that Cross has fairly represented two differing ideologies of kingship as presented by the biblical texts. However, one may ask in respect to the conditional kingship ideal, who in fact subscribed to this ideology? Cross himself recognizes that it may actually have been a political commitment kept alive only in prophetic circles.[114] Indeed there is little evidence to suggest that the populace in general sought to maintain such an ideal, or that the king and his royal court embraced it. To the contrary, the evidence suggests that from the time kingship was first instituted in the Israelite State the royal court as well as the people in general accepted the principle of unconditional dynastic succession.

Such a claim can be supported even for Saul's kingship which both Alt and Cross regarded as the pattern followed later in the Israelite State. Evidently, as Saul's attempts to insure the succession of his son Jonathan demonstrate, Saul did not embrace a concept of limited or conditional kingship. As for the people, their true attitude towards Saul's kingship is most clearly perceptible in their support of the Saulide dynasty at the succession of Ishbaal. Similarly, both Jeroboam I and Baasha were succeeded by their sons, but though the biblical authors report the early demise of both dynasties, they suggest neither that Israel opposed these dynastic claimants, nor that Israel put forward different candidates on the grounds that Jeroboam or Baasha had violated the conditions of their kingship.

Only the prophets, if anyone, kept alive the ideal that kingship in the Israelite State should be subject to conditions. Only the prophets appear to have made any attempt to limit kingship. Yet even here the evidence is meager. In the long succession of nineteen kings of the Israelite State the sources have only two instances to report where a prophet actually designated a person to take the kingship of Israel, namely Ahijah's designation of Jeroboam (1 Kgs 11:29-39) and the unnamed prophet's designation of Jehu (2 Kgs 9:1-10). Only in these two cases did prophetic

---

[114] *Canaanite Myth and Hebrew Epic*, 260.

activity actually effect the emergence of a new king. Yet if the ideology of conditional kingship had actually had a constitutional basis, or even if it had had secure support from significant constituents of the kingdom, one would expect to find some organized body capable of imposing limitations on the king. The prophets certainly do not act consistently enough to be considered candidates for this office.

It follows then that one must reject the explanation that the Israelite State sought to maintain an ideal of conditional kingship and that this ideal provided the motivation for the frequent *coup d'états* in Israel. Such an ideology could at most account for the rise to power of Jeroboam I and Jehu. More satisfactory explanations for the instability of kingship in the Israelite State may be brought forward. Since the overthrow of the Israelite kings consistently came about through a military *coup d'état* one may reckon with the likelihood that most were motivated either by dissatisfaction with the performance of the existing king or by personal ambition. Baasha may have disposed of Jeroboam's dynasty out of dissatisfaction with the war at Gibbethon; Zimri, the commander of the chariotry, may have overthrown his predecessor out of personal ambition; Omri and Jehu were both high ranking officers in the army and personal ambitions could account for their conspiracies. Possibly intertribal rivalry also accounts somewhat for the changes in dynasties. For instance, Jeroboam I was Ephraimite (1 Kgs 11:26), but his dynasty was overthrown by Baasha from Issachar (1 Kgs 15:27).[115]

The argument that Jeroboam may have pursued a policy of decentralized government in order to remain in harmony with Israelite ideologies of kingship and statehood falters in view of the foregoing considerations. It is unlikely that Jeroboam or any other Israelite king embraced an Israelite ideal of conditional or limited kingship. Nor does the evidence suggest that the population of the Israelite State advocated such an ideal. Rather, the eventual outcome of the kingship in the Israelite State in the relatively stable dynasties, first, of the Omrides and, then, of the Jehuites, suggests that a dynastic and centralized administration was the goal all along.

### 3. Shechem as a Religious and Political Administrative Center

For the question of why Jeroboam would establish both Bethel and Dan as royal sanctuaries when neither became his capital, the explana-

---

[115] On the possible causes behind the usurpations see Ishida, *Royal Dynasties*, 173-75.

tion that Jeroboam had adopted a policy of decentralized power fails. Another explanation, quite opposite to this one, is also possible. One could account for the little information the biblical text offers concerning city building and sanctuary appointments (1 Kgs 12:25, 29-30) with the explanation that Jeroboam followed the model of centralized government, that he established his central administration in Shechem, and that he appointed various sanctuaries as royal sanctuaries (with Bethel and Dan among them) to represent the jurisdiction of God and king in their respective areas. This explanation requires that one give plausible reasons for concluding that Shechem may have functioned as capital.

The note in 1 Kgs 12:25 appears to offer some confirmation for this explanation. It says that Jeroboam fortified Shechem and that he dwelt there. This may signify that Shechem became the capital for Jeroboam.[116] Then 1 Kgs 12:25 taken together with 14:17 could be interpreted to mean that this arrangement endured only for a time, that Jeroboam during the course of his reign established his capital first at Shechem, then moved it to Penuel, and finally, to Tirzah.[117] However, it is just as probable that 12:25 does not signify a transfer of residence at all. In fact, 12:25 says neither that Jeroboam lived in Penuel nor that he administered the State from there. The report may simply mean that while maintaining his residence in Shechem Jeroboam also fortified Penuel. In fact, a comparison of 1 Kgs 12:25 to the rather similar formulation of 2 Chr 11:5 supports such an interpretation:

1 Kgs 12:25
*wayyiben yārobʿām ʾet-šĕkem bĕhar ʾeprayim wayyēšeb bāh wayyēṣēʾ miššām wayyiben ʾet-pĕnûʾēl*
Jeroboam fortified Shechem in the hill country of Ephraim, and he dwelt in it; and he went out from there and he fortified Penuel.

2 Chr 11:5
*wayyēšeb rĕhabʿām bîrûšālāim wayyiben ʿārîm lĕmāṣôr bîhûdâ*
Rehoboam dwelt in Jerusalem and he fortified cities as fortresses in Judah.

---

[116] The archaeological data permits an interpretation that is consistent with this reading of 1 Kgs 12:25. R. G. Boling and E. F. Campbell ("Jeroboam and Rehoboam at Shechem," in *Archaeology and Biblical Interpretation*, 269-70) reconstruct that the destruction of the unfortified Shechem as evidenced in stratum X was accomplished by Shishak in 918 BCE, and that stratum IX contains the remains of the city which Jeroboam rebuilt on a more substantial scale, probably with fortifications.

[117] So Noth, *Könige*, 280-81. Noth thinks that Jeroboam abandoned Shechem to flee Shishak's invasion of Israel (cf. 1 Kgs 14:25-28) and that after Shishak withdrew he returned to the west side of the Jordan, but to Tirzah rather than to Shechem.

The purpose of the fortification of Penuel will have been to "secure the influence of Israel over the remnants of David's empire in Transjordan, and to prevent the coercion of North Israelite elements there by Judah."[118] As for the datum that 1 Kgs 14:17 gives Tirzah as the location of Jeroboam's residence, probably this should be accepted as an indication that Jeroboam moved his capital from Shechem to Tirzah at some time during the course of his reign.

The choice of Shechem as political center for the new Israelite State may have been dictated by Jeroboam's previous political experience under Solomon. Jeroboam's high level office as overseer of the Josephite corvée in Solomon's administration will have prepared him with an intimate knowledge of the political structures in the North. It is quite probable that he did not build up totally new administrative structures to govern the emergent Israelite State but that he adopted structures already existing in the North.[119] The strength and independence of these existing institutions is apparent in the narrative about the assembly at Shechem (1 Kgs 12). On the one hand, Rehoboam recognized their strength and independence in that he went to Shechem to receive kingship; and on the other hand, the assembly at Shechem demonstrated its political power in that it successfully withstood Rehoboam's bid for kingship. The fact that the assembly occurred at Shechem rather than at some other city indicates the ongoing importance of that city as a center of religious authority and political influence in the North. It should occasion no surprise, then, if under Jeroboam Shechem should begin to function as the political base of a new centralized government.

To speak of centralized government from Shechem as capital city for the Israelite State implies that Jeroboam held power over an integrated and unified Israel. Against this Olivier has argued that Jeroboam had a limited power base "only in the central hill area, i.e. the territory of the tribes of Ephraim and Manasseh," and that Shechem held prestige and political power only for that area.[120] According to this argument, when the Israelites made their break with Jerusalem, the Canaanite city states in the valleys followed suit; but then they re-established their indepen-

---

[118] Gray, *Kings*, 314. Cf. Würthwein, *Könige*, 151.

[119] Cf. Alt, "Israels Gaue unter Salomo," in *Kleine Schriften zur Geschichte des Volkes Israel*, 3 vols (München: C. H. Beck, 1953) 2: 76-89.

[120] Olivier, "In Search of a Capital," 126.

dence from Israel as well, reverting to their former form of self-government.[121]

However, one may wonder whether David and Solomon had not wholly integrated the city states of the plains before the end of the period of the United Kingdom. Furthermore, though the biblical texts give no direct evidence for the extent of political control which the new Israelite State exercised in the major cities of the plains, they do offer some telling bits of information that show that its political jurisdiction reached well beyond the Ephraimite and Manassite hill country. 1) Jeroboam had influence in the Transjordan as is evident from the fact that he fortified Penuel (1 Kgs 12:25). 2) Jeroboam held jurisdiction as far north as Dan as is evident from the fact that he refurbished the sanctuary there. 3) Shortly after Jeroboam's death his son Nadab laid siege to the Philistine city of Gibbethon just west of the Israelite-Philistine border (1 Kgs 15:27). One would expect this kind of military expedition only after the Israelite State had been consolidated internally. 4) Nadab's successor, Baasha, had political jurisdiction as far north as Ijon, Dan, Abel-bethmaacah, and Chinnereth, as is confirmed by the report of 1 Kgs 15:20-21 that Ben-hadad encroached on Baasha's territory there.

Furthermore, though the biblical texts do not give much explicit evidence for the extent of Shechem's political influence during the period of Jeroboam, the Amarna letters illustrate from an earlier period the potential power that this city in the hill country could wield over the cities of the plain. The letters tell of the complaint of one as far north and west as King Biridiya of Megiddo that King Labayu of Shechem was threatening his sovereignty,[122] and of another as far south as Shuwardata, prince of the Hebron region, who knew very well of Labayu's imperialistic policies.[123] Then one can hardly argue, as Olivier does, on "mere ecological, topographical, economical and security grounds" that the hill country areas and Shechem in particular "would hardly have contact with the more urban orientated and prosperous communities of the coastal plains and major valleys, and so also with the other communities

---

[121] In this connection Olivier ("In Search of a Capital," 127) draws on P. C. Salzman's ("Ideology and Change in the Middle Eastern Tribal Societies," MAN Ns 13 [1978] 618-37) concept of "reserve ideology" to speak of the rather general phenomenon of the resurgence of older political configurations when a newly imposed central government loses control.

[122] ANET, 485, EA # 244, cf. EA # 250.

[123] ANET, 487, EA # 280.

in the Galilee and in Transjordan."[124] To the contrary, it is quite conceivable that Jeroboam could have attempted to establish a central administration in Shechem for an integrated, unified Israelite State reaching from Dan to Bethel and from the Transjordan to the Mediterranean.

Even if the argument holds that Jeroboam exercised political jurisdiction from Shechem, that does not automatically warrant calling it his capital, at least not according to the definition employed above. By that definition, if Shechem had been Jeroboam's capital, it must have functioned both as the political and as the religious center of the kingdom. However, in addition to the problem posed by the fact that 1 Kgs 12:29 appears to say that Jeroboam established Bethel and Dan as royal sanctuaries for his kingdom, the biblical sources yield no explicit evidence regarding a sanctuary in Shechem at this time. Archaeologists have succeeded in locating remains of two temples dating to the Late Bronze age, but these temples were destroyed before the end of the twelfth century BCE.[125] One might expect that the Israelites would have continued to use these sacred areas, but the archaeological data indicates that they did not build temples at these places.

However, the fact that no Israelite temples were built where the Late Bronze age temples once stood does not exclude the possibility that an Israelite sanctuary existed elsewhere in or near Shechem. Biblical references appear to refer to sacred areas located both inside and outside the city of Shechem.[126] Moreover, recent excavations on Mt. Ebal have located an installation which A. Zertal interprets as an Israelite sanctuary from approximately the mid-thirteenth to mid-twelfth centuries BCE.[127] This site was abandoned long before the time of Jeroboam and

---

[124] "In Search of a Capital," 126.

[125] See Boling and Campbell, "Jeroboam and Rehoboam at Shechem," 267; R. J. Bull, J. A. Callaway, E. F. Campbell, J. F. Ross, and G. E. Wright, "The Fifth Campaign at Balâṭah (Shechem)," *BASOR* 180 (1965) 11-15; and Wright, *Shechem*, 80-122.

[126] So Gottwald, *The Tribes of Yahweh*, 564-65. Gottwald distinguishes between the Canaanite holy place inside the city, apparently referred to in Judg 9:4, 6, and 46, and the Israelite holy place outside the city as indicated by the location of its sacred tree in Gen 12:6, 33:18b-20, 35:4, Deut 11:30, Josh 24:26, and Judg 9:37. Cf. also Haran, *Temples and Temple Service*, 50-51.

[127] "An Early Iron Age Cultic Site on Mount Ebal," *TA* 13-14 (1986-87) 105-65; idem, "Has Joshua's Altar Been Found on Mt. Ebal?" *BARev* 11 (1985) 26-43. Zertal's interpretation of the main structure as an altar was contested by A. Kempinski, "Joshua's Altar—An Iron Age I Watchtower," *BARev* 12 (1986) 42, 44-49; but reasserted by Zertal, "How Can Kempinski Be So Wrong?" *BARev* 12 (1986) 43, 49-

consequently could not have been the sanctuary for his capital. However, the attestation of this sanctuary together with the attestation of the two temple areas inside Shechem during the Late Bronze age indicates the multiplicity of sacred sites at Shechem over the course of time. Hence it is plausible that an Israelite sanctuary existed in or near Shechem in Jeroboam's time, though at a location not yet discovered.[128]

A few additional considerations suggest that Shechem continued to function as a cultic center for Israel after the twelfth century BCE. Probably it was due to Shechem's strong covenantal associations from earliest Israelite times (Josh 8:30-35, 24:1-28, cf. Deut 27) that Rehoboam went there to be confirmed as king over Israel (1 Kgs 12:1). That Shechem was considered an appropriate location for the confirmation of Rehoboam probably indicates the continuing existence of a sanctuary there. Presumably Israel would have made Rehoboam king by entering a covenant with him "before Yahweh" just as the elders of Israel made a covenant with David "before Yahweh" at Hebron (1 Sam 5:3). According to M. Haran the phrase "before Yahweh" is technical terminology signifying the abode of the deity, that is, it is an "indication of the existence of a temple at that site."[129] If Israel intended to make a covenant with Rehoboam "before Yahweh" at Shechem, there must have been a sanctuary there. Furthermore, two prophetic texts, Hos 6:9 and Jer 41:5, though from a much later time, imply the continued existence of Shechem as a cult center.[130]

On the basis of the foregoing considerations it appears probable that an Israelite sanctuary existed at Shechem during Jeroboam's time. Probably Jeroboam established it as his central royal sanctuary, as part of his central administration in his capital at Shechem. This conclusion follows from the foregoing argument regarding the Israelite ideology of kingship and from the recognition that 1 Kgs 12:25 attests to Shechem as the center of Jeroboam's political administration, at least for the first part

---

53. Cf. M. D. Coogan's ("Of Cults and Cultures," 2) tentative acceptance of Zertal's interpretation.

[128] Cf. comments by Boling and Campbell, "Jeroboam and Rehoboam at Shechem," 267-68.

[129] Temples and Temple Service, 26.

[130] On Shechem as a cult center in Hos 6:9 see J. L. Mays, Hosea (OTL; Philadelphia: Westminster, 1969) 101; and H. W. Wolff, Hosea (Hermenia; Philadelphia: Fortress, 1974) 122. In Jer 41:5, Shechem appears as one of three Israelite cities (all prominent sanctuary cities of the past) from which pilgrims come bearing sacrifice to offer at the destroyed temple in Jerusalem. See R. P. Carroll, Jeremiah (OTL; Philadelphia: Westminster, 1986) 710.

of his reign. That the biblical sources fail to report about a central sanctuary in Shechem is not at all remarkable. After all, the author of 1 Kgs
12:26-32 writes with the intent of disparaging the political and religious
institutions of the Israelite State and, consequently, only offers information selectively to accomplish that end. With regard to the sanctuaries
that intent was evidently realized by the report concerning the installation of the two calf images at Bethel and Dan.

In establishing Bethel and Dan among his royal sanctuaries,
Jeroboam probably intended to signify the extension of his jurisdiction
into the areas they served. Royal sanctuary cities served the purpose of
representing the power of both god and king in the area within which
they lay.[131] Thus, Bethel and Dan stood in relationship to Shechem in the
same way that the temple at Arad would have stood in relationship to
Jerusalem, that is, as outlying administrative cities representing the
interests of the capital both politically and religiously. The fact that
during the time of Jeroboam II Bethel could still be referred to as *miqdaš
melek* and *bêt mamlākâ* when Samaria was capital city in Israel (and of its
status as capital there can be no doubt in contrast to the status of
Shechem during the time of Jeroboam I) lends confirmatory evidence for
this interpretation.

## C. The Appointment of a Priesthood
### for the New State

### 1. *An Evaluation of the Pertinent Biblical Texts*

There are four biblical texts that pertain to the priesthood which
Jeroboam appointed for the new Israelite state: 1 Kgs 12:31-32; 13:33-34;
2 Chr 11:13-15; and 13:8-9. Each of these requires evaluation.

According to 1 Kgs 12:31b Jeroboam "appointed priests from among
all the people who were not of the Levites." It has been argued in chap-

---

[131] So Y. Aharoni, *The Land of the Bible: A Historical Geography*, rev. and enlarged
ed., trans. and ed. A. F. Rainey (Philadelphia: Westminster, 1979) 323. As a demonstration of this point Aharoni mentions the sanctuary at Arad which Solomon established at the southern border of Judah to represent the power of the king there. Similarly, Ahlström (*Royal Administration*, 1-42) has recently offered substantial data in
support of his contention that "[b]ehind the phenomenon of establishing temple
forts is the idea that they symbolize the power of the country, namely, god and
king" (p. 11). For an opposing view see Haran, *Temples and Temple Service*, p. 56, n.
22.

ter II of this study that though possibly this information ultimately depends on an annalistic source from the Israelite State, certainly in its present formulation it exhibits an attitude strongly critical of Jeroboam's priesthood in its claim that the new priests were not levitical. This is to be expected given its context (vv. 26-32) that shows a marked Jerusalemite bias. After making allowance for this bias, one may still inquire to what degree 1 Kgs 12:31b reflects the actual historical situation, first, in its statement that Jeroboam appointed new priests and second, in its further qualification that these priests were not Levites. These questions will require consideration below.

1 Kgs 12:32c adds that Jeroboam "placed in Bethel the priests of the high places which/whom[132] he had made." This note, which would seem to belong with v. 31b, appears somewhat out of place because it stands isolated from v. 31b by an intervening comment about Jeroboam's festival. Furthermore, its claim is rather odd because it seems to imply that Jeroboam moved priests from the high places which he had just refurbished (v. 31a) and where he had just installed them as priests (v. 31b) in order to have them serve in Bethel.[133]

However, read from the perspective of the prophetic legend that follows in 1 Kgs 13:1-32, the note in 12:32c functions appropriately as preparation for that legend. The note names Bethel as the geographical setting, and it suggests that Jeroboam brought priests together from various localities to Bethel to help officiate in the festival which, according to 12:33, provided the occasion for the events the prophetic legend narrates. Then probably the statement at v. 32c belongs with 12:33 as a redactional bridge[134] to the story in 1 Kgs 13:1-32 rather than with the

---

[132] The relative particle followed by ʿāśâ could refer to either the priests or the high places as its antecedent since both appear as the object of ʿāśâ in v. 31. The ambiguity does not yield to clear resolution, and perhaps the ambiguity is intentional to underline that both high places and priests are merely of Jeroboam's making.

[133] The sequence of thought in vv. 31-32 is rather confusing, probably because vv. 31-32 is not a literary unity (as will be explained subsequently). If the bêt bāmôt built by Jeroboam (v. 31a) in fact denote several sanctuaries of the kingdom (a probability argued in section III.B), and if v. 31b refers to the appointment of priests (the most probable interpretation of ʿāśâ kōhănîm) for these refurbished sanctuaries, then v. 32c either contradicts v. 31 by saying that the priests were all installed at Bethel rather than at the various sanctuaries, or it suggests the sequence of events as explained above. In any case, v. 32c itself, by its reference to high places (pl.), suggests that priests came from other sanctuaries to officiate at Bethel.

[134] For v. 33 as a redactional bridge see section IV.A. Its character as a bridge passage is clear from the way in which it takes up material from vv. 31-32, often

material that precedes it in vv. 25-32. As such it is doubtful that any historical value can be attached to the nuances it offers.

1 Kgs 13:33-34 is another redactional bridge that also takes up material from 12:31, reiterating its criticism of Jeroboam and his newly appointed priesthood but omitting to explicitly deny the levitical status of the priests. It develops further the criticism put forward in 12:31 by judging Jeroboam's action in establishing the new priesthood as a capital offence. Aside from this more severe attitude which it exhibits, it offers nothing new over 12:31b.

A paragraph at 2 Chr 11:13-15 adds the information that besides installing his own priests, Jeroboam and his sons actually expelled the existing priests *and the Levites* from service at Israelite sanctuaries and that the priests and the Levites then went to Judah. 2 Chr 13:8-9 essentially repeats this but designates the expelled functionaries more specifically as "the priests of Yahweh, the sons of Aaron, and the Levites." Thus the Chronicler makes a distinction between the priests (which for the Chronicler are the sons of Aaron) and the Levites that is not present in 1 Kgs 12:31.

As has been concluded in chapter II, these particular sections in which the Chronicler presents material that has no direct parallel in 1 Kings are probably the Chronicler's own free composition incorporating reworked material from 1 Kgs 12:26-32. Thus, from the note in 1 Kgs 12:31 that Jeroboam installed new priests, the Chronicler inferred that Jeroboam must have expelled the old priests first. Adding to this, the Chronicler introduced the distinction between the priests (i.e., the sons of Aaron) and the Levites, an anachronism that presupposes the Chronicler's own setting in the post-exilic period when Zadokite priests claiming Aaronic descent secured an exclusive privilege to the priesthood.[135] By means of the new compositions in 11:13-15 and 13:3-20 the Chronicler apparently intended to expose and to underscore the apostasy of the Israelite cult over against the true worship practised in Judah.[136] In particular, the Chronicler created the speech by Abijah the righteous king of Judah to serve this interest (13:4-12). Nonetheless, even

---

verbatim, and rearranges it slightly in order to give it a new emphasis as a preparation for the account that follows in 13:1-32. Hence v. 33 could hardly offer any information from an independent source.

[135] On this development see Cross, *Canaanite Myth and Hebrew Epic*, 195-215, especially p. 208; and A. Cody, *A History of Old Testament Priesthood* (AnBibl 35; Rome: Pontifical Biblical Institute, 1969) 146-74.

[136] Williamson, *Chronicles*, 243 and 251.

though the Chronicler's material is excluded as evidence because it does not derive from a source independent of 1 Kings, one may still ask whether the Chronicler might not have inferred correctly regarding Jeroboam's expulsion of the existing priests.

## 2. Jeroboam's Reorganization of the Priesthood

The foregoing evaluation of the biblical texts has served to isolate two questions for further consideration. The first concerns the reliability of the claim in 1 Kgs 12:31b that Jeroboam appointed new priests and its further qualification that these priests did not derive from levitical pedigree. The second concerns the correctness of the Chronicler's inference that Jeroboam expelled the existing priests from serving in the cult of the Israelite State (2 Chr 11:14 and 13:9a). Certainly if one could offer plausible explanations for Jeroboam's motivation in taking such actions, that would argue in favor of an affirmative response for both questions.

Before seeking out such explanations it is necessary to inquire in what way 1 Kgs 12:31b may present a distortion because of the author's bias. It is evident that all of the texts discussed above were written from a Judahite or a Jerusalemite perspective. In view of their common inclination to derogate the religious policies and the cult of the Israelite State one can hardly accept without suspicion their less than flattering claims that Jeroboam installed priests indiscriminately from among the people without paying attention to their pedigree. Rather, one may recognize that certain criteria determinative for the legitimacy of priests were applicable in the time and place in which these authors wrote, and that they have applied those criteria to judge the legitimacy of Jeroboam's priesthood even though it belonged to another time and place. Thus, when the author of 1 Kgs 12:31b takes pains to point out that Jeroboam's priests were not levitical, that author has probably evaluated their credentials in a wholly anachronistic way. It appears that for the earliest monarchical period the appointment of priests was a royal prerogative, and levitical status was not a necessary criterion of a legitimate priestly appointment. Thus David installed his own sons and Ira the Jairite as priests (2 Sam 8:18 and 20:26). Similarly, Solomon appointed Zabud the son of Nathan to his cabinet as priest (1 Kgs 4:5). It appears that none of these appointees had levitical pedigree, yet they escape criticism in the biblical text. It is somewhat remarkable, then, that Jeroboam should be criticized for exercising his prerogative in selecting priests unless one recognizes that the criticism comes from the perspective of a later period when different criteria of legitimacy applied.

Though 1 Kgs 12:31b may actually tell the truth in saying that Jeroboam appointed non-Levites as priests, one may judge that the author has nuanced it unfairly by applying the levitical criterion anachronistically.

Considering the question of whether Jeroboam actually appointed new priests, one could explain that such action was necessitated for purely religious reasons. A. Cody thinks that levitical circles, because they clung to the spirit of Shiloh and to the old religious ideals of Israel which it typified, objected to the cult that Jeroboam sponsored, and hence they were unwilling to serve in Jeroboam's royal sanctuaries.[137] Consequently Jeroboam had no choice but to appoint new priests. However, such an explanation can at best provide only a partial answer. Its weakness is that it presupposes that Jeroboam made innovations of such magnitude in the Israelite cult that priests who formerly had served in it could no longer conscientiously do so. It is very doubtful that Jeroboam would have pursued such major innovations at a time of relative political insecurity such as would have existed in the Israelite State while he was in the process of establishing its new independent political institutions.

For a more satisfactory explanation of Jeroboam's motivation for installing new priests one may begin by observing that in Israel, as elsewhere in the ancient Near East, the priesthood exercised significant political influence.[138] This is evident in that the three biblical texts which list David's and Solomon's cabinet officials each name priests as part of the cabinet (2 Sam 8:15-18; 20:23-26; 1 Kgs 4:1-6). Then one could surmise that at the time of Israel's secession from the United Monarchy one of Jeroboam's administrative priorities will have been to install priests loyal to himself for official religious service in the new state. Probably Jeroboam also had to expel certain of the priests already in office because he could not count on their loyalty to his kingship since they had previously served the interests of the Davidic monarchy in Jerusalem.

Such action on Jeroboam's part would have been analogous to 1) the measures Saul took against the priests at Nob when he perceived that

---

[137] *A History of Old Testament Priesthood*, 108-111. Cody points to Exod 32:25-29 in its context as evidence that Levites objected to the cult established in the Israelite State. However, as will be argued in section IV.c, this passage dates from much later than Jeroboam and does not offer a reliable picture of attitudes toward Jeroboam's cult before or during his time.

[138] See Ahlström, *Royal Administration*, 3-8.

they had entered into conspiracy with David and therefore posed a threat to the security of his kingship (1 Sam 22:9-19), 2) Solomon's expulsion of Abiathar from the Jerusalem priesthood because he had supported Adonijah's claim to the throne (1 Kgs 1:5-8 and 2:26), and 3) Jehu's massacre of the (presumably high-ranking) priests who served under the Omrides (2 Kgs 10:11). The fact that these kings took such strong action against priests whom they perceived as loyal to political rivals should be taken as an indicator of the potential power wielded by the priests. The incident in which Jehoiada the priest in Jerusalem took the initiative to elevate Joash to the throne and to depose Queen Athaliah illustrates well how politically influential the priests could be (2 Kgs 11:4-20). Similarly, one may note how Amaziah the priest at Bethel guarded the interests of Jeroboam II when he opposed Amos (Amos 7:10-13).

Further support for the thesis that Jeroboam expelled certain priests because of their political loyalties may be sought in the findings of modern investigations regarding the functions of the Levites and the purpose of the levitical cities during the period of the United Monarchy. W. F. Albright argued that the lists of levitical cities in Joshua 21 and 1 Chronicles 6 are historical documents that reflect an actual historical situation from the period of the United Monarchy.[139] Building on this foundation B. Mazar argued on the basis of 1 Chronicles 23 that David, towards the end of his reign and during the vice-regency of Solomon, organized the Levites as royal servants for the purpose of centralizing the royal administration and cult.[140] In particular Mazar took note of the responsibilities given to the Kohathite family from Hebron, a family that he surmised would have been active in support of David's coronation at Hebron. According to 1 Chr 26:30-32 David gave this family *"the oversight* of Israel westward of the Jordan for all the work of Yahweh and *for the service of the king"* (v. 30) and *"the oversight* of the Reubenites, the Gadites, and the half-tribe of the Manassites for everything pertaining to

---

[139] *Archaeology and the Religion of Israel*, 121-25; and *idem*, "The List of Levitic Cities," in *Louis Ginzberg Jubilee Volume* (New York: American Academy for Jewish Research, 1945) 49-73. For a contrasting view on the dating, cf. A. Alt ("Bermerkungen zu einigen judäischen Ortslisten des Alten Testaments," in *Kleine Schriften zur Geschichte des Volkes Israel*, 3 vols [München: C. H. Beck, 1953] 2: 294-95, 305) who thinks the lists reflect a post-Josianic situation.

[140] "The Cities of the Priests and Levites," in *Congress Volume* (vrs up 7; Leiden: E. J. Brill, 1960) 193-205. See similarly Aharoni, *The Land of the Bible*, 301-305.

God and *for the affairs of the king*" (v. 32). Thus the text itself explains that the Levites worked in an official capacity as servants of the king.

According to Mazar, David and Solomon settled loyal Levites strategically in areas where the authority of the central administration needed undergirding, and the Levites served there in cultic capacities but also on behalf of the king, presumably to collect taxes and to manage royal estates. In this connection Mazar points out that the levitical cities are located in groups which have no geographical continuity between them, and that what can be learned about the several locations indicates that they were areas of non-Israelite or mixed population where David or Solomon may well have found it expedient to settle loyal Levites who would help in securing the administration of these areas.[141] If this understanding of the function of the Levites is correct, one may concur with Mazar that Jeroboam probably had to expel Levites from the cult in the emergent Israelite State because of their loyalty to the Davidic dynasty.

One may note, however, that Mazar draws evidence regarding the function of the Levites in the levitical cities primarily from 1 Chronicles 23-26. In these texts Chronicles offers material that has no parallel in 1 & 2 Kings. Probably these chapters reflect the elaborate levitical organization of the post-exilic period and artificially connect that with the time of David. Nevertheless, Mazar has given plausible reason to believe that the Chronicler's material at least at some points reflects the political and religious organization of levitical cities in the time of the United Monarchy.[142] Given the datum that during the post-exilic period, prior to the Maccabees, the Transjordan did not fall under Judaean jurisdiction, it would seem somewhat odd that the Chronicler should make reference to levitical activity in that area (v. 32). In this respect the mate-

---

[141] Mazar, "The Cities of the Priests and Levites," 199ff. Hence the cities in the southern hills of Judah all fall into the districts of the Calebites and the Kenizzites. Two other cities which are mentioned in connection with Judah, namely Libnah and Beth Shemesh, lie near the western border with the Philistines. Other levitical cities were established 1) west of Jerusalem in the former territory of Dan where the heavy Canaanite population was dominated by the Philistines until the rise of David, 2) in the North, often in Canaanite cities first conquered by David, e.g., Taanach, Ibleam, and Jokneam, 3) in Benjamin where the royal house held substantial estates inherited from the house of Saul, and 4) east of the Jordan.

[142] "The Cities of the Priests and Levites," 198-99; cf. Braun, *Chronicles*, 254; and Williamson, *Chronicles*, 173.

rial does not reflect circumstances of the Chronicler's own time,[143] but rather, circumstances in the period of the United Monarchy. Of particular significance is the Chronicler's mention of Levites in the city of Jazer (v. 31) which the lists of levitical cities locate in the territory of Gilead (Josh 21:39; 1 Chr 6:66=Eng 6:81). If the levitical lists date from the time of the United Monarchy, the reference to Jazer in 1 Chr 26:31 adds a sense of historical credibility to what the Chronicler reports in 1 Chr 26:30-32.

Mazar's analysis suggests that during the period of the United Monarchy the Levites served an integrated cultic and civil function as royal servants. In addition to the evidence 1 Chr 26:30-32 offers in support of this conclusion, one may note that generally in the ancient Near Eastern context cultic officials served in civil functions. On this point Ahlström writes:

> It should be noted that the distinction between priests and other officials of the crown was not as sharp as has usually been thought. For example, it was not unknown for a high priest to be appointed vizier. On the other hand, a Pharaoh might appoint a favorite civil servant to the office of high priest.[144]

Ahlström also argues from various biblical texts that the Levites served as administrators and/or as police force (pĕquddâ, 1 Chr 23:11), as instructors and enforcers of the law, both civil and religious (2 Chr 17:7-10), and as tax collectors (2 Chr 24:11).[145]

---

[143] Unless this material was actually added to Chronicles as late as the Maccabean period.

[144] *Royal Administration*, 46.

[145] *Ibid.*, 47-49. As an ancient Near Eastern parallel Ahlström draws attention to the guard duty required of the Hittite temple officials as evidenced by "Instruction for Temple Officials," in *ANET*, 209. Cf. R. de Vaux, *Ancient Israel*, vol 1: *Social Institutions* (New York: McGraw-Hill, 1965) 133.

See also C. Hauer ("David and the Levites," *JSOT* 23 [1982] 33-54) who has applied anthropological theory to test the thesis that levitical cities formed part of a royally instituted ecclesiastical establishment. In the context of this study he cites with approval the following from M. Harris:

> Ecclesiastical bureaucracies are usually associated with state-level political forms. In most instances the leaders of the ecclesiastical hierarchy are members of the ruling class and, in some instances, a state's political and ecclesiastical hierarchies are indistinguishable. (M. Harris, *Culture, People, Nature: An Introduction to General Anthropology*, 2d ed. [New York: Thomas Y. Crowell, 1975] 523).

In view of the evidence that priests wielded significant political influence, and in consideration of Mazar's argument that Levites (levitical priests) functioned both in political and cultic capacities, one may reasonably conclude that in as much as Jeroboam actually expelled priests (who may have been levitical) from service in the Israelite State, it was because they were loyal to the Davidic dynasty. But if Jeroboam expelled priests he would have had to install new priests loyal to himself in order to fill the resulting vacancies. These explanations give plausible motives for two of the measures Jeroboam reportedly took regarding the priests. Thus the claim of 1 Kgs 12:31b that Jeroboam installed new priests and the inference of 2 Chr 11:13-15 and 13:8-9 that he expelled the existing priests finds confirmation.

However, one need not simply conclude on the basis of 2 Chr 10:13-14 and 13:9 that all the existing priests in the territories embraced by the new Israelite State faced expulsion when Jeroboam became king, nor that all the existing priests maintained loyalty to the Davidic dynasty. On the contrary, one should recognize that for the Chronicler, who considered David as the founder of the only legitimate and true Israelite cult, those cultic functionaries who formerly had served under David could hardly have continued to serve in the apostate cult of the Israelite State. Consequently the Chronicler had to assume that the priests and Levites all moved south to Judah. Surely the Chronicler has overstated the case at this point.

Probably a significant number of the religious leaders living in the territory of the emergent Israelite State threw their support behind Jeroboam and remained in their posts. Justification for this claim comes from two biblical texts which indicate that there had been tension between Solomon and religious leaders in the North and so suggest the probability that not all these religious leaders would have remained loyal to the king in Jerusalem. According to the first text (1 Kgs 2:26-27) Solomon expelled Abiathar, a priest of the Elide line (1 Sam 14:3 and 22:20), from the priesthood in Jerusalem. This would probably have resulted in the alienation of other priests who considered themselves close of kin to Abiathar. According to the second text (1 Kgs 11:29-39) Ahijah of Shiloh designated Jeroboam to be king of Israel in place of Solomon. Probably one should take this event as an indication of support for Jeroboam from the religious leadership at Shiloh. Then perhaps Jeroboam enjoyed fairly wide-spread support from the existing priesthood in the new Israelite State despite the Chronicler's note to the contrary.

Probably the required re-organization of the priesthood for the Israelite State entailed only the removal and replacement of certain Davidic loyalists while the majority of the priests supported Jeroboam and retained their positions. Of course, the political independence of the new Israelite State would also have entailed the establishment of an independent priesthood, and this would have meant that Jeroboam had to select individuals loyal to himself for new top level appointments.

### 3. *The Priestly Families at Dan and Bethel*

By denying the levitical pedigree of Jeroboam's new appointments to the priesthood, the author of 1 Kgs 12:31b evokes the further query concerning the identity of these priests. It may very well be that not all of the priests serving under Jeroboam can be identified with groups known elsewhere from the Hebrew Bible. However, one can hardly conclude that Jeroboam simply ignored priestly lineage and replaced the priests he expelled with persons simply chosen from the laity. In any case, there is some biblical evidence that may help to decide the identity of the priestly families that served at Dan and Bethel during the time of Jeroboam.

According to the note in Judg 18:30, Jonathan ben Gershom ben Moses[146] and his sons were priests at the Danite sanctuary from the time of its establishment "until the day of the captivity of the land." The "day of the captivity of the land" must refer either to the exile by Tiglath-Pileser III in 732 BCE or to the exile by Sargon II after 721 BCE. Thus the text suggests that an unbroken line of priests claiming descent from Moses served the sanctuary at Dan throughout the period it functioned as an Israelite sanctuary, presumably including the time of Jeroboam. As to the reliability of Judg 18:30, though it appears to have a secondary connection with the story that precedes it,[147] its claim probably corresponds to the actual historical situation. Evidently, even though the traditions associated with the cult at Dan could be shaped in a manner thoroughly critical of that cult as Judges 17-18 attests, yet as Judg 18:30 shows, it could not be denied that from ancient times the sanctuary at Dan boasted an honorable priesthood tracing its lineage from Moses.

---

[146] One should regard the suspended *nûn* in the MT of Judg 18:30 as an attempt to safeguard the name of Moses from association with the cult at Dan which the preceding story has described as exceedingly corrupt. See R. C. Boling, *Judges* (AB, 6A; Garden City: Doubleday, 1975) 266.

[147] On this point see section IV.B.

The identification of the priesthood at Bethel presents a somewhat more complex problem because no biblical tradition makes so explicit a claim regarding its priesthood as Judg 18:30 does for the priesthood at Dan. According to Judg 20:26-28, Phinehas the grandson of Aaron served as priest at Bethel. In addition, Josh 24:33 says that Eleazar the son of Aaron was buried at Gibeah, the town of Phinehas his son, in the hill country of Ephraim. This note locates the home of Phinehas in Ephraim in whose territory Bethel also lay. Since Josh 24:33 offers a tradition totally independent of the accounts of the tribal allotments, it probably should be trusted and accepted as a secure reference in locating the home of Eleazar and Phinehas.[148] Consequently the identification of Eleazar and Phinehas as Ephraimite priests and the connection of Phinehas with Bethel seems quite secure.

It could be concluded on the basis of these texts (Judg 20:26-28 and Josh 24:33) that since both Eleazar and Phinehas appear in the lineage of Aaron, the priesthood at Bethel must have been Aaronide. Even so, further considerations are required because the objection could be brought forward that Aaron in the oldest traditions was not a priestly figure and that he, in fact, belongs in the South.[149]

However, in support of the view that priests living at Bethel actually traced their lineage to Aaron, one should note the prominence of the sons of Aaron in the lists of levitical cities. As a document reflecting the historical situation in the time of the United Monarchy, it attests to the early significance of the sons of Aaron. Though most of the cities of the sons of Aaron are located south of Jerusalem, several appear north of

---

[148] So K. Möhlenbrink, "Die levitischen Überlieferungen des Alten Testaments," ZAW 11 (1934) 216-17.

[149] So Cody, A History of Old Testament Priesthood, 146-74. Cody recognizes Aaron as a very ancient figure but as a leader rather than as a priest (p. 150). He argues that this figure became the antecedent on the basis of which the post-exilic P author constructed the figure of Aaron as priest. Nevertheless, he recognizes that persons known as the sons of Aaron already functioned as Levites at rural sanctuaries localized in Judah in pre-exilic times, and that it was they who sought admission to priestly functions in the Jerusalem temple after Josiah centralized the cult there (pp. 165-67). In response to Cody, one surely must wonder at the strange datum that a group that exercised priestly functions in the pre-Josianic time should be named after Aaron if Aaron himself had not already been recognized as the priestly ancestor in whose name the sons of Aaron could ground their claim to legitimacy and honor.

Jerusalem (Gibeon, Anathoth, Almon, and Geba), giving evidence that Aaronides lived in the vicinity of Bethel.[150]

Probably from very early times Aaron had a secure association with Bethel, and priests tracing their lineage to him served at Bethel.[151] But 2 Chr 13:9 claims that Jeroboam expelled the sons of Aaron from serving as priests in the Israelite State. One must inquire, then, whether that claim corresponds to the historical circumstances or whether the Chronicler as a pro-Aaronide merely sought to guard the reputation of the Aaronide priestly group by removing from their history the possible tarnish of service in the cult established by Jeroboam.

B. Halpern evaluates that 2 Chr 13:9 reflects the actual historical situation, explaining that till Jeroboam the Bethelite priesthood had been Aaronide but that Jeroboam replaced it with a Mushite priesthood.[152] He reasons that Mushite Levites whom Solomon had settled in the levitical cities in northern Israel (1 Chr 6:71-76, Josh 21:27-33) and whom Solomon had alienated even to the extent of expelling their representative Abiathar from the priesthood in Jerusalem, became a powerful force of rebellion, electing and supporting Jeroboam as king for the secessionist state of Israel as evidenced in 1 Kgs 11:29-39.[153] Hence Jeroboam owed a tremendous debt to these supporters of his kingship, and consequently he installed them as priests at Bethel where Aaronides loyal to the Davidic dynasty had served till this time.

However, Halpern's thesis rests very heavily on several rather tenuous connections and insecure identifications. It is not at all certain that

---

[150] If the lists of levitical cities reflect a situation from the time of the United Monarchy, then the Israelite-Judahite border cannot come into consideration here as a dividing line between Bethel and the four levitical cities north of Jerusalem. Nor should the datum that the Aaronide levitical cities all appear within either Judahite or Benjaminite borders be taken to signify that the sons of Aaron belonged to those two tribal entities and therefore could not have been associated with the Ephraimite sanctuary at Bethel. The arrangement of the levitical cities according to tribal territories is probably secondary to the division according to the levitical groups of the Kohathites, Gershonites, and Merarites as one may infer from the fact that these levitical groups do not appear each in its own well-defined and distinct tribal area. Cf. Cody, *A History of Old Testament Priesthood*, 160; and Noth, *Das Buch Josua*, 2d rev. ed. (HAT 1, 7; Tübingen: J. C. B. Mohr [Paul Siebeck], 1953) 97.

[151] So Cross, *Canaanite Myth and Hebrew Epic*, 198-99; and B. Halpern, "Levitic Participation in the Reform Cult of Jeroboam I," *JBL* 95 (1976) 34.

[152] "Levitic Participation," 31-42; and "Sectionalism and the Schism," *JBL* 93 (1974) 519-32.

[153] Halpern also considers the Shilonite priesthood to have been Mushite and Ahijah the Shilonite to have been one of its representatives.

the Gershomites/Gershonites who were settled in northern Israel (1 Chr 6:71-76 and Josh 21:27-33) were in fact descendants of Moses. Such an identification requires that the Gershomites/Gershonites who along with the Kohathites and the Merarites are always connected directly to Levi in genealogical tables (Gen 46:11, Exod 6:16, Num 3:17, 26:57, 1 Chr 5:27, 6:1, etc.) should rather be recognized as descendants of Moses by Gershom (cf. Judg 18:30 and 1 Chr 23:15). But even if such an identification were accepted, it would still be uncertain that these Gershomites/Gershonites were kin with the Elide Abiathar because the identification of Eli, and therefore also of his descendant Abiathar, as Mushite can appeal only to one very ambiguous reference in 1 Sam 2:27. Though several scholars understand its reference to Eli's ancestor as a reference to Moses,[154] at least some others have taken it as a reference to Levi or possibly even to Aaron.[155] Since this ambiguous text constitutes the most direct evidence available for the ancestry of Eli, his lineage remains in question. On the other hand, some considerations weigh strongly against identifying Eli as Mushite. According to 1 Kgs 2:26 Solomon banished Eli's descendant Abiathar to his estate (śādeh) in Anathoth. But Anathoth was a levitical city given to the Aaronides (Josh 21:18, 1 Chr 6:45). If Abiathar had been Mushite it seems improbable that he would have had an estate in an Aaronide levitical city. Furthermore, recognizing the Mushite sympathies of DtrH,[156] it seems rather odd that they would use a tradition so strongly anti-"Mushite" as that concerning the fall of the Elide house to support the Zadokite claim to pre-eminence in Jerusalem. One may suspect, therefore, that DtrH did not perceive Eli as a descendant of Moses.

Quite possibly Abiathar was not Mushite. In fact it is just as conceivable that he was Aaronide. Then one may suppose that certain Aaronides were alienated by Solomon's expulsion of Abiathar. Consequently, it is quite conceivable that certain Aaronides supported

---

[154] Halpern ("Levitic Participation," 33) confidently identifies the Shilonites as Mushites; and Cross (*Canaanite Myth and Hebrew Epic*, 196-97) presents an argument for this identification in agreement with J. Wellhausen, *Prolegomena to the History of Ancient Israel* (Meridian Books; Cleveland: World Publishing, 1957) 126.

[155] H. P. Smith, *The Books of Samuel* (ICC; Edinburgh: T & T Clark, 1899) 22; K. Budde, *Die Büche Samuel* (KHAT 8; Tübingen: J. C. B. Mohr, 1902) 23; H. J. Stoebe, *Das erste Buch Samuelis* (KAT 8; Gütersloher Verlagshaus Gerd Mohn, 1973) 116; and H. W. Hertzberg, *I & II Samuel* (OTL; Philadelphia: Westminster, 1964) 37.

[156] This sympathy or, rather, absolute allegiance is clearly evidenced in the foundational place these authors give to the law of Moses in their work. Cf. Halpern, "Levitic Participation," 33.

Jeroboam and continued on as priests in Bethel whereas Mushites continued to serve at Dan.[157]

## 4. Summary of Results

In general the foregoing investigation has found no evidence to suggest that Jeroboam undertook far reaching or innovative measures for the re-organization of the priesthood of the Israelite State. On the contrary, all considerations point to the probability that he retained the existing priests in their positions and maintained traditional policies in as far as that was politically expedient.

Thus the evidence suggests that Mushite priests remained in service at Dan and that Aaronide priests continued on at Bethel even after Jeroboam became king. Other lines of evidence also point toward the conclusion that many priests who were already in office in the territories that became the Israelite State supported Jeroboam as he became king and retained their offices. At the same time one must reckon with the likelihood that Jeroboam had to expel some priests, perhaps both Aaronides and Mushites among them, because of their loyalty to the Davidic kings. To replace these, Jeroboam would have installed new priests who would conform to the new political realities under his kingship. Also, since an independent Israelite State required its own independent religious and political administration, Jeroboam would have had to find new appointees for top level positions.

---

[157] Cross (*Canaanite Myth and Hebrew Epic*, 196-99; and "Reuben, First-Born of Jacob," 53-54) also thinks that Jeroboam actually confirmed the existing Mushite priesthood in Dan and the existing Aaronide priesthood in Bethel, thus appointing an official dual priesthood so as to alienate neither. However, his argument that Exodus 32 in its present form reflects a polemic by the Mushite priesthood of Shiloh (later of Nob) against the calf cult which the Aaronides of Bethel served encounters several difficulties: 1) As argued above, it is questionable that the Shilonites were actually Mushite. 2) If Mushites had objected to the bull cult at Bethel, it would seem odd for them to serve in the sanctuary at Dan which used the same iconography. 3) As will be argued in section IV.C, the polemic against the calf cult in Exodus 32 did not, in fact, arise in the Shilonite (or even Israelite) context prior to the fall of Samaria, but rather from a context in Jerusalem after 721 BCE. 4) Considering the possibility that the epithet *ʾăbîr yaʿăqōb* had connections with the Ark in the cult at Shiloh (Ollenburger, *Zion, the City of the Great King* 41-42), it is possible that calf iconography also had a place at Shiloh. If that were the case, the priests at Shiloh would hardly have criticized the calf iconography at Bethel.

These conclusions lend further confirmation to the thesis being
developed that Jeroboam sponsored religious initiatives firmly rooted in
Israel's most ancient traditions.

## D. The Institution of A Festival

The text in 1 Kgs 12:32 offers one brief comment about the festival
held by Jeroboam. For the present context it raises two significant issues.
First, if one reads v. 32 in light of the comments in v. 33 it appears that
Jeroboam, in respect to at least one important festival, unilaterally
changed the cultic calendar for the Israelite State. If such is the case it
would be of significance to know the reasons for this action. Second,
considering that religious festivals in the ancient Near East functioned in
part to celebrate and undergird the political institutions, one would like
to know the content of the particular festival which Jeroboam established and to inquire in what way it undergirded his kingship.

However, before these questions can be considered the text of 1 Kgs
12:32-33 requires closer analysis in order to evaluate to what extent it
might have claim to historical probability, or to what extent its
emphases may derive from polemical or editorial intent.

The text appears rather repetitive in that it points out twice the
location "in Bethel" and in that it takes up once again from v. 31b the
subject of the priests whom Jeroboam had installed. Repetition also
occurs in that a series of clauses and phrases found in v. 32 appears
again in almost identical wording in v. 33. V. 33 offers something new
over v. 32 only in the details that the date of Jeroboam's festival was
"one which he invented of his own heart"[158] and that it was in order "to
burn incense" that Jeroboam went up to the altar.

By means of all its repetition v. 33 serves an apparent editorial function, preparing for the narrative of the denunciation of Jeroboam's altar
at Bethel which follows in 1 Kings 13. It connects that story to the material preceding it by taking up already familiar ideas from vv. 31-32ab
(reading v. 32ab up to *laʿăgālîm*, "to the calves," but without *kēn ʿāśâ
bĕbêt-ʾēl*, "so he did at Bethel," which is editorial as will be argued below)
and by altering their emphases to suit as introduction to the next

---

[158] Reading the *qĕrēʾ*, *millibbô* instead of the *kĕtîb*, *millĕbad*.

story.[159] The apparent intention of the editor in v. 33 is to underline the illegitimacy of the Jeroboam's service of worship by stressing that in so far as he himself made the altar and determined the time of the festival, the initiatives had come from Jeroboam alone (rather than from God, one might presume). The editor insinuates that the initiatives were Jeroboam's to the extent that he even assumed the function of the priests for himself.

The editor responsible for v. 33 must also have modified v. 32 with the result that it now has a function similar to that of v. 33. This is evident in the phrase *kēn ʿāśâ běbêt-ʾēl* which intrudes between the main clause, "He went up to the altar," and the purpose clause, "to sacrifice to the calves." The purpose of the intruding phrase is evidently to point an accusing finger at Jeroboam, "That's what he did." Similarly, the twice-repeated use of the phrase *ʾăšer ʿāśâ* in v. 32bc accentuates that Jeroboam acted on his own. It follows that this phrase (like the phrase *kēn ʿāśâ běbêt-ʾēl*) must also derive from the editor who wrote v. 33. Thus the editor's additions to v. 32bc and the new editorial formulation in v. 33 emphasize what the editor already found to be implicit in the use of the verb *ʿāśâ* in vv. 31-32a.

The intruding phrase in v. 32b serves a second purpose. It prepares for the prophetic legend in 1 Kings 13 by specifying its geographical setting at Bethel whereas the comments in vv. 25-32ab have concerned the cult of the Israelite State with reference to its sanctuaries in general (v. 31), including both Bethel and Dan in particular (v. 29). The location at Bethel is specified a second time in v. 32c where the editor takes up from v. 31b the subject of the priests whom Jeroboam had installed, evidently with the purpose of underlining again the illegitimacy of Jeroboam's cult in preparation for the coming denunciation in 1 Kings 13.

One may reconstruct v. 32 without these editorial additions as follows: "And Jeroboam held a festival on the fifteenth day of the eighth month like the festival in Judah, and he went up to the altar to sacrifice to the calves." According to this reconstruction the location for the festival instituted by Jeroboam is not specified and one need not understand that its observance occurred only at Bethel. Probably it was observed in various sanctuaries, including the royal sanctuary at Dan, though Jeroboam, of course, will only have attended at one place and

---

[159] The criterion by which one may judge that v. 33 depends on vv. 31-32a rather than *vice versa* is that v. 33 presents the same material as vv. 31-32a but in a way suited to lead into 13:1-32 as will be explained subsequently.

approached the altar there. Furthermore, in this reconstruction v. 32 offers no explicit reproach against Jeroboam. The disapproval implied by the words, "he went up to the altar to sacrifice to the calves," may not be subtle at all, but the technique of implied criticism is consistent with what has already been observed in vv. 25-31. Certainly v. 32 contains no explicit criticism concerning the date of the festival. That first arises in the editorial bridge passage at v. 33.

Nevertheless, the claim of v. 33 that Jeroboam set his own date for the festival warrants further consideration. Judging from the date given for the festival, i.e., the fifteenth day of the eighth month (v. 32a), the festival in question must have been the autumn festival, i.e., the Feast of Tabernacles, which was celebrated at the completion of the harvest. The author of v. 33 presupposes that the proper date for its observance was one month earlier in the seventh month, as in Jerusalem (cf. 1 Kgs 8:2). Building on the assumption that during the time of the United Monarchy Jerusalem actually observed the fifteenth day of the seventh month as a fixed date for this festival, scholars have offered various explanations as to why Jeroboam might have set another date.

First, a few scholars think that the festival in Jerusalem posed a problem for Jeroboam in that it attracted many pilgrims from among his subjects. These scholars explain that Jeroboam tried to make his festival competitive by moving it up one month so that those who had earlier made the pilgrimage to Jerusalem could attend his festival as well.[160] However, one must wonder whether Israelite farmers would have spent the time and resources to observe the festival instituted by Jeroboam if they had already attended the harvest festival at Jerusalem.

Second, some scholars argue that Jeroboam reverted to an older cultic calendar that Israel had followed before the time of the Davidic and Solomonic Kingdom. J. Morgenstern claims that Israelites originally followed a pentacontad calendar (an old agricultural calendar based on seven fifty-day-cycles that corresponded to successive stages of annual crops), but when Solomon introduced his kingdom to international politics and commerce he adopted the more universal solar calendar, largely under the influence of his ally, Hiram of Tyre. Jeroboam, then, took the initiative to restore the old agricultural calendar for the people of the Israelite State.[161] Morgenstern's reconstruction does not appear to have convinced many scholars.

---

[160] So Šanda, *Könige*, 346; and Kraus, *Worship in Israel*, 55.
[161] J. Morgenstern, "The Festival of Jeroboam I," *JBL* 83 (1964) 109-18.

In an argument that leads to a similar result, S. Talmon reasons that the time of the harvest festival originally was not the same for all regions in Palestine but that in each region it was set according to the completion of the fruit harvest. Due to climatic differences harvest in Ephraim could be about a month later than in the Shephalah of Judah. The centralized administration of the United Monarchy, however, synchronized the observance of the harvest festival. Jeroboam, then, reacted against the synchronization imposed by Jerusalem and allowed the Israelite State to follow its old agricultural timetable.[162]

Many scholars have denied the existence of such climatic differences between Jerusalem and Bethel/Samaria (or between Judah and Israel) that the harvest festival would have been observed a month later in Israel than in Judah.[163] But Talmon's data pertains to the timing of the grape harvest specifically in the Judaean Shephelah as compared to the hill-country of Ephraim, and to the timing of the olive harvest in the district of Lydda-Ramleh (of the Shephelah) as compared to the region around Shechem.[164] He appears to be arguing that a divergence existed between the calendars followed by the rival sanctuaries at Shechem and at Hebron, and he implies that Jerusalem would have followed the calendar from Hebron.

It may be true that in various places the celebration of the harvest festival occurred at different times, possibly depending on differences in climate as well as on differences in local customs.[165] The cultic calendars in Exod 23:14-17; 34:18, 22; and Deut 16:1-17 may actually reflect the existence of such variability in that they do not specify a date for the observance of the Feast of Tabernacles (Ingathering) though they do, by way of contrast, specify the month of Abib for the Passover festival.[166] Only P's cultic calendar specifies a date, namely, the fifteenth day of the seventh month, as the beginning of the Feast of Tabernacles (Lev 23:34, 39; Num 29:12). This date corresponds with the date given for Solomon's

---

[162] S. Talmon, "Divergences in Calendar-Reckoning in Ephraim and Judah," *VT* 8 (1958) 48-74.

[163] So Šanda, *Könige*, 346; Montgomery, *Kings*, 260; Kraus, *Worship in Israel*, 152; de Vaux, *The Bible and the Ancient Near East*, 107; Noth, *Könige*, 286; and Gray, *Kings*, 318.

[164] "Divergences in Calendar-Reckoning," p. 56, n. 2.

[165] Judg 21:19 may imply a difference in festival times between Shiloh and Mizpah. Compare the comments by Noth, *Könige*, 286.

[166] Similarly they do not set a time for the Feast of Weeks because it is determined by the ripening of the grain.

observance of it in 1 Kgs 8:2, and it seems to be presupposed by the criticism of Jeroboam in 1 Kgs 12:33. It may be that the fifteenth day of the eighth month only became a fixed date for the Feast of Tabernacles in the Judahite cult at a time considerably later than Jeroboam, that the author of 1 Kgs 12:33 knew this as the "correct" date and therefore judged Jeroboam by it anachronistically.

Alternatively, the centralized administration in Jerusalem may have required a fixed date for the festival, especially if the festival came to be connected with the New Year celebration or with the celebration of Kingship. In that case, Jeroboam may have broken with the new customs of Jerusalem and re-instituted older customs that had been followed in territories that became the Israelite State.

Another possible explanation regarding the date of the festival is that Jeroboam actually carried on the tradition that was being followed in Jerusalem. According to 1 Kgs 6:38 Solomon completed the temple in the month of Bul, that is, in the eighth month. Presumably the dedication of the temple will have occurred after its completion, and one might expect that dedication to have happened within the context of the autumn festival (as 1 Kgs 8:2 suggests). Then possibly the date that 1 Kgs 8:2 gives for the dedication of the temple in the seventh month is an adjustment to the text from a later period when the Feast of Tabernacles had a fixed time in the seventh month. Perhaps Jeroboam actually held a feast like the one in Jerusalem, both in respect to its time in the eighth month and in respect to its nature, but the author of 1 Kgs 12:33 criticized him on the grounds of a later cultic calendar.

The problem posed by the apparent divergence between the date of Jeroboam's festival and that of the corresponding festival in Jerusalem does not yield readily to resolution because the Hebrew Bible offers very little evidence directly pertinent to the question. However, having recognized the late provenance and the editorial character of 1 Kgs 12:33, it appears most likely that the negative insinuations it makes regarding the timing of Jeroboam's festival arise from a failure or refusal to appreciate the ancient and venerable traditions that informed Jeroboam's appointed date.

Regarding the content of Jeroboam's festival, one may seek a clue in the claim made by 1 Kgs 12:32 that Jeroboam's festival was *like* the one in Jerusalem. Nevertheless, one must approach this comparative statement critically and inquire about the extent of that likeness. Beyond that question lies the problem of determining the content of the Jerusalem festival.

The festival in question, i.e., the autumn festival or the Feast of Tabernacles, was certainly a very prominent festival in Jerusalem during the period of the monarchy. Though the content of this festival has been a matter of intense debate among modern scholars,[167] it is probable that the festival included as its main components 1) the celebration of Yahweh's kingship, 2) the celebration of Yahweh's election of David and Jerusalem, and 3) the celebration of the Exodus and Conquest.[168]

Now certainly Jeroboam's festival will not have celebrated Yahweh's election of David and Jerusalem. But it would have required only a substitution of the names Jeroboam and Shechem in place of David and Jerusalem so that the festival in the Israelite State could also celebrate God's election of its king and capital. For this surmise, however, one can appeal to no liturgical texts of the cult of the Israelite State that can give evidence corresponding to that given by Psalm 132 for the Jerusalem cult. Nor can one be certain that Jeroboam's Israel had a royal ideology that could be celebrated the way it was in Jerusalem. One could argue with greater probability that Jeroboam's autumn festival included celebration of Yahweh's election of king and capital as one component if one could show evidence that it included the other two components present in the Jerusalem festival as listed above, namely, the celebration of Yahweh as king and the celebration of Yahweh's deliverance and victory for Israel in the Exodus and Conquest.

Then it must be inquired whether the celebration of Yahweh's kingship can be demonstrated as a probable component in the cult sponsored by Jeroboam. One may begin by observing that the concept of the kingship of Yahweh had a place in Israelite thought even in the pre-monarchic period. Already at Shiloh El=Yahweh was honored as king enthroned above the cherubim. The Song of the Sea, an old hymn dating back to the era of the league,[169] reaches the climax of its exultation over

---

[167] Among many others, S. Mowinckel, *The Psalms in Israel's Worship* (Oxford: Basil Blackwell, 1962); A. Weiser, *The Psalms* (OTL; Philadelphia: Westminster, 1962) 23-52; and H.-J. Kraus, *Psalms 1-59* (Minneapolis: Augsburg, 1988) especially pp. 86-89; *idem, Die Königsherrschaft Gottes im Alten Testament* (Tübingen: J. C. B. Mohr, 1951); *idem, Worship in Israel*. For a recent discussion of the literature pertaining to this topic see J. Gray, *The Biblical Doctrine of the Reign of God* (Edinburgh: T & T Clark, 1979) 1-38.

[168] See the summary observations on the autumn festival by P. D. Miller, "Israelite Religion," in *The Hebrew Bible and Its Modern Interpreters*, ed. D. A. Knight and G. M. Tucker (Philadelphia: Fortress, 1985) 221-22.

[169] Cross, *Canaanite Myth and Hebrew Epic*, 124 and 137. Further to the date of this hymn see chapter I above.

Yahweh's victory at the sea in its proclamation of the eternal kingship of Yahweh (Exod 15:18). Alongside this reference one may consider Num 23:21 from another old Israelite (not Judahite) text[170] which celebrates at one and the same time both the kingship of El and El's deliverance of Israel in the Exodus. Thus both Exod 15:1-18 and Num 23:21-22 show a correspondence with the old mythic pattern of the march of the divine warrior in which the manifestation of the god's kingship occurs by virtue of his victory over the enemy.[171] If, as the cultic formula in 1 Kgs 12:28e attests, the celebration of victory at the Exodus held a central place in Jeroboam's Israelite cult, it follows that that cult probably also culminated in the acclamation of God as king. One may note, furthermore, that Num 23:21 in speaking of El's deliverance of Israel at the Exodus compares the might of El to that of a wild bull. In this way it brings together the concept of El as king and the symbol of the bull to signify El's strength in battle. In comparison with this association one may note the Ugaritic designation of Bull El as king.[172] Above it has already been argued that the calf iconography in the cult sponsored by Jeroboam symbolized El=Yahweh's might in the deliverance of Israel from Egypt. Now one may add to that the further refinement that the calf image in the cult of the Israelite State probably signified the might of God as king.

In ancient Near Eastern theology the election of an earthly king was the prerogative of the heavenly king. Thus the former concept presupposes the concept of the god as king. It would be quite reasonable to think that Jeroboam took advantage of this common ancient Near Eastern ideology and supported his claim to kingship over the Israelite State by making the claim that the Divine King had elected him. The old tradition of Jeroboam's designation as king over Israel by the prophet Ahijah probably provided the necessary propaganda to support this claim.[173] The datum that Ahijah came from Shiloh where El=Yahweh had been honored as the Divine King enthroned above the cherubim may suggest that Ahijah himself perceived the designation of Jeroboam as the designation of a vice-regent to El=Yahweh.

---

[170] On its dating see section III.A above.

[171] On the old mythic pattern of the march of the Divine Warrior see Cross, *Canaanite Myth and Hebrew Epic*, 147-63.

[172] *KTU* I.3.v.35-36; I.4.i.4-5; I.4.iv.38-39, 47-48; cf. I.14.i.40-43.

[173] For discussion and references concerning this old tradition see section II.A above.

It is probable that Jeroboam's autumn festival included as one component the celebration of God's kingship. Furthermore, the formula in 1 Kgs 12:28e clearly attests that the commemoration of the historical traditions of the Exodus held a central place in that festival. If in these respects it resembled the autumn festival in Jerusalem, it is probable that it also corresponded with that festival in celebrating God's choice of king over Israel, in this context naming Jeroboam as king. Then this festival would have served to undergird the political institutions of the new Israelite State.

In summary, with respect to its central components, the biblical author has probably represented Jeroboam's festival altogether correctly in saying that it was like the festival at Jerusalem. Again it appears likely that Jeroboam's initiatives in the area of religion favored the ancient traditions.

# CHAPTER IV

# An Inquiry Regarding Opposition by Jeroboam's Contemporaries to His Initiatives for Religion

The inquiry of the preceding chapter into the purpose and significance of Jeroboam's policies and initiatives for religion serves to confirm that Jeroboam consistently drew on old Israelite traditions rather than introducing new religious practices. Nevertheless there are a few texts that appear to show evidence of opposition to Jeroboam's initiatives by his contemporaries. The purpose of this chapter is to investigate these texts in an attempt to determine how contemporary Israelites (or even Judahites) responded to the cult sponsored by Jeroboam. Presumably, if Jeroboam did sponsor the old Israelite traditions, the Israelite religious leaders and the populace in general would not have opposed his policies.

The first text to be considered in this context is 1 Kgs 13:1-32 which, by all appearances, responds with much censure to Jeroboam's sanctuary and festival at Bethel. A second text at Judges 17-18 forms a companion piece to 1 Kgs 13:1-32 in that it holds up the sanctuary at Dan for reproach. Though Judges 17-18 makes no explicit reference to Jeroboam's activity there, this text requires consideration as possibly an indirect polemic against Jeroboam's sanctuary at Dan. A third text in Exodus 32 issues a stern invective against the calf cult, and thus it comes into consideration as a possible criticism of Jeroboam because the biblical historian remembers Jeroboam primarily for his reprehensible calf cult. A fourth text at 1 Kgs 14:1-18 tells of the oracle of death for Jeroboam's son given by Ahijah the Shilonite, and of Ahijah's stern oracle of doom for Jeroboam's entire household on account of Jeroboam's evil in making other gods. Each of these texts requires examination to determine whether it actually reflects opposition to Jeroboam and his measures for religion from a time contemporary with Jeroboam.

## A. 1 KINGS 13

The prophetic story in 1 Kings 13 tells of the proclamation of a word of judgment against Jeroboam's altar in Bethel by a man of God from Judah. From this representation it would appear that Jeroboam's contemporaries in Judah offered strong opposition to his measures for the cult at Bethel. Whether or not there is a measure of truth to this historically, at least in the case of 1 Kings 13 this impression arises as a result of its editorial revision and redactional placement in its present context.[1] As will be argued below, the composition of this material probably did not arise out of an historical incident in the time of Jeroboam, and probably the original traditions had nothing to do with Jeroboam's activity at Bethel. The apparent censure of Jeroboam's religious measures in 1 Kings 13 derives from a time considerably later than Jeroboam.

In order to develop such an argument about the prophetic story that has been incorporated at 1 Kings 13 one must first isolate the original story. It is evident that a new narrative sets in with its own plot and its own slate of characters at 1 Kgs 13:1.[2] The material immediately preceding 13:1 in 12:32c-33 takes up ideas and phrases from 12:26-32b and reshapes them to provide a linkage between 12:26-32b and the narrative that follows in 1 Kings 13 by introducing Bethel as its geographical setting, by specifying Jeroboam's feast as the occasion of which it relates, and by placing Jeroboam at the scene in the act of offering incense on the

---

[1] On the interpolation of 1 Kings 13 into its present context see comments in section II.B above.

[2] Quite possibly this narrative originally began with something even before 13:1. W. Gross ("Lying Prophet and Disobedient Man of God in I Kings 13," *Semeia* 15 (1979) 100-101) claims that a *wĕhinnēh* construction such as the one which opens 13:1 never opens an independent unit. The editor responsible for 12:32c-33 may have discarded the original beginning that preceded 13:1 in the interests of the new introduction and linking passage in 12:32c-33.

altar. It follows, then, that 12:32c-33 does not belong as an original part of the narrative in 1 Kings 13 but merely serves to introduce it,[3] and it also follows that the original setting of the narrative in 1 Kings 13 was not necessarily as 12:32c-33 specifies (i.e., at the festival held by Jeroboam with Jeroboam himself standing at the altar).

Furthermore, as preparation for 1 Kings 13, the editor in 12:32c-33 apparently intends to draw attention to particular faults in Jeroboam that call for judgment. By heaping up comments that underline what Jeroboam did (e.g., "he went up to the altar which he had made" 33a, and "he went up to the altar to burn incense" 33b) the editor reproaches the altar and the cult attached to it as one arising solely from Jeroboam's initiative rather than from Yahweh's. Since the phrase in 13:1b, "and Jeroboam was standing at the altar in order to burn incense," ties back into and repeats these ideas from 12:32c-33, one should also assign it to the editor. Similarly, the name "Jeroboam" and the localization "from the altar" in 13:4a pick up on the setting as established by 12:32c-33, and therefore they reflect the same editor's work. Originally 13:4a may have said, "When the king heard the saying of the man of God . . . *he* stretched out his hand, saying . . . ."

In 1 Kgs 13:2b the following pronouncement of judgment against the altar appears:

> A son is about to be born to the house of David. Josiah will be his name. He will sacrifice upon you the priests of the high places who burn incense upon you and human bones will be burned upon you.

This is a *vaticinium ex eventu* regarding Josiah's destruction of the altar at Bethel (2 Kgs 23:15-20). At least this part of the text must have been composed after Josiah's reform.

One may note the particularly close correspondences between 1 Kgs 13:2b and 2 Kgs 23:15-20. The correspondence is such that 2 Kgs 23:16 absolutely presupposes the narrative of 1 Kings 13 with its particular prediction in v. 2b. This suggests that either the *vaticinium ex eventu* in v. 2b was interpolated into the pre-existing narrative of 1 Kings 13 in order to prepare specifically for 2 Kgs 23:15-20, or that at least parts of 2 Kgs 23:15-20 originally belonged with 1 Kings 13 as its conclusion and that the whole text was only composed after Josiah's reform.[4] However,

---

3 Also see the argument in section III.D above.

4 A. Jepsen ("Gottesmann und Prophet: Anmerkungen zum Kapitel I Könige 13," in *Probleme biblischer Theologie. Gerhard von Rad zum 70 Geburtstag* [München: Chr

against the latter assessment there are weighty arguments: 1) the story in
1 Kings 13 finds full resolution in 13:32 and does not require a completion such as 2 Kgs 23:15-20 might offer;[5] 2) the datum that the prophet
identified as one from Bethel in 1 Kings 13 is identified as one "who
came out of Samaria" in 2 Kgs 23:18 suggests two independent traditions; and 3) the datum that the part of the judgment pronouncement
against the altar in 1 Kgs 13:3b finds no correspondence in the story of
fulfillment in 2 Kgs 23:15-20 indicates that 2 Kgs 23:15-20 could not have
originally formed a conclusion to 1 Kings 13. In view of these considerations, the original composition in 1 Kings 13 must have been independent of and older than 2 Kgs 23:15-20. In that case, it may be concluded
that 13:2b is an interpolation into 1 Kings 13 that serves to prepare for 2
Kgs 23:15-20, and probably the interpolation as well as the latter text
derive from the editor.[6]

But if 1 Kgs 13:2b is recognized as secondary, the same must be true
of v. 3a because after v. 2b is removed v. 3a obtrudes between the
address to the altar in v. 2a[b] and the actual judgment pronouncement in
v. 3b. Thus vv. 2a[b]+3b alone remain as the original word against the
altar. This assessment finds confirmation in the fact that v. 3b is the only
part of the judgment speech against the altar that has no corresponding
sentence to indicate its fulfillment in 2 Kgs 23:15-20. Thus, following
upon the narrative introduction supplied by vv. 1a+2a[a], the original
pronouncement of the man of God against the altar must have read:

> Oh Altar, Oh Altar, thus says Yahweh,
> "Behold the altar will be torn apart and the ashes
> upon it will be spilt out."

If, as has been argued, v. 3a is judged as secondary, then v. 5 must
also be secondary because it refers back to the sign of which v. 3a
speaks. Another decisive consideration for the secondary nature of this
verse lies in the fact that once v. 5 has reported the immediate fulfillment of the judgment announced in v. 3b it renders purposeless the
remainder of the story in which the authenticity of the judgment oracle
and of the man of God is tried. Furthermore, if v. 5 indeed belonged to

---

Kaiser, 1971] 171-72) holds to the latter view, though he considers only 2 Kgs 23:15-
18 as conclusion to the 1 Kings 13 story. He argues that 1 Kings 13 is incomplete
without the story of the fulfillment of the prediction in 2 Kgs 23:16-18.

[5] So also T. B. Dozeman, "The Way of the Man of God from Judah: True and
False Prophecy in the Pre-Deuteronomistic Legend of I Kgs 13," *CBQ* 44 (1982) 382.

[6] Cf. McKenzie, *The Trouble with Kings*, 52 and 54; O'Brien, *The Deuteronomistic
History Hypothesis*, 263; Nelson, *The Double Redaction*, 82; and Noth, *Könige*, 293.

the original story, then the concluding word of the prophet in v. 32 which affirms the certain and coming fulfillment of the oracle against the altar would have no meaning.

The narrative builds to its conclusion in v. 32. There the old prophet from Bethel can finally decide the issue that has been at stake throughout the story, namely, whether or not the oracle pronounced by the man of God is authentic. Thus the old prophet gives as a reason for his request to be buried in the same tomb with the man of God that "the pronouncement which he (the man of God) cried by the word of Yahweh against the altar in Bethel will surely come to pass." Without this concluding sentence the old prophet's request would remain an unexplained puzzle.[7] However, the remaining part of v. 32 broadens the application of the pronouncement of judgment spoken by the man of God from simply the altar at Bethel to "all the houses of the high places in the cities of Samaria," and therefore it must stem from an editor.

At this point one may summarize the findings of the discussion above. Before its placement at 1 Kings 13 the narrative probably included the following: 1a, 2a, 3b, 4 (without the name "Jeroboam" and the localization "at the altar"), and 6-32a.

The foregoing literary analysis has weakened the connection between 1 Kings 13 and Jeroboam by its argument that all of the references which would give the story a setting in Jeroboam's festival or that would give Jeroboam a part in the story (12:32c-33, 13:1b and the term "Jeroboam" in v. 4) are secondary and derive from the editor who joined the narrative to the material regarding Jeroboam in 12:25-32b. One could

---

7 See also Dozeman ("The Way of the Man of God from Judah," 382) who argues that "the theme of I Kings 13 is resolved by 13:32a." The claim that the story in 1 Kings 13 finds its resolution in v. 32a presupposes that 1 Kings 13 comprises an original literary unity. In support of this view one may note that 1 Kings 13 is woven together tightly 1) by pervasive thematic terminology, e.g. *bidbar yhwh* in vv. 1, 2a, 9, 17, 18, 32a; *derek* in vv. 9, 10, 12, 17, 24, 25, 26, 28; and *šûb* in vv. 7, 9, 10, 16, 17, 18, 19, 20, 22, 23, 26, 29; and 2) by a tight progression of plot wherein the first episode (about the man of God from Judah, the word against the altar, and the king, vv. 1-10) is bound securely to the second section (about the testing of the authenticity of the man of God from Judah and of his message, vv. 11-32a) by the recurring motif of returning, eating, and drinking (vv. 7-9, 15-19). See similarly Gross, "Lying Prophet," 102-103; and Lemke, "The Way of Obedience," 306. But contrast Würthwein (*Könige*, 168; and "Die Erzählung vom Gottesmann aus Juda in Bethel: Zur Komposition von I Kön 13," in *Wort und Geschichte: K. Elliger Festschrift* [AOAT 18; Neukirchen: Butzon & Bercker Kevelaer, 1973] 181-89) who finds two originally independent legends in vv. 1-10 and 11-31.

add to this argument another based on form. The story shows little interest in concrete details that would tie it to a historical setting. It does not name its two main characters, neither the man of God from Judah nor the prophet from Bethel. Similarly, in most of its references to the king he is unnamed (4a, 6a, b, 7a, 8, 11). This formal consideration renders even the two existing references to Jeroboam in v. 1b and v. 4 highly suspect.[8] Thus it is very doubtful that the original story in 1 Kings 13 had anything to do with Jeroboam. *what a doubt!!!*

Yet even if the argument is granted that 1 Kings 13 has only a redactional connection with the material regarding Jeroboam and that the editor entered the name of Jeroboam into the text, it is still conceivable that the story could be old enough to reflect a contemporary criticism of the religious institutions established by Jeroboam. However, certain elements in the story suggest another more probable historical setting. When the story in 1 Kings 13 is isolated as has been done above, when it is stripped of all allusions to Josiah's action at Bethel in vv. 2b-3a, then the oracle of judgment against the altar can be understood on its own terms. The oracle in itself offers no indication as to the source from which the judgment shall come, but one may seek an answer to the question thus raised by asking from where Amos and Hosea expected judgment to come against Israel's sanctuaries (Amos 3:13-15, 5:5, 7:8-9, 10-13, 9:1; Hos 8:6, 10:5-6, 8). Probably one should understand for 1 Kgs 13:3b as in the case of Amos and Hosea that the destruction of the altar will be due to foreign conquest.[9] It is highly improbable that 1 Kgs 13:3b originally anticipated the desecration of the royal sanctuary at Bethel from some source within Israel or Judah. Indeed, the story about the man of God from Judah has its strongest parallel precisely in the account about Amos, another prophet from Judah who also pronounced a word of judgment against the altar in Bethel during the time of another king named Jeroboam (Amos 3:13-15; 5:5; 7:8-9, 10-13; 9:1). Though one probably should not go so far as to identify the two prophets,[10] and though

---

[8] Similarly, Dozeman, "The Way of the Man of God from Judah," 382; Noth, *Könige*, 293-94; and Gross, "Lying Prophet," 101.

[9] Noth (*Könige*, 295), though he does not make reference to the Amos and Hosea parallels, thinks that "the threat against the altar at Bethel evidently anticipates an enemy invasion, an overthrow of Israel . . . ."

[10] Such an identification is made by J. L. Crenshaw, *Prophetic Conflict: Its Effect upon Israelite Religion* (New York: Walter de Gruyter, 1971) 42; and by J. Morgenstern, *Amos Studies*, 2 vols. (Sigmund Rheinstrom Memorial Publications 2; Cincin-

the strong parallels do not necessarily constitute evidence that the two prophets worked contemporaneously with each other, the Amos story suggests a possible historical setting for 1 Kings 13 in the period of political instability after the rise of the Assyrian threat.

Since the connection of 1 Kings 13 to Jeroboam I has proven to be extremely tenuous on a literary basis, and since the oracle of judgment against the altar at Bethel in v. 3b is most easily understood in a context when foreign threat against the Israelite State looms large, the time of Amos and Hosea presents a plausible and perhaps even a probable historical setting for 1 Kings 13 whereas the time of Jeroboam I appears improbable. Though the story in 1 Kings 13, by its oracle against the altar at Bethel, indeed signified a judgment on the cult the Israelite State, it did not specifically oppose Jeroboam I or his initiative for religion in Israel. The connection of 1 Kings 13 with Jeroboam I derives from a late period and is accomplished through the editing of the story and through its placement in its present context.

The editing and placement of 1 Kings 13 served to emphasize a key point. The story could now be utilized to present the cult and sanctuary at Bethel as one under divine condemnation and judgment from the very beginning of Jeroboam's reign because it was a sanctuary chosen and established out of Jeroboam's own initiative rather than out of Yahweh's.

## B. Judges 17-18

The narrative in Judges 17-18 offers an account of how an Israelite sanctuary came to be established at Dan, and it describes the founding of that sanctuary in highly polemical language. In view of the claim in 1 Kgs 12:29-30 that Jeroboam installed a golden calf in the sanctuary at Dan, one may inquire about the possible connections between the account about the Danite sanctuary in Judges 17-18 and Jeroboam's activity there. Does Judges 17-18 offer relevant information regarding the sanctuary at Dan antecedent to Jeroboam's initiatives there, and/or is it meant as an indirect criticism against the cult Jeroboam sponsored there?

As the narrative in Judges 17-18 now stands there can be no doubt about its intent to ridicule or to criticize the religious ventures of which

nati: Hebrew Union College Press, 1941) I: 164-79. Contrast Lemke, "The Way of Obedience," 315-16.

it tells. The assertion, "In those days there was no king in Israel; every-one did what was right in one's own eyes" (17:6, cf. 18:1a), makes this evident. This assertion intends to say that events such as those reported here could only take place in the absence of an appropriate, regulative authority and that if there had been a king in Israel these things would not have been allowed.

But what are the things that stand under this negative judgment? In view of the position of the formula at v. 6 one must presume that the first five verses already tell about such a thing that should not have occurred. Probably an element of ridicule lies in the explanation that the silver which was once stolen by Micah and put under the curse by his mother had now been melted down to form a sacred image. However, the activities that the authority of the king could be expected to regulate must be first and foremost the manufacture of graven images, the erec-tion of "houses of gods", and the appointment of priests. In all these respects the statement of v. 6 appears to place a negative judgment on the religious ventures of Micah and his mother.

Yet the reproach of v. 6 also pertains to what is narrated in the text that follows it, as does the similar insinuation of 18:1a, and so one must understand that even in the appointment of the Levite (17:7-13) proper order has not been observed. If in this way the entire cultic arrangement set up by Micah stands under such negative evaluation, then the shrine which the Danites established using the Levite and the cultic parapher-nalia which they had stolen from Micah must stand under the same negative judgment. Since the whole story moves toward the moment of the establishment of the Danite sanctuary, one must conclude that the primary intention of the narrative is to point out the illegitimacy of the sanctuary at Dan.[11]

Given that Judges 17-18 raises a polemic against the sanctuary at Dan, and given Jeroboam's connections with that sanctuary, it would be of interest to inquire regarding the source and date of that polemical composition in order to determine whether and how it pertains to Jeroboam. Possibly the polemical composition predates Jeroboam and does not pertain to Jeroboam at all, or perhaps someone composed it

---

[11] For discussion of the many literary subtleties whereby the story ridicules and disparages the cult of Micah and thereby, even more so, the cult at Dan see M. Noth, "The Background of Judges 17-18," in *Israel's Prophetic Heritage: Essays in Honor of James Muilenburg*, ed. B. W. Anderson and W. Harrelson (New York: Harper and Row, 1962) 68-85; and D. R. Davis, "Comic Literature—Tragic Theology: A Study of Judges 17-18," *WTJ* 46 (1984) 156-63.

during the time of Jeroboam as a criticism of Jeroboam's official cult at Dan or of some other contemporary Danite cult, or it could be that the author prepared this composition at a time much later than Jeroboam with the intention not to criticize specifically Jeroboam's religious policies at Dan but, rather, to criticize the cult at Dan much more broadly over the entire period of its existence.

Judges 17-18 and 19-21 are frequently recognized as appendices to the book of Judges because they interrupt the continuity between the deliverer stories that precede, on the one hand, and the account of the last deliverer with the transition to the monarchical period in 1 Samuel 1-7, on the other hand. If one accepts a Josianic date for the first edition of the Deuteronomistic History,[12] that sets the earliest possible time for the incorporation of Judges 17-18 and 19-21 into the Deuteronomistic History at the end of the seventh century BCE. The actual composition of these appendices could have occurred at approximately this same time, or it could have occurred much earlier.

Judges 17-18 offers several temporal indicators to assist in the determination of the date of its composition, namely 1) the twice repeated assertion that "in those days there was no king in Israel" (17:6, 18:1a), 2) the statement that the priesthood in Dan remained with the line of Jonathan, the son of Gershom until "the day of the captivity of the land" (18:30), and 3) the claim that Micah's image stood at Dan "for the whole time that the house of God was at Shiloh" (18:31).

If one were to date the composition on the basis of these indicators, then the reference in 18:30 would require a date after the Assyrian conquest and exile of the northern and Transjordanian regions of Israel in 732 BCE (2 Kgs 15:29) at the earliest, or alternatively after the conquest and exile of Samaria in 721 BCE. However, it could be argued that one or more of the temporal indicators listed above are the product of editorial revisions to the text and that the story actually predates them.[13] Hence each of them requires consideration on its own merits.

Most likely the formulae in Judg 17:6 and 18:1a have had an integral place in this narrative from the time of its composition. Noth has offered

---

[12] Cross, *Canaanite Myth and Hebrew Epic*, 284; and Nelson, *The Double Redaction*, 120-22; McKenzie, *The Trouble with Kings*, 133-34; O'Brien, *The Deuteronomistic History Hypothesis*, 288; cf. Provan, *Hezekiah and the Book of Kings*, 153-55.

[13] So, for instance, G. F. Moore (*A Critical and Exegetical Commentary on Judges* [ICC; New York: Charles Scribner, 1895] 369) considers the formulae in 17.6 and 18.1a secondary; and Noth ("The Background of Judges 17-18," 83) considers 18.30b redactional.

a persuasive argument in this regard by pointing out that whereas in Judg 19:1a and 21:25 the same formulae appear at the very beginning and at the very end of a narrative, precisely where one might expect to find redactional additions, the formulae in 17:6 and 18:1a mark junctures where one theme gives way to another, at places where one would be less likely to expect redactional formulae.[14] Thus the original narrative in Judges 17-18 appears to have been composed with the intention of illustrating the disarray in religious affairs in the absence of a regulative monarchical authority. Hence the polemical composition must date from monarchical times.[15]

Since Judges 17-18 devotes a great deal of attention to the establishment of Micah's shrine and to the Danite plundering of that shrine, it requires a resolution of that theme at the end to show what became of the Levite and of the sacred objects which the Danites had taken with them. Such a resolution first occurs at 18:30-31. Judging from the repetitious nature of this section, part of it must be secondary to the original composition. Since 18:30 rather abruptly offers the identification Jonathan the son of Gershom the son of Moses for the priest who to this point has been unnamed,[16] one may suspect that it is secondary. Consequently it does not supply any evidence for dating the composition. It

---

[14] Noth, "The Background of Judges 17-18," 79.

[15] Contrast R. G. Boling (*Judges* [AB 6A; Garden City: Doubleday, 1975] 254-67) who finds in this narrative mostly "preformed units" (p. 257) dating from the premonarchical period and critical of the anarchy in the cult practices of that period. However, one may question to what extent cult practices such as those reflected in Judges 17-18 would actually have come under criticism during the pre-monarchic period. In the earliest period of Israelite religion various iconographies appear to have found acceptance (e.g., the bronze serpent fashioned by Moses [Num 21:6-9, cf. 2 Kgs 18:4] and Gideon's ephod [Judg 8:24-27]) and priests other than Levites could function without apparent criticism (e.g., David's sons [2 Sam 8:18], Ira the Jairite [2 Sam 20:26], and Zabud the son of Nathan [1 Kgs 4:5]). The criticisms offered against Micah's religious ventures in Judges 17 could hardly derive from the pre-monarchical period.

[16] Contrast C. F. Burney (*The Book of Judges* [Library of Biblical Studies; New York: KTAV, 1970] 415) and J. A. Soggin (*Judges* [OTL; Philadelphia: Westminster, 1981] 266) who reconstruct "Jonathan son of Gershom" from "traces" in *wĕhûʾ gār šām* at Judg 17:7. However, there is no textual evidence for such a reconstruction. Furthermore, the primary interest of the author apparently lies in the evaluation of religious practices rather than in the presentation of historical detail such as names. Therefore, one should accept the MT as it stands. (It may be suggested that even the name Micah, rather than preserving some actual historical detail, was chosen to serve the interests of the story since the name *mîkāyĕhû* ["Who is like Yahweh?"] stands in ironic contradiction to the creation of an image to represent Yahweh.)

seems most probable, then, that 18:31 with its claim that the Danites set up Micah's graven image for the whole time the house of God was at Shiloh must be the original conclusion to the story.

If the formulae in 17:6 and 18:1a and the note referring to the house of God at Shiloh in 18:31 are accepted as original to the story, the date of its composition must be after the destruction of the Temple at Shiloh (ca. 1050) and after the emergence of the monarchy in Israel. From this point one may proceed by the process of elimination to locate the most likely historical context for the composition of Judges 17-18.

First one might consider the period of the United Monarchy on the grounds that the formulae in 17:6 and 18:1a indicate that the material is promonarchical and apologetic, that it offers an argument that the strong central authority of David or Solomon was necessary to regulate affairs in the country.[17] However, this suggestion raises a serious difficulty in that it presupposes that already during the period of the United Monarchy the impetus towards centralization of worship in Jerusalem was so strong as to occasion a polemic against rival sanctuaries. Yet it is evident from several sources that other sanctuaries continued to play a vital role for this period. Clearly Hebron continued to function as an important sanctuary during this period as is evident from Absalom's resorting to its sanctuary (2 Sam 15:7). Similarly Gibeon continued as the greatest high place till at least the beginning of Solomon's reign (1 Kgs 3:4). Furthermore, considering the fact that David also had a teraphim (1 Sam 19:13), consulted the ephod (1 Sam 30:7-8), and made his own sons and Ira the Jairite priests (2 Sam 8:18, 20:26), the criticisms offered in Judges 17-18 could be turned against David himself. Therefore they appear quite inappropriate and quite unlikely in the context of the Davidic-Solomonic court.

Second, one might consider Noth's point of view, that Judges 17-18 derives from the new priesthood installed by Jeroboam at Dan and is directed against the old tribal sanctuary with its silver statuette and its vagabond priesthood.[18] However, this conclusion is impossible since one of the chief criticisms in the narrative concerns the graven and molten image which Micah had made, and this criticism would have applied as much to Jeroboam's calf iconography as to the old image used in the cult at Dan. Furthermore, Noth's argument presupposes that

---

[17] So A. E. Cundall, "Judges—An Apology for the Monarchy?" *ExpTim* 81 (1970) 178-81; and cf. Davis, "Comic Literature," 157.

[18] Noth, "The Background of Judg 17-18," 81-82.

Jeroboam chose new iconography, a new priesthood, and a new cult center at Dan. As has been argued above in chapter III, it is highly unlikely that Jeroboam made any such radical breaks with tradition.[19]

It is much more likely that the composition in Judges 17-18 originates in Judah at a time concurrent with or shortly after the writing of the first edition of the Deuteronomistic History. The story betrays a Judahite setting in its notation that the camping spot of the Danites in Judah near Kiriath Jearim[20] is called Mahaneh-dan "to this day" (18:12), a tradition that has little relevance to the story and would have little interest to anyone outside of Judah.[21] Furthermore, the story at several points presupposes the Deuteronomistic perspective which found its final expression in the Judahite context. This is true for 18:31 which contrasts the illegitimate sanctuary at Dan with the true sanctuary at Shiloh. That verse probably means to say, "[At Dan] they set up the graven image which Micah had made (even though) for that whole time the (legitimate) house of God was at Shiloh."[22] Also, the formulae in 17:6 and 18:1a presuppose Deut 12:8[23] with its impetus for centralization of the cult. It bears emphasizing that Judg 17:6 and 18:1a in their context

---

[19] See further the argument by M. Goulder, *The Psalms of the Sons of Korah* (JSOTSup 20; Sheffield: JSOT Press, 1982) 52-53.

[20] The mention of Kiriath-Jearim as a city of Judah might also be taken as an indicator of the earliest time at which the story could have been written because Kiriath-Jearim at first entered into league with Benjamin (Josh 9:17, cf. Josh 18:28 and the note in BHS) and probably passed into the possession of Judah only when Judah's northern border was redrawn after the break-up of the Solomonic kingdom. So also Noth, "The Background of Judges 17-18," p. 71, n. 9.

[21] So also W. Hertzberg, *Die Bücher Josua, Richter, Ruth* (ATD; Göttingen: Vandenhoeck & Ruprecht, 1953) 237-38; contrast Noth, "The Background of Judges 17-18," 70-71. In agreement with Noth one should recognize the strong connection of Judges 17-18 to the sanctuary at Dan. However, as will be argued below, that pertains to an even earlier stage of the traditions that have been taken up into the composition of Judges 17-18.

[22] One may infer from the respect given to Shiloh in 1 Samuel 1-4 and from the "Deuteronomistic" words of Jeremiah in Jer 7:9, "Shiloh, where I made *my name dwell*," that the Deuteronomists considered Shiloh as the central sanctuary for the period before David. The writer at Judg 18:31 apparently shares this opinion. Cf. the comments on Judg 18:31 by G. Ahlström, *Aspects of Syncretism in Israelite Religion* (Horae Soederblomianae 5; Lund: C. W. K. Gleerup, 1963) 26-27; and Boling, *Judges*, 267.

[23] Specifically, Judg 17:6 shares with Deut 12:8 the negative evaluation of cultic conduct in a period lacking regulation when "everyone did whatever was right in one's own eyes."

concern precisely matters of the cult and so correspond very closely with the concern of Deut 12:8.

Thus the story in Judges 17-18 with its polemical orientation probably originated in the late monarchical period in Judah at the hand of an author closely aligned with the perspectives of the DtrH.[24] The composition in Judges 17-18, aside from its incorporation into the Deuteronomistic History, served to explain why the Yahweh sanctuary at Dan suffered destruction in the Assyrian conquest. It was because the sanctuary from its inception had involved the use of reprehensible graven images and ill-gotten cultic paraphernalia. Such a story could be incorporated appropriately into the Deuteronomistic History because it fit in with DtrH's own special theme concerning Jeroboam as the root cause of apostasy in Israel. To serve this theme the story presented the sanctuary at Dan, which at a later time the apostate Jeroboam would choose as an important shrine of his kingdom, as an illegitimate cult center from its very foundation. In this way the story threw the whole history of worship at Dan, including its use during the period of Jeroboam, under negative judgment.

However, it appears that in creating this polemical composition the author of Judges 17-18 made use of much older traditions that had their original setting at the sanctuary at Dan. The fact that Judges 17-18, even in its present shape, exhibits knowledge in some detail concerning the old city of Laish and preserves a significant tradition of how the Danites came to live there argues for the existence of such old traditions. These traditions concerned the Danite conquest and the Danite aetiology for the shrine at Dan. The shape these traditions originally took and the incidents of which they told are no longer fully accessible to the reader on account of the late polemical reshaping of the traditions, but the stories must have related with pride certain facts about how God had given the city of Laish into the hands of the Danites and about how cultic objects and a levitical priest were brought from Ephraim to establish this sanctuary at Dan.[25] The comment in 1 Kgs 12:30 that the people

---

[24] Similar conclusions are offered by Ahlström, *Aspects of Syncretism*, 26-27; Soggin, *Judges*, 269 and 277; and Goulder, *The Psalms of the Sons of Korah*, 53.

[25] A. Malamat ("The Danite Migration and the Pan-Israelite Exodus-Conquest: A Biblical Narrative Pattern," *Bib* 51 [1970] 1-16) has shown rather convincingly how Judges 17-18 shares the pattern of the all-Israelite conquest narrative. It offers a small version of the larger pattern including as common elements the episodes of the spies, of the campaign, and episodes involving the priesthood and the cultic objects.

made procession before one of the calves as far as Dan may very correctly reflect a traditional cultic re-enactment of the circumstances by which cultic objects were originally moved from a shrine in Ephraim to establish the sanctuary at Dan.

It may be concluded, then, that a pre-literary, positive cult-aetiology that told about the fashioning of a cult image and appurtenances and about their establishment at Dan lies behind the narrative in Judges 17-18 with its present polemical orientation. The probability of such a reconstruction can be argued further by drawing analogies from several other biblical accounts of the creation of cult objects which originally appear to have held an acceptable place in Israelite religion but eventually came to be viewed as illegitimate. Such an analogy may be demonstrated most clearly in the case of the bronze serpent, the construction of which tradition attributed to Moses (Num 21:6-9).[26] The tradition that tells of its construction does so in a wholly positive way, and it has survived as such within the Hebrew Bible. Evidently this bronze serpent continued to hold a place in the Jerusalemite cult as an acceptable iconographic item until the reign of Hezekiah at which time someone determined its illegitimacy in the cult of Yahweh and required its removal from the temple (2 Kgs 18:4). A second analogy may be drawn from the account concerning Gideon's ephod (Judg 8:24-27). One may note that Judg 6:11-8:23 consistently presents Gideon sympathetically as one faithful to Yahweh and that the account in Judg 8:24-27a tells of Gideon's manufacture of the golden ephod in neutral terms. It comes as somewhat of a surprise, then, that Judg 8:27b should criticize Gideon's ephod as a cause for Israel's "harlotry" and as a "snare" for Gideon's family. In all probability this criticism entered the tradition at a secondary level[27] and represents a later evaluation of what at first functioned as an acceptable cultic item. A third analogy may be derived from the text of Exod 32:1-6. To anticipate the argument in section IV.c, that text probably originated as a positive cult-aetiology for the calf image in Israelite worship, but, of course, that cultic image eventually also came to be rejected.

Behind the disparaging criticisms, the underlying traditions of Judges 17-18 offer a veiled glimpse into the cult at the sanctuary of Dan antecedent to Jeroboam's activity there. It is doubtful that the propriety of its cult or the legitimacy of its sanctuary ever came into question

---

This in itself suggests that an underlying, positive story has undergone polemical revision.

[26] Cf. the comments by Mettinger, "The Veto on Images," 17.

[27] Probably it originated with DtrH. So Mettinger, "The Veto on Images," 16.

before or during the time of Jeroboam, and in all likelihood the literary disparagement of the sanctuary and its cult in Judges 17-18 only came about in the attempt to explain its demise after the Assyrian conquest.

## C. Exodus 32

Exodus 32 stands in close relationship with 1 Kgs 12:26-32 as one may judge on the basis of several points of contact between the two narratives. In both contexts the calf image occupies a central place, and the cry *hinnēh*[28] *ʾĕlōhêkā yiśrāʾēl ʾăšer heʿĕlûkā mēʾereṣ miṣrāyim* ("Look, your god[s], oh Israel, who brought you out of the land of Egypt") is spoken in reference to the image. In both cases an altar is set up before the calf, and in both cases sacrifice is offered in front of it. Both texts, moreover, refer to the appointment of a festival.[29] One could cite more points of contact,[30] but these are sufficient to demonstrate the close relationship between the texts and to justify consideration of Exodus 32 in connection with an investigation regarding calf iconography in the religion of the Israelite State.

In seeking to determine more closely the relationship between the two texts,[31] the explanation lies close at hand that Exodus 32 is intended to censure the cult of the Israelite State for its use of calf iconography as instituted by Jeroboam. To this end, it portrays that cult as idolatrous, and it sets Israel's first departure into this idolatry into the context at Sinai in order to bring it under condemnation by Moses.[32] As for the question of whether this text intends to condemn Jeroboam in particular, it may be noted that Exodus 32 makes no specific reference to Jeroboam. Of course, such a reference should not be expected if the author has

---

[28] Exod 32.4 has *ʾēlleh* at this point.

[29] Exod 32:5 describes it explicitly as a festival to Yahweh. 1 Kgs 12:32 does not say for whom the festival is held, although the argument in section III.D above indicates that it was in honor of Yahweh.

[30] M. Aberbach and Leivy Smolar ("Aaron, Jeroboam, and the Golden Calves," *JBL* 86 [1967] 129-140) list thirteen "points of identity or contact" (p. 129) in support of their claim that the texts are interdependent. Several of the comparisons, however, are rather forced.

[31] Regarding the various possible construals, see Moberly, *At the Mountain of God*, 162-63.

[32] So Noth, *Exodus* (OTL; Philadelphia: Westminster, 1962) 246; and *idem*, *A History of Pentateuchal Traditions* (Chico, California: Scholars Press, 1981) 143-44. Cf. S. Lehming, "Versuch zu Ex. xxxii" *VT* 10 (1960) 21.

indeed shifted the setting of the account of the manufacture of the calves back to an ancient time. However, if the author intended to condemn Jeroboam for the manufacture of the calves, one might expect that the responsibility for their manufacture would have been laid on an individual who could conceivably stand as representative of Jeroboam. But the text usually places the responsibility for the fashioning of the calves with the people of whom it is repeatedly said that "they made" the calf (vv. 7, 20, 31, and 35). Only twice does the text attribute responsibility to Aaron (vv. 4, 35b). Even if the text had consistently made Aaron responsible for fashioning the calf, one would have to ask in what sense Aaron could possibly stand as a representative of Jeroboam. This shows that the story does not intend to respond first and foremost to Jeroboam's action in making the golden calves,[33] but rather, that it responds to a people who, with or without Jeroboam's initiative, have chosen the calf image as iconography for their cult.

Consequently, to explain that the composition of Exodus 32 arose as a polemic against the installation of the golden calves by Jeroboam as reported in 1 Kgs 12:26-32 does not suffice. The relationship of Exodus 32 to 1 Kgs 12:26-32 does not consist in their having a common historical referent in Jeroboam's action of making the golden calves. Rather, Exodus 32 responds in a broad sense to the subject of calf iconography in the Israelite cult while 1 Kgs 12:26-32 contributes to that same subject by affording but one brief glimpse of that cult under the official sponsorship of Jeroboam at one particular point in the history of the religion of the Israelite State.

Granting that points of contact exist and that the two texts bear this kind of relationship to each other, the preponderance of evidence points to the probability that Exodus 32, like 1 Kgs 12:26-32, pertains to calf iconography in the cult of specifically the Israelite State. All other biblical references to the calf iconography (Hos 8:4b-6, 10:5-6, 13:1-3) pertain to the cult of the Israelite State (never to the cult in Judah). Furthermore, the divine epithet ʾăbîr yaʿăqōb ("Bull of Jacob," e.g., in Gen 49:24) indicates that the taurine imagery had a specific association with Israelite territory since Jacob traditions adhere to Israelite localities such as Bethel, Shechem, and Penuel. However, with respect to Exod 32:1-6 one may look even more specifically to Bethel as the geographical setting behind the narrative. One may argue that the figure of Aaron in

---

33 Cf. the argument by Mettinger, "The Veto on Images," 17.

Exod 32:1-6 connects the narrative with Bethel since Aaronide priests held office there.[34]

If Exodus 32 is intended to censure the cult of the Israelite State for its use of calf iconography, one may inquire regarding the source of this censure and whether Exodus 32 reflects opposition by groups that might have been contemporaries or near contemporaries with Jeroboam.

In analyzing the text of Exodus 32, it quickly becomes evident that the text is multi-layered. Its various layers appear to represent various voices that arose in opposition to the calf iconography, possibly at different times. Following upon the initial account of the fashioning of the golden calf and of the sacred festival held in honor of Yahweh (vv. 1-6), the text offers six different and in some ways irreconcilable responses to that action: 1) Yahweh intends to destroy the people for making the calf, but when Moses intercedes Yahweh repents of the evil (vv. 7-14); 2) Moses responds angrily, breaking the tables of the covenant, destroying the golden calf, and forcing the people to drink the water into which the dust of the pulverized image has been thrown (vv. 15-20); 3) Moses scolds Aaron for making the calf (vv. 21-24); 4) Moses summons the sons of Levi to massacre their guilty kinfolk (vv. 25-29); 5) Yahweh threatens to punish the people at some future time (vv. 30-34); 6) Yahweh sends a plague to punish the people for making the calf (v. 35).

A significant tension exists between these various responses. It comes as a surprising turn of affairs that Moses, after having persuaded Yahweh not to reject Israel (vv. 7-14), should himself break the "tables of the testimony" signifying thereby the dissolution of the covenant between Yahweh and Israel (vv. 15-20); or that after having merely reproved Aaron (vv. 21-24), Moses should call on the Levites to massacre the guilty among the people (vv. 25-29); or that after the massacre by the Levites there should still be need for Moses to seek to make atonement for Israel's sin (vv. 30-34); or that after having threatened that punishment would come at some future time (v. 34) Yahweh should send a plague in the present time (v. 35). One may explain these tensions by saying that the various responses represent independent layers of tradition, each of which exhibits an attitude critical of the calf iconography as employed in the cult of the Israelite State.[35]

---

34 Regarding Aaronide priests at Bethel see section III.c above.

35 Further to the literary criticism of Exodus 32 see W. Beyerlin, *Origins and History of the Oldest Sinaitic Traditions* (Oxford: Basil Blackwell, 1965) 19. In support of the analysis of Exodus 32 given above one may also point to the repetitive nature of the story. It contains two accounts of the making of the golden calf, one in vv. 1-6

For the task of identifying these several voices of opposition (i.e., vv. 7-14, 15-20, 21-25, 26-29, 30-34, 35)[36] with one or another of the penta-teuchal sources, the texts of these units offer very few and very ambigu-ous points of reference. The clearest decision can be made for vv. 7-14 on the basis of the phraseology it shares only with the Deuteronomistic material[37] and on the basis of its agreement with the parallel account in Deut 9:8-29 that no punishment followed upon Israel's sin with the golden calf. Consequently one may assign vv. 7-14 to a Deuteronomistic source[38] or more precisely to a pre-deuteronomistic source since its par-allel in Deut 9:12-14, 25-29 clearly depends literarily on Exod 32:7-14 and develops it further.[39]

For source identification in the remaining units which respond to the initial account, the diversity of assessments offered by scholars under-lines the complexity of the task.[40] Nevertheless, the texts of these units

---

and the other in vv. 21-24. Moses learns in two different ways about Israel's sin in making the calf image, once in vv. 7-8 where Yahweh tells him about it while he is yet on the mountain, and once in vv. 15-20 where Moses, in his descent from the mountain, remains unaware of the circumstances till he comes in view of the calf. Also, Moses intercedes twice on behalf of the people, once successfully with the re-sult that Yahweh repents of intended evil against Israel (vv. 11-14), and once appar-ently without success in that Yahweh merely postpones the punishment (vv. 30-34).

The foregoing analysis does not claim to set out fully the literary complexities of Exod 32. At vv. 17-18, for instance, where Joshua quite without warning suddenly appears alongside Moses on the mountain, one should probably recognize interrup-tive material, but for the present purposes further refinements in the analysis offer no advantage. Lehming ("Versuch zu Ex. xxxii," 16-50) has pursued the source critical analysis of this text in much greater detail though at points one may question the adequacy of his criteria and whether the resulting presentation of Exodus 32 is not overly fragmented.

[36] The basic narrative in vv. 1-6 and the question of its source will receive consideration later.

[37] For details see Hahn, Das "Goldene Kalb", 112, and J. W. Davenport, "A Study of the Golden Calf Tradition in Exodus 32" (Ph. D. dissertation, Princeton Theologi-cal Seminary, 1973) 35-36. The distinctively Deuteronomistic usages are *šiḥēt* used without an object (v. 7, cf. Deut 9:12, 32:5), *mahēr* as adverb (v. 8, cf. Deut 4:26, 7:4, 22, etc.), *sārû min-hadderek* (v. 8, cf. Deut 11:28, 31:29, etc), and *bĕyād ḥăzāqâ* (v. 11, cf. Deut 11:2, 26:8, etc), *šûb mēḥărôn ʾappĕkā* (v. 12, cf. Deut 13:18, Josh 7:26, 2 Kgs 23:26).

[38] So Jaroš, *Die Stellung des Elohisten*, 375; cf. Noth, *Exodus*, 244 who includes only vv. 9-14.

[39] On this point see Hahn, Das "Goldene Kalb", 243-45; and J. Loza, "Exode xxxii et la redaction JE," *VT* 23 (1973) 34.

[40] See Hahn (Das "Goldene Kalb", 142-43) for a review of (mostly German) com-mentators from 1857-1978.

avail several points of reference to allow for the determination of their provenance and the time of their composition at least in general terms.

As a first point of reference, one may note the absence of polemic against the Israelite State such as one might have expected from authors writing from a Judahite perspective during the period in which the two kingdoms existed side by side and in rivalry with each other. In none of the layers of tradition does the accusing finger point unequivocally at the Israelite State, at Ephraim, at Jacob, or at Jeroboam, but rather the responsibility for the sin with the golden calf is referred in a general way to "the people".[41] If Exodus 32 were a polemic from Judahite sources directed against the cult of the Israelite State *while that cult was still in existence*, one would expect the identification of the offending party to be clearer and less ambiguous. As the composition now stands with its general references to "the people", the Judahite authors would have implicated the people of Judah as well as the people of Israel for an offence attributable only to Israel. Therefore, as the materials in Exodus 32 stand, it would appear either that the authors were from the Israelite State, writing in and for an Israelite context, and that in speaking of "the people" their reference to the citizens of the Israelite State would have been clear to their audience or readers; or, as is more probable, that the authors wrote at a time when it was possible for elements of both Israel and Judah to identify with each other in a common story and that the reference to "the people" implies an "all Israel" conception which embraces Judah as well. The earliest time when such an attitude would have been possible would be after the fall of Samaria, perhaps in the time of Hezekiah, when refugees from Israel moved down to Jerusalem. At that time the Jerusalemite monarch perceived in the new circumstances an opportunity where he could present himself as the only remaining hope for the survivors from the Israelite State, and where he could venture to work for a re-unified Israel under the authority of the Davidic monarchy in Jerusalem.[42] This period provides a suitable setting

---

[41] See Exod 32:1, 3, 7, 9, 11, 12, 14, 17, 21, 25, 28, 31, 34, 35. Only v. 20 identifies the people as Israel, and so also the cultic formula in vv. 4 & 8, but here even the term Israel hardly allows itself to be read unambiguously as a reference to the Northern State.

[42] Hezekiah's ambitions for the re-establishment of the Davidic state may be perceived in his efforts to centralize power in Jerusalem through the suppression of worship at sanctuaries outside of Jerusalem (2 Kgs 18:4 and 18:22), in his efforts to reclaim territory from the Philistines (18:6), and in his invitation to remaining elements in what was formerly Israel to make pilgrimage to Jerusalem to celebrate the passover (if 2 Chr 30:1 reflects an actual event of Hezekiah's time). The passover

for the revival of an all-Israelite dream and for Judahite tradents *to absorb as part of their own story* some of the experience of the Israelite State. The period of Hezekiah's reform, with its zealous rejection of country shrines in Judah and with its iconoclastic thrust, may have proved an appropriate context for religious leaders in Judah to identify Judah with Israel in its sin of idolatry and apostasy.

Furthermore, in reference to the attitude displayed in Exodus 32, one may detect a conciliatory spirit in at least the two components which recount Moses' intercession on behalf of the people (vv. 7-14, 30-34). Again, this attitude hardly suits Judahite authors writing against the cult of the Israelite State during the period of rivalry between the two states. Certainly Israelite authors criticizing the cult of their own people might have adopted such a conciliatory attitude, and similarly, authors living in Judah and writing in a time when rivalry between Israel and Judah had ended after Israel lost its political independence.

A final point of reference for the tradition-history of the various units in Exod 32:7-35 may be established on the evidence that one unit among them evaluates the calf cult as the cause of Yahweh's rejection of Israel that *has already occurred* and presupposes that the punishment for the sin *has already come*. Thus vv. 15-20 tells of the shattering of the covenant symbols and of the destruction of the calf image.

Exod 32:20 reports the destruction of the calf image. Probably these lines reflect events during the time of Assyrian incursion into the Israelite State. Though historically the conquering Assyrians probably carried off the golden calves of Dan and Bethel as booty (cf. Hos 10:6), the biblical author, in order to present a narrative consistent with the adopted framework of the Sinai story, reported the fate of the golden calf differently. According to Exod 32:20 Moses burnt (*šrp*) the image with fire, ground (*ṭḥn*) it to powder, and scattered (*zrh*) it upon the water. The verbs employed in this description correspond remarkably with those used in a scene from the Ugaritic texts in which Anat, fighting on behalf of Baʿal-Haddu, burns (*šrp*) the body of Mot, crushes (*ṭḥn*) it, and scatters (*drʿ*) it in the field where birds eat its flesh (*KTU* I.6.ii.33-36; cf. I.6.v.14-18).[43] Of course, this sequence of activities does not work realis-

---

festival, because it commemorated Israel's liberation from Egypt, could be expected to fan hopes among the Northerners for a new national liberation, this time from the oppression of the Assyrians, and this time by the agency of the Davidic king in Jerusalem. See further B. Oded, "Judah and the Exile," in *Israelite and Judaean History*, ed. J. H. Hayes and J. M. Miller (OTL; Philadelphia: Westminster, 1977) 442-44.

43 This verbal correspondence has been noted and discussed by S. E. Loewenstamm, "The Ugaritic Fertility Myth—the Result of a Mistranslation," *IEJ* 12 (1962)

tically. Having burned Mot's body, Anat would not be able to crush it or to scatter it in the fields for birds to eat. Loewenstamm explains that the author has employed this sequence of tangible images without regard for realism in order to emphasize the total annihilation of the adversary Mot.[44] At Exod 32:20 the author, by employing the corresponding Hebrew verbs, picks up on a conventional mode of expression[45] and makes a similar departure from realism. An image cast from gold could hardly be burned with fire nor could it be ground to powder after having been burned. Here also the evocative language signifies that the calf image, viewed as a hostile deity, has now been wholly overcome.

Considering other biblical texts, Moses' action toward the image corresponds most closely with the requirements first set forward in Deut 7:5, 25, 12:3 with respect to how Israel must deal with Canaanite altars, pillars, asherahs, and graven images. It may be argued from this that because Exod 32:20 has Moses fulfilling a requirement first given written formulation in Deuteronomy (though the law itself may have been somewhat older) Exod 32:15-20 must be a relatively late composition.[46]

Since vv. 15-20 presupposes that the calf image has disappeared, one may conclude that the time of its authorship must be sought after the beginning of Assyrian annexations of Israelite territories in 732 BCE (2 Kgs 15:29). But the note in v. 19 offers further clues regarding time of authorship. Moses' action in shattering the tablets of the covenant signifies that the apostasy of the people has resulted in the dissolution of God's covenant with Israel. In this one may see an allusion to the events of the destruction of the Israelite State. If so, the interpretation of those events as offered by Exod 32:19 corresponds with Hosea's perception that "put[ting] an end to the kingdom of the house of Israel" (Hos 1:4) meant that Yahweh had dissolved the covenant relationship with the people (1:9).

It is hardly conceivable that the brief narrative in vv. 15-20 could ever have existed on its own as a story of judgment that spells an abso-

---

87; and *idem*, "The Making and Destruction of the Golden Calf," *Bib* 48 (1967) 481-490. See also P. L. Watson, "The Death of 'Death' in the Ugaritic Texts," *JAOS* 92 (1972) 60-64; and Albright, *Yahweh and the Gods of Canaan*, 38.

44 "The Making and Destruction of the Golden Calf," 484-85.

45 Though Exod 32:20 apparently presupposes familiarity with traditional motifs, that does not necessarily constitute evidence that the text is extremely old. Rather one must recognize, as is often the case, that literature of a later period takes up extremely old traditions and motifs.

46 Cf. Hahn, *Das "Goldene Kalb"*, 124.

lute end to Israel's relationship with Yahweh.[47] Rather, the account in Exod 32:15-20, with its focus on the broken tablets, immediately opens forward to the possibility of covenant renewal about which Exodus 34 relates. Hence the account of vv. 15-20, within which the narration regarding the broken tablets occurs, must stem from a time when circumstances forced the conclusion upon the author that the covenant had been dissolved, but also from a time in which circumstances allowed for the hope of its future renewal. Such circumstances would have presented themselves after the fall of Samaria in 721 BCE and during the time of Hezekiah when an author writing in Jerusalem could look forward with some hope to a future for Israel together with Judah as people of Yahweh.

Beginning with this as a point of anchorage, and observing the inter-relationships between the various components in Exodus 32, one may reconstruct some basic chronological relationships between those components. Vv. 1-6 constitutes the basic narrative. All other components of Exodus 32 presuppose this narrative. After vv. 1-6 the section vv. 15-20 appears to hold priority in terms of composition history because it answers the question, "What became of the calf?" All the other units that respond to the narrative of vv. 1-6 presuppose the answer to this question. It is doubtful that any one of these other units could have stood after vv. 1-6, either to speak of Moses interceding for the people, or of Moses commissioning the sons of Levi to carry out their massacre, without this fundamental question first finding its answer.[48]

If one assesses vv. 15-20 as the oldest layer of the materials contained in vv. 7-35, and if one dates its composition to the period after 721 BCE, then all the remaining materials in vv. 7-35 must originate at that time or even later.[49] The fairly common attribution of vv. 7-14 to a

---

47 This would be just as inconceivable as Noth's explanation concerning the purpose and perspective of the Deuteronomistic Historian, that is, that the historian took on the massive task of composing the theological history of Israel solely with the intent of explaining the reason for the final disaster of Israel, without entertaining any hope for the future of Israel as a nation or as God's people (see Noth, *The Deuteronomistic History*, 97-99).

48 Others also recognize in vv. 15-20 an old layer of the story. See Beyerlin, *Oldest Sinaitic Traditions*, 19-20; Loza, "Exode xxxii," p. 51, n. 1; but cf. Davenport, "A Study of the Golden Calf Tradition," 154ff.

49 It may be added that the units vv. 21-24, 25-29, and 30-34 also presuppose vv. 15-20 simply in terms of development of the story line. Moses had to descend from the mountain before he could reprove Aaron, or before he could give the Levites their charge, or before he could again ascend the mountain to intercede on behalf of

Deuteronomistic or, more precisely, to a pre-Deuteronomistic source corresponds with this conclusion. The pre-Deuteronomistic author, as J. Loza argues,[50] probably worked during the time of Hezekiah, seeking to explain to the survivors of the fallen Israelite State that Israel's unfaithfulness, particularly in the matter of the calf image, was the reason for Yahweh's rejection of the Israelite State, that punishment was not Yahweh's last word, but that Israel could again live as the people of Yahweh under a renewed covenant.

If the foregoing conclusions regarding Exod 32:15-20 are granted, then further considerations concerning date and provenance of the units vv. 7-14, 21-24, 25-29, 30-34, and 35 are unnecessary in this context. If all these materials derive from after the end of the period of the Israelite State, their critical perspective with regard to the calf iconography has no relevance for the inquiry concerning the reception of Jeroboam's religious policies by his contemporaries.

Returning to the initial account in vv. 1-6, one may now inquire what attitude it exhibits toward the calf iconography. The very first verse appears to set up the entire account in negative terms. It says that the people assembled themselves against (*yiqqāhēl ʿal*) Aaron. Probably this terminology connotes rebellion as in the murmuring traditions (Num 16:3, 19; 17:7=Eng 16:41; 20:2).[51] V. 1 goes on to say that the people requested of Aaron to make *ʾĕlōhîm* to lead them in the place of Moses who had been absent for a long time. In this request the people appear to abandon the God of Moses in favor of gods.

After v. 1 there follows an account which describes in rather neutral terms the collection of earrings as material for making an image, the fashioning of the calf image itself, the proclamation of a cultic affirmation over the image, the making of an altar, and the celebration of a festival to Yahweh. Possibly one should interpret that the formula *ʾēlleh ʾĕlōhêkā yiśrāʾēl ʾăšer heʿĕlûkā mēʾereṣ miṣrayim* (v. 4d) connotes more than one deity. It may be that in using this formula the author intended to

---

the people. Unless one or more of these units originally belonged with the composition of vv. 15-20 (as may actually have been the case with vv. 30-34), they must have been composed after vv. 15-20.

[50] "Exode xxxii," 31-55, especially 51-55. Loza designates this pre-Deuteronomistic writer RJE and recognizes the work of this writer in Exod 32:7-14, (perhaps 21-24), 30-34, 33:12-23, 34:1b, 6-10, Num 9:11-15, 14:11-23. According to Loza, RJE deserves the credit for the present structure in Exodus 32-34 of covenant establishment, covenant breaking, and covenant renewal.

[51] For further discussion see G. W. Coats, *Rebellion in the Desert* (Nashville: Abingdon, 1968) 188 and 24-25.

mark the cult as polytheistic even though in this literary context the formula creates an inconsistency in view of the fact that the account speaks of only one calf image. On the other hand, one may also interpret the plurals in this formula as *pluralis maiestatis* in reference to the one god of Israel.[52]

Scholars have also found other features in the text of vv. 1-6 which, according to their assessment, imply a negative evaluation of the event narrated there. Thus some commentators have sensed a contemptuous tone in the choice of the term ʿēgel.[53] However, this term need not have had and probably did not have such a connotation.[54] Commentators have also interpreted that lĕṣaḥeq (v. 6) intends to disparage the festivities as vile sexual orgies, but, as has already been argued above, the verb probably denoted a quite acceptable celebrative activity in the context of Israelite worship (cf. 2 Sam 6:5=1 Chr 13:8; 2 Sam 6:21=1 Chr 15:29).[55] Thus the account in vv. 1-6 bears marks of a critical or polemical attitude only in v. 1 and possibly in the formula in v. 4d.

Considering vv. 1-6 as a literary unit, it quickly becomes evident that it could not have existed as an independent piece. Having portrayed the people as rebellious, apostate, and perhaps as idolatrous and polytheistic, the account given in vv. 1-6 requires resolution to explain the out-

---

52 Further to this question, refer back to section III.A.1.

53 Rather than the designation ʿēgel, i.e. calf, the author could have chosen the term šôr, i.e. bull. See Noth, *Exodus*, 248, and *Könige*, 284; Montgomery, *Kings*, 257; and other references in Hahn, *Das "Goldene Kalb"*, p. 17 n. 28.

54 To the contrary, according to Albright the term ʿēgel has a complimentary and positive significance in that it refers to a young two or three year old bull in the prime of its strength (*From the Stone Age to Christianity*, 300). That the terminology in itself did not have disparaging connotations can be seen from the ways in which the term ʿēgel has been used in biblical literature and in epigraphic sources from Syria-Palestine: 1) In Ps 106:19-20 ʿēgel occurs in parallel with šôr which is cognate to Ugaritic ṯr, often used as an epithet of El (*KTU* I.4.iv.38-39, I.14.i.40-42, I.14.iv.6). 2) Samaria Ostraca #41 attests the personal name ʿglyw (Y. Aharoni, *The Land of the Bible*, trans. and ed. A. F. Rainey [Philadelphia: Westminster, 1979] 361). The name may mean "Yahweh the young bull" or "the calf of Yahweh" (Noth, *Die Israelitischen Personennamen*, 150; and De Vaux, *The Bible and the Ancient Near East*, 102). If the former interpretation is correct, the parent who gave the name must have considered the association of ʿēgel with Yahweh quite appropriate. 3) According to 1 Kgs 10:19, if one corrects the pointing of the MT rôʾš ʿāgôl to rāʾšê ʿēgel (as presupposed by the LXX), Solomon's throne had calf heads as iconography along the back, presumably to signify the power of the throne (Montgomery, *Kings*, 231; Noth, *Könige*, 204; Gray, *Kings*, 263; DeVries, *I Kings*, 147).

55 Refer back to section III.A.3.b.

come of this state of affairs. Vv. 15-20 provide exactly such a resolution. Hence it could be concluded that vv. 1-6 belongs integrally with vv. 15-20 as a literary unit. If such is the case, then in view of the conclusions reached above regarding the provenance and date of vv. 15-20, it follows that vv. 1-6 also derives from the period after the collapse of the Israelite State. In that case this section, like all the materials that follow it in Exodus 32, can offer no evidence of opposition to the official Israelite cult from the time of Jeroboam or from the time shortly after it.

However, vv. 1-6 also yields to another possible analysis. Regarding v. 1a it may be noted that it ties the account into the Sinai context by linking up with Exod 24:12-18. One may suspect that its association with the rest of vv. 1-6 is secondary, that it was introduced at this point only to make this connection.[56] Perhaps v. 1b should also be reckoned with v. 1a in this way. On the other hand, the request of the people in v. 1b could mean that in the absence of Moses as leader they desired a visible symbol of Yahweh's presence. The fact that the people later proclaim a Yahwistic cultic formula over the image and celebrate a feast to Yahweh before it suggests such an interpretation. As for the cultic formula in v. 4b, if indeed it intends the connotation of polytheism, it may be that the actual formula used in the cult unambiguously referred to one god, *zeh ʾĕlōhêkā ʾăšer heʿelkā mimmiṣrāyim* ("This is your God who brought you up from Egypt"—Neh 9:18 with reference to the golden calf), but that Exod 32:4b attests a formula that has been polemically altered under the influence of 1 Kgs 12:28e where the connotation of polytheism better fits the context.[57]

Thus one may argue that vv. 1-6 exhibits a pejorative attitude towards the calf iconography only as a result of editorial addition and revision. In its present form this section requires the resolution offered by vv. 15-20 as has been explained above, and one may explain that the writer responsible for vv. 15-20 introduced these pejorative editorial changes to vv. 1-6. However, when loosed from its editorial preface in v. 1a and freed from the possibly pejorative connotation in v. 4b, vv. 1b-6 can stand quite independently of the material that follows in vv. 15-20 as an account complete in itself. On its own vv. 1b-6 appears to be an aetiology for the use of calf iconography in the cult, claiming the authority

---

[56] So Jaroš, *Die Stellung des Elohisten*, 378; Davenport, "A Study of the Golden Calf Tradition," 50. Cf. Beyerlin, *Oldest Sinaitic Traditions*, 127.

[57] So Noth, *Exodus*, 248; Childs, *Exodus*, 559-60; Cross, *Canaanite Myth and Hebrew Epic*, 73-74.

of so venerable a figure as Aaron for its institution.[58] In consideration of Aaron's association with Bethel one may suggest Bethel as the origin of this aetiology.

A further argument for Exod 32:1b-6 as an aetiology for a cultic object derives from the parallels provided by several other aetiologies preserved in the Hebrew Bible. Aaron's request for golden rings and his subsequent fashioning of a cult object from them finds a parallel in Gideon's request for golden earrings and his fashioning an ephod from them (Judg 8:24-27).[59] A second parallel may be sought in the P narrative of the offerings of gold, silver, etc., that Moses solicited for the construction of the ark and the tabernacle with all its appurtenances (Exod 35).

In addition to the correspondence in the solicitation of jewelry or precious metals as construction material, Exod 32:1b-6 also parallels other aetiologies in the way it authorizes the cultic object through an important figure. Aaron fashioned the golden calf just as Gideon fashioned the ephod, and just as Moses made the bronze serpent (Num 21:6-9) still venerated in the Jerusalem temple under the name Nehushtan till the time of Hezekiah (2 Kgs 18:4), and just as Moses commissioned and oversaw the construction of the ark and the tabernacle with all its appurtenances (Exod 35:30-39:43). Probably one should conclude that the role of Aaron as one who fashioned the image was not simply invented, but rather that it arose from the historical circumstance that priests who considered themselves of Aaronic descent served in the cult employing the calf iconography and considered it an integral part of their tradition.

Exod 32:1b-6 probably derives from an old aetiology pertaining to the calf image in the Bethelite cult. The aetiology will have been preserved by tradents in the Israelite State. After the fall of the Israelite kingdom in 721 BCE this tradition found its way to Judah, probably borne by Israelite refugees. There it was taken up by the author respon-

---

[58] A long list of scholars either view vv. 1-6 as a positive cult aetiology or recognize this unit as a polemical reworking of an originally positive cult aetiology. So Th. J. Meek, *Hebrew Origins*, rev. ed. (New York: Harper, 1950) 136; Beyerlin, *Oldest Sinaitic Traditions*, 127; Coats, *Rebellion*, 184; Cross, *Canaanite Myth and Hebrew Epic*, 74; Loza, "Exode xxxii," p. 51, n. 1; Davenport, "A Study of the Golden Calf Tradition," 50-82; Jaroš, *Die Stellung des Elohisten*, 380; and Mettinger, "The Veto on Images," 17. For more references, see Hahn, *Das "Goldene Kalb"*, p. 215, n. 19.

[59] Again one may judge that the negative evaluation (v. 27b) of Gideon's cult object belongs to a late (Deuteronomistic) strata of the tradition.

sible for vv. 15-20 and reworked into a composition that evaluated the cult of the Israelite State as an apostate cult which eventually led to the fall of Israel. Possibly some other units such as vv. 30-34 also belonged to this first stage of the growth of Exodus 32, and other materials accrued in time. The present compilation in Exodus 32 shows evidence of several stages of development, the precise nature of which it was not necessary to clarify in this context.

In summary, the various components of Exodus 32 that judge the calf iconography and the cult in which it serves as idolatrous and apostate derive from a time after the collapse of the Israelite State, from a time much later than Jeroboam. Exodus 32 does not offer any evidence of contemporary or near contemporary opposition to Jeroboam's installation of the golden calves in Bethel or in Dan.

## D. 1 KINGS 14:1-18

1 Kgs 14:1-18 reports an explicit repudiation of Jeroboam by one of his own contemporaries, namely, the prophet Ahijah from Shiloh. Moreover, this text singles out Jeroboam's making of the cult images as the specific sin that warrants his absolute rejection by Yahweh, and it spells out the consequent judgment as the eventual, total annihilation of Jeroboam's house, on the one hand, and the immediate death of his son Abijah, on the other. This text in its present form certainly appears to depict an early renunciation of the kingship of Jeroboam and of the cult established by Jeroboam.

However, the simple story line of this prophetic legend, which begins with great economy of words to set forward the problem of Abijah's illness and to describe Jeroboam's strategy for making an inquiry of Ahijah regarding the outcome of that illness (vv. 1-6), gives way to a complex and massively overburdened oracle in response to that inquiry (vv. 7-16). Much of that oracle evidently derives from a late, secondary revision of the text, as will be argued below. Therefore it holds no value as evidence of opposition to Jeroboam by his contemporaries. So the basic task in this context will be to determine whether the text, when stripped of these secondary revisions, shows any evidence of opposition to Jeroboam from the time contemporary with Jeroboam. However, before that task can be taken up it will be necessary to ascertain the extent of the secondary revisions and to discover the original text.

It may be observed, to begin, that the text does not have literary homogeneity. Though in the present state of the text attention is focused primarily on the oracle regarding Jeroboam's house—an oracle that is constructed in rather pragmatic terms—one may observe quite another interest at the beginning of the text (vv. 1-6) in which the author appears to have employed the art of story-telling for the sake of the story.

In vv. 1-6, after the introduction of the plot, the writer describes in a rather artful way the stratagem by which the inquirer seeks to conceal her identity, presumably from the prophet. In the course of the story this stratagem turns out to be of no avail because the prophet though blind perceives her identity anyway by means of special insight given to him by Yahweh. In this way the text exhibits its marked interest in the person of Ahijah, in his clairvoyance, and—if one may anticipate vv. 17-18—in the reliability of his prophetic word. This skillfully told story could hardly have come from the same hand that composed the ponderous judgment oracle that follows after v. 7.

The material of the judgment oracle in vv. 7-11 appears to interrupt the continuity between vv. 1-6 in which Jeroboam's wife comes to inquire regarding the health of her son and vv. 12-13 in which Ahijah responds specifically to that inquiry. Even so it is possible, as Noth claimed, that the story could have been constructed in this way so that the prophet would first respond to Jeroboam's wife with an indictment and judgment concerning the whole of Jeroboam's house and then move on to a specific response concerning the prince Abijah.[60] In that case, perhaps vv. 7-11 constitutes a thorough reworking of the material that originally stood at this place.

Then regarding the material in vv. 7-11 one must inquire further whether in part or in whole it belongs integrally to the story begun in vv. 1-6. Considering vv. 7b-9 first, this section is made up almost entirely of motifs and phrases that appear elsewhere in 1 & 2 Kings, always in contexts heavily marked by Deuteronomistic editing. Vv. 7b-8 recall the account of the designation of Jeroboam in 11:29-39 and the note about its fulfillment in 12:15. Also, v. 7b has a formulation very similar to that in 1 Kgs 16:2a. V. 8b plays on one of DtrH's key themes concerning Yahweh's loyal servant David who kept the commandments with all his heart (cf. 3:3, 9:4, 11:32, 15:3-5, 15:11).[61] V. 9 develops DtrH's

---

[60] Könige, 310-11; and cf. Gray, Kings, 333.
[61] On this as a theme see Cross, Canaanite Myth and Hebrew Epic, 281-85.

other key theme concerning the sin of Jeroboam.[62] DtrH repeatedly applies the indictment of v. 9 to other kings of the Israelite State (though with some variation in terms of the components included) that 1) the king has done evil above all that were before him (16:19, 25, 30), 2) that the evil consists of making or serving other gods (16:13, 26), and 3) that the king has provoked Yahweh to anger (15:30; 16:2, 7, 13, 26, 33; 22:53). Since the themes in vv. 8b-9 are peculiar to the DtrH, and since their formulation here corresponds closely in wording with the other appearances of these same themes, one may confidently conclude that this material derives from the DtrH.

With vv. 10-11 the matter stands slightly differently because the motifs that comprise this material are not peculiarly Deuteronomistic, nor do the formulaic phrases used here appear exclusively in Deuteronomistic contexts. Thus the motif of the extermination of the *maštîn běqîr* ("every male") occurs also in the non-Deuteronomistic context of 1 Sam 25:22, 34; the phrase *ʿaṣûr wěʾazûb* ("bond and free"), in the possibly non-Deuteronomistic Deut 32:36; and the motif of human corpses lying in the field unburied as food for birds and animals, in 1 Sam 17:44, 46; Jer 7:33; 16:4; 19:7; 34:20; Ezek 29:5; and Ps 79:2. H. Seebass has argued plausibly that these motifs have their primary home in the military setting.[63] Hence one might argue, as Seebass has done, that because these motifs do not bear any characteristic imprint of DtrH they belong to the pre-Deuteronomistic narrative as part of an oracle threatening military catastrophe for Jeroboam and Israel.[64] This possibility requires further consideration.

---

[62] Again, see Cross, *Canaanite Myth and Hebrew Epic*, 278-81.

[63] "Tradition und Interpretation bei Jehu ben Chanani und Ahia von Silo" *VT* 25 (1975) 175-90.

[64] "Tradition und Interpretation," 175-90. Seebass actually builds on the argument by Noth (*Könige*, 310-11) that vv. 10-11 preserve some original material. Noth offers as his basic argument that if vv. 7-11 and 13-16 were all secondary, "what significance could there have been in the incident of the illness of an otherwise unknown, still child-aged son of Jeroboam, in the inquiry of the prophet concerning this matter, in the announcement of death, and in the actual death of the sick child that it occasioned the composition and transmission of this story?" However, this does not serve as a useful criterion for determining what originally belonged to the legend in 14:1-18 because the prophetic legend probably was occasioned neither out of concern for the sick child Abijah nor out of any concern about Jeroboam. Rather, its central purpose was to illustrate the clairvoyance of prophets and the reliability of the prophetic word (so Würthwein, *Könige*, 179). One can readily multiply examples of prophetic stories that serve little purpose other than to glorify the prophets (cf. 1 Kgs 20:1-21, 22-34; 2 Kgs 2:23-24; 4:1-7).

Three other texts in the Deuteronomistic history bring together the motifs under discussion in practically identical wording. For the sake of comparison, the texts are presented on page 139 in parallel columns together with the text of 1 Kgs 14:10-11. The four motifs have been numbered in order to display more clearly the relative sequences in which they appear and in order to highlight how particular ones have been selected for each context.

Each of these texts comes from the context of a prophetic denunciation of a king of the Israelite State. Though the motifs under consideration in these texts appear to have had their original function in descriptions of military engagements, it is remarkable that only one of these texts, namely 1 Kgs 21:21-24, actually has a report of a military engagement and catastrophe for the Israelite State following it.[65] Following upon each of the other texts one finds accounts of usurpers rising against and decimating only the royal household. Furthermore, with the exception of the prediction concerning Jezebel (1 Kgs 21:23, cf. 2 Kgs 9:30-37), none of the catastrophes predicted in these texts actually finds fulfillment in a subsequent report in which human corpses lie out in the open, unburied, as food for birds and dogs. Hence, it appears that in these literary settings the motifs have been adapted to serve a function other than their original or normal function. The motifs are not precisely suited to the manner in which they are employed here. They are not integral to their contexts.

---

Seebass ("Tradition und Interpretation"), following upon Noth's suggestion, isolated vv. 7, 8a, 9bb, 10ab, 11a, 12, 13, and 15aa as part of the old tradition which had been reworked by the Deuteronomists. The old tradition, then, contained an oracle that predicted an imminent military catastrophe for the Israelite State, and alongside this prediction it also included a specific word regarding prince Abijah. The problem with this analysis is that the reconstructed narrative lacks unity. In it the death of the child has no connection with the predicted military catastrophe. Rather, the death occurs as a result of illness when Jeroboam's wife enters the gate of her home town.

[65] But even here, the outcome of the battle as reported in 1 Kgs 22:32-36 does not correspond at all with the prediction of 1 Kgs 21:21-24 since of the house of Ahab only Ahab himself is reported to have died.

| 1 Kgs 14:10-11 | 1 Kgs 16:3-4 | 1 Kgs 21:21-24 | 2 Kgs 9:8 |
|---|---|---|---|
| 1) *lākēn hinĕnî mēbî ʾ rāʿâ ʾel-bêt yārobʿām* | *hinĕnî* | 1) *hinĕnî mēbî(ʾ) ʾēlêka rāʿâ*<br>3) *ûbiʿartî ʾahărêka* | |
| 2) *wĕhikrattî lĕyārobʿām maštîn bĕqîr ʿāṣûr wĕʿāzûb bĕyiśrāʾēl* | | 2) *wĕhikrattî lĕʾahʾāb maštîn bĕqîr wĕʿāṣûr wĕʿāzûb bĕyiśrāʾēl . . .* | 2) *wĕhikrattî lĕʾahʾāb maštîn bĕqîr wĕʿāṣûr wĕʿāzûb bĕyiśrāʾēl* |
| 3) *ûbiʿartî ʾahărê bêt-yārobʿām kaʾăšer yĕbaʿēr haggālāl ʿad-tummô* | 3) *mabĕʿîr ʾahărê baʿšāʾ wĕʾahărê bêtô . . .* | [for motif #3 see above] | |
| 4) *hammēt lĕyārobʿām bāʿîr yōʾkĕlû hakkĕlābîm wĕhammēt baśśādeh yōʾkĕlû ʿôp haššāmayim* | 4) *hammēt lĕbaʿšāʾ bāʿîr yōʾkĕlû hakkĕlābîm wĕhammēt baśśādeh yōʾkĕlû ʿôp haššāmayim* | 4) *hammēt lĕʾahʾāb bāʿîr yōʾkĕlû hakkĕlābîm wĕhammēt baśśādeh yōʾkĕlû ʿôp haššāmayim* | |
| 1) Therefore I am about to bring evil to the house of Jeroboam. | 1) I am about | 1) I am about to bring evil upon you,<br>3) and I will consume you. | |
| 2) I will cut off from Jeroboam every male, both bond and free, in Israel. | | 2) I will cut off from Ahab every male, both bond and free in Israel. | 2) I will cut off from Ahab every male, both bond and free in Israel. |
| 3) I will consume the house of Jeroboam just as one burns dung until none is left. | 3) to consume Baasha and his house . . . | | |
| 4) Anyone belonging to Jeroboam who dies in the city, dogs will devour; and anyone who dies in the field the birds of heaven will devour. | 4) Anyone belonging to Baasha who dies in the city, dogs will devour; and anyone who dies in the field the birds of heaven will devour. | 4) Anyone belonging to Ahab who dies in the city, dogs will devour; and anyone who dies in the field the birds of heaven will devour. | |

Since each of the four narratives in whose contexts these combinations of motifs appear has its independent tradition-history, one may reasonably attribute the motifs they exhibit in common to the person responsible for collecting and editing the four narratives into the Deuteronomistic History, i.e., to DtrH. Yet one could also argue that DtrH found these motifs already drawn together in 1 Kgs 14:10-11 as part of the original text of that narrative and that DtrH took them up from there and applied them in the other three contexts.

Against this it should be noted that the three texts 1 Kgs 16:3-4, 21:21-24, and 2 Kgs 9:8 do not slavishly take up the same combinations of motifs or the same sequence in their presentation as 1 Kgs 14:10-11, as if it were merely a matter of copying existing material from that text. Yet the individual motifs in themselves appear in verbally identical formulations from one text to another. Thus the combinations must be comprised of discrete motifs which DtrH feels at liberty to select and arrange in various ways. Even 1 Kgs 21:21-24, which corresponds most fully to 1 Kgs 14:10-11, does not use all the same motifs or present them in the same order. Furthermore, at one point the historian takes the freedom to select only one of these motifs, i.e., the one concerning the extermination of the *maštîn bĕqîr*, to speak about the fulfillment of the oracle regarding Baasha (1 Kgs 16:11). These data suggest that DtrH did not find these motifs gathered together in an already set pattern at 1 Kgs 14:10-11, but rather that DtrH pulled together discrete motifs, exercising selectivity and a limited creativity in the use of them, and that DtrH introduced these motif combinations into each of the four texts under consideration here.

One may also argue on the basis of formal considerations that vv. 10-11 do not have an integral place in 1 Kgs 14:1-18. First, if vv. 7b-9 are removed as addition by DtrH, then the announcement of punishment in vv. 10-11 lacks the grounding of an indictment, and it is formally an incomplete judgment oracle. Second, the narrative in 1 Kgs 14:1-18 as a whole has the form of a prophetic legend with an obvious interest in the pattern of "prophetic announcement of an oracle—verification of the reliability of the prophetic word" (cf. 1 Kgs 13:1-32*, 20:1-21, and 20:22-34). However, the fulfillment in vv. 17-18 pertains only to the prediction given in vv. 12-13 regarding prince Abijah's death and funeral. The formula that explicitly underlines this as the fulfillment of the prophet Ahijah's words (v. 18b) concludes the story without making any reference to the part of the oracle predicting military catastrophe for the Israelite State and judgment on the house of Jeroboam. Thus the prediction in 14:10-11 has no corresponding statement of its fulfillment within the narrative. It cannot be original or integral to the narrative.

As a conclusion regarding 14:10-11, the evidence favors the explanation that DtrH, having several stock motifs available, applied them at this point in a revision of 14:1-18*. This conclusion can be supported on the positive side by showing why DtrH would want to add this material at 1 Kgs 14:10-11. One of the two prominent themes in DtrH's account of the kings is the theme of the evil perpetrated by the kings of the Israelite State in following after the example of the sin of Jeroboam. Thus DtrH portrays Jeroboam ben Nebat as the "archetypal *Unheilsherrscher*" for the Israelite State.[66] In the text presently under discussion, this perspective comes into view in the clause in 14:9, "You have done evil above all that were before you . . . ." This stock formula is wholly unsuited in application to the first king in the Israelite State who has no antecedents. Even so, DtrH employs it here in order to make emphatic the negative evaluation under which Jeroboam stands. DtrH uses the same formula to evaluate Omri (1 Kgs 16:25) and Ahab (16:30), marking each of them for special notice in this way. Just as DtrH has described Jeroboam as the worst of all kings, so DtrH requires an emphatic way of speaking about his judgment. DtrH used the hyperbolic combination of the motifs in 14:10-11 because it suited this purpose well.

Having argued that 14:7b-11 in their totality stem from revision by DtrH, one may locate the beginning of the original oracle by Ahijah in v. 12 because there the actual response to the woman's inquiry occurs in the expected manner. Since Ahijah in v. 12 gives the woman no message to deliver to Jeroboam, the messenger formula of v. 7a must also be reckoned with vv. 7b-11 as part of the revision by DtrH. Furthermore, if the theme of the non-burial of the persons of Jeroboam's household in v. 11 is secondary, then the explanation in v. 13b that prince Abijah alone will come to the grave because "something pleasing to the Yahweh" was found in him must also be secondary. Such an explanation was required because the old story had reiterated twice that Israel honored Abijah with mourning and customary burial (vv. 13a and 18a), and this datum demanded reconciliation when the theme of non-burial was introduced at v. 11.

---

[66] See development of this point by C. D. Evans, "Naram-Sin and Jeroboam: The Archetypal *Unheilsherrscher* in Mesopotamian and Biblical Historiography," in *Scripture in Context II*, edited by W. W. Hallo, J. C. Moyer, L. G. Perdue (Winona Lake: Eisenbrauns, 1983) 97-125. Cf. also J. Holder, "The Presuppositions, Accusations, and Threats of 1 Kings 14:1-18," *JBL* 107 (1988) 27-38.

Regarding the section vv. 14-16, one may note that it also disrupts the continuity of the narrative by introducing unrelated material between the oracle of Ahijah in vv. 12-13a and the statement of its fulfillment in vv. 17-18. In addition, v. 14 corresponds to and betrays common authorship with the report about the fulfillment of the announcement of judgment against Jeroboam by Baasha in 15:29 which is literarily independent of 14:1-18*. Hence 14:14 must be secondary. Vv. 15-16 build on the theme of Jeroboam's sin as the root cause of the exile, a theme already introduced at 13:33-34 and 14:9, and therefore they must also be attributed to DtrH.

Thus the pre-Deuteronomistic prophetic legend appears in 14:1-6, 12-13a, 17-18.[67] The old oracle responded only to the inquiry regarding the health of prince Abijah. The pronounced and explicit opposition to Jeroboam appears altogether in the editorial additions.

Turning to the pre-Deuteronomistic legend as isolated above, one could understand the old oracle with its announcement of death for prince Abijah as a sign of opposition to Jeroboam from Shilonite prophetic circles. However, such a conclusion lacks warrants from the text. Contrary to such a conclusion, one may argue on the basis of formal considerations that the prophetic legend has little to do with Jeroboam or with any conflict between Jeroboam and Ahijah. Instead its primary concern is to illustrate the clairvoyance of prophets and the trustworthiness of the prophetic word. Indeed, in order to highlight the prophet's clairvoyance the story puts him at a double disadvantage by having the Jeroboam's wife disguise herself and by presenting the prophet as blind on account of his age.[68] Also, if the story actually did intend to portray a

---

[67] So also Dietrich, *Prophetie und Geschichte*, 51-53; similarly McKenzie, *The Trouble with Kings*, 62-63; DeVries, *Kings*, 177-79; and Würthwein, *Könige*, 172-78.

[68] Of course, this argument presupposes that the theme of disguise in vv. 1-6 is original and integral to the legend. Contrast Würthwein (*Könige*, 179) who considers it a later accretion. The reason for the disguise is not necessarily that Jeroboam, expecting a negative response from Ahijah because of conflict between the two of them, wishes to trick the prophet into giving a positive response by means of this strategy. In fact, that interpretation has several weaknesses: 1) It assumes that Jeroboam does not know the prophet well enough to recognize that the disguise strategy is unnecessary because of the prophet's blindness. 2) It fails to ask why Jeroboam would consult this particular prophet if he fears a negative response. (Cf. Ahab in 1 Kings 22 who chose not to consult Micaiah ben Imlah because of such a reason). 3) The text itself does not give a reason for the disguise so other explanations are possible. That one is immediately inclined to think that Jeroboam fears a negative response is due to the context of the story in the material beginning with

clash between royal and prophetic interests, one would expect a reason to be given as grounds for the negative oracle (cf. 1 Kgs 20:35-43, 2 Sam 12:1-14). However, as has been argued above, the section in vv. 7b-9 that supplies such a "reason" does not belong to the original legend. Finally, the mere fact that a prophet announces a negative word to the king need not mean that the prophet stands in stiff opposition to that king or that the prophet has repudiated the king. Certainly the example of Nathan's rebuke of David and announcement of the death of his son after David's affair with Bathsheba illustrates this point.

The argument presented above leads to the conclusion that the explicit denunciation of Jeroboam in 1 Kgs 14:1-18 derives altogether from secondary revisions to the original legend and that when the original legend itself is isolated it is hardly suited as a source for evidence regarding Jeroboam's relationship to prophetic circles at Shiloh.

---

11:26 which all along conditions the reader to expect judgment from a divine spokesperson. However, the story of Saul disguising himself to go to see the medium at Endor suggests that other factors may motivate the inquirer to self-concealment. Possibly Saul concealed his identity because he had made mediums and wizards illegal in Israel and would now be seen in violation of his own principles, or perhaps kings considered it beneath their dignity to consult with mediums, wizards, or certain prophets. The intent at this point is not to argue that Jeroboam's motivation was the same as Saul's but simply to say that the question allows at the very best for an extremely conjectural answer. 4) As a final and perhaps as the most important consideration, to ask why Jeroboam requested of his wife to disguise herself probably presumes that the story is more historical than in fact it is. Very likely the motif of disguise is only a literary device, like the prophet's blindness, to accentuate the prophet's clairvoyance.

Thus the fact that the legend has Jeroboam sending his wife to Ahijah in disguise can hardly be taken as implicit evidence of conflict between Jeroboam and Ahijah.

# CHAPTER V

# Conclusions Drawn from Chapters Three and Four

G enerally this investigation has confirmed that Jeroboam officially sponsored a cult that followed in line with Israel's ancient
traditions. According to all indications he encouraged the
traditional Israelite devotion to El=Yahweh. Above, this conclusion has
been argued both positively and negatively. It has been argued
positively beginning with the evidence of the cultic cry *hinnēh ʾĕlōhêkā
yiśrāʾēl ʾăšer heʿĕlûkā mēʾereṣ miṣrāyim* on the grounds that in the Hebrew
Bible formulae concerning the Exodus only attribute that act of
deliverance either to Yahweh or to El. It has been argued negatively on
the grounds that evidence of opposition to Jeroboam's religious policies
by his contemporaries is completely lacking. If Jeroboam had abandoned the ancient traditions of Israel one would expect opposition to
have arisen, and if Jeroboam in his initiatives with the calf iconography
had sponsored an innovatively "Baalized" cult one would expect evidence of opposition on that account from persons such as Ahijah, Elijah,
Jehu, or Dtrн.

Furthermore, Jeroboam's calf iconography probably carried on an
ancient, pre-monarchic Israelite tradition. This has been argued on the
basis of evidence from archaic biblical texts that use taurine symbols in
reference to Israel's deity. Num 23:22 and 24:8 attribute to El the
strength of a wild ox in connection with El's deliverance of Israel from
Egypt, and Gen 49:24 applies to Israel's deity the epithet "Bull of Jacob"

(*ăbîr ya‛ăqōb*), an epithet which probably first had its connections with the ark at Shiloh. Further confirmatory evidence may be sought in the datum that the old cult aetiology of Exod 32:1-6 claims an ancient provenance for the iconography.

The judgment that the calf iconography belonged to the cult of Yahweh rests primarily on the basis of the Yahwistic cultic formula proclaimed over it (1 Kgs 12:28e). The more precise determination that its associations derived from El whom the biblical traditions identify with Yahweh found substantiation in the ancient poetic traditions of Num 23:22 and 24:8, and in the comparative study of the Ugaritic representations of El with a particular stream of biblical representations of Israel's deity.

The foregoing investigation has emphasized, furthermore, that Jeroboam fostered a very significant continuity with ancient Israelite tradition in his selection of royal sanctuaries at Bethel and Dan, and of a royal capital at Shechem, all of which had already served since the time of Israel's emergence in the land as sanctuaries for Israelite worship of El=Yahweh. Even with respect to Jeroboam's autumn festival, the biblical evidence suggests the probability that Jeroboam carried on earlier Israelite practice. Though little can be said about the content of this festival, the one bit of evidence available in the cultic formula *hinnēh ᵊĕlōhêkā yiśrā᾿ēl ᾿ăšer he‛ĕlûkā mē᾿ereṣ miṣrāyim* indicates the central place that the ancient, constitutive Israelite traditions of the Exodus had in the cult sponsored by Jeroboam.

Given the political realities of the monarchic tradition now firmly established since the time of Saul, one can hardly doubt that modified configurations of certain religious institutions would have been required in the new Israelite State. The royal administration of the new state needed the ideological undergirding that an official state religion could provide, and it required the loyal support of religious leaders. Hence Jeroboam will have required royal sanctuaries where the ideology of the emergent kingdom could be fostered and the unity of the citizen population could be promoted in the annual festivals. For this purpose he chose, probably among others, the sanctuaries in Bethel and Dan which he elevated to the status of royal sanctuaries. Also, Jeroboam will have had to expel those priests, whatever their lineage, who were loyal to the Davidic dynasty, and he will have installed new priests or elevated those of the existing priesthood who were loyal to him to key positions of religious leadership.

One could scarcely assume that any political administration, regardless of how well grounded in tradition and regardless of how positive its popular reception, would completely escape criticism or opposition in its contemporary time. However, the biblical texts which one might consider as the most likely sources of evidence of opposition to Jeroboam by his contemporaries (1 Kgs 13, Judg 17-18, Exod 32, 1 Kgs 14:1-20) offer no convincing evidence of the like, but only of a programmatic editorial and redactional effort to render evaluation and judgment on the cult sponsored by Jeroboam from a perspective obtained after the fall of Samaria. Thus the analysis of the prophetic legend in 1 Kings 13 has concluded that the original legend had nothing to do with Jeroboam. Rather an editor, by means of several editorial additions and by giving the legend its place after 1 Kgs 12:26-32, reshaped the legend as a repudiation of the sanctuary at Bethel which Jeroboam had raised to a new status. Similarly, in Judges 17-18, old Danite traditions of conquest and of the founding of the sanctuary at Dan have been taken up by a post-Deuteronomistic editor in Judah who worked them into a disparaging composition to show how the cult at that sanctuary had been illegitimate from its very foundation. As for Exodus 32, it is unlikely that it reflects an intra-Israelite critique of the Bethelite iconography from the time of Jeroboam or shortly thereafter. Rather, in Exodus 32 an ancient Israelite aetiology for the calf iconography (vv. 1-6) prefaces a miscellany of units which offer the judgment that the Israelite State has breached the covenant and brought about its own ruin in 721 BCE through its reverence of the golden calf. Finally, and especially important in this connection are the conclusions regarding the prophetic legend in 1 Kgs 14:1-18. The foregoing investigation has determined that the words of condemnation and judgment against Jeroboam within this composition belong in total to editorial additions attributable to DtrH, and furthermore, that the original legend provides no evidence that the prophet Ahijah opposed the religious or political policies of Jeroboam.

In summary the conclusion reached by this investigation is that the religious policies and institutions advocated by Jeroboam drew upon ancient Israelite traditions, that they were Yahwistic, and that they were perceived as legitimate practice in the Israelite State during the period of Jeroboam and probably for a long time thereafter, perhaps until the time of Hosea.

The conclusion that Jeroboam sponsored an authentic Israelite, Yahwistic cult, of course, contradicts the biblical evaluation of Jeroboam's religious policies and institutions. The report in 1 Kgs 12:26-

32, by implication, suggests that Jeroboam forsook the ancient, legitimate traditions of Israel, that he made far-reaching innovations, and that he, by his own initiative, established his own iconography, sanctuaries, priests, and a new cultic calendar. What 1 Kgs 12:26-32 says only by implication concerning the abandonment of legitimate Israelite traditions becomes explicit in the evaluation DtrH offers concerning Jeroboam through the mouth of the prophet Ahijah in 1 Kgs 14:9:

> But you have done evil more than all who preceded you. You have gone and made for yourself other gods, molten images, provoking me to anger, and me you have cast behind your back!

From the perspective of DtrH, Jeroboam, by making the calf images, went after "other gods" and rejected Yahweh; he had established an un-Israelite, un-Yahwistic, and illegitimate cult. From this point on to the fall of Samaria, DtrH punctuates the historical narrative concerning the Israelite State with a repeated and regular refrain in which each successive king of the Israelite State receives a negative evaluation for following the example of Jeroboam with respect to the cult. Furthermore, a post-Deuteronomistic editor adapted the prophetic legend in 1 Kings 13 so that it should express Yahweh's judgment on Jeroboam's sanctuary and cult in Bethel, and another author in Judges 17-18 demonstrated that the royal sanctuary and cult at Dan were also illegitimate and idolatrous from their inception. As for the golden calves themselves, the authors of Exod 32:7-35 placed this iconography under severest condemnation as the offence by which the Israelite State had broken its covenant with Yahweh and placed itself under judgment.

As has been argued in chapters II and IV, the authors of these materials all wrote from a perspective after the catastrophe of 721 BCE. Furthermore, one may argue that their experience of that catastrophe placed on them an urgent question which they sought to address in their work. These authors wrote in order to render that event meaningful, in order to provide an explanation regarding the root causes of that disaster. Its cause, according to their determination, lay in the illegitimate cult of the Israelite State which they claimed Jeroboam had inaugurated. They judged that this cult had been idolatrous, un-Israelite, and un-Yahwistic in every respect, and this had called forth punishment by Yahweh in the catastrophe of 721 BCE. Thus DtrH presents Jeroboam as an archetypal *Unheilsherrscher*, or as the perpetrator of that original sin which eventually led to the death of the nation.[1] This perspective finds clearest expression in 1 Kgs 14:15-16:

> Yahweh will smite Israel, as a reed is shaken in the water, and root up Israel from this good land which Yahweh gave to their fathers and scatter them beyond the Euphrates because they made their asherahs, provoking Yahweh to anger. *And Yahweh will give Israel up on account of the sins of Jeroboam which he sinned and which he caused Israel to sin.*

If the biblical materials critical of Jeroboam and his cult were finally written or redacted only in the period following upon the disaster of 721 BCE with the aim of explaining the cause of that disaster, it follows that the attitude these materials exhibit belongs to a period two centuries removed from the time of Jeroboam. Hence, one could justify the total exclusion of these materials as evidence regarding the orthodoxy or unorthodoxy of Jeroboam's religious policies for his own time, unless there were reason to believe that the authors were in some respects heir to traditions critical of Jeroboam that derived from closer to the time of Jeroboam.

Though the investigation pursued in chapter IV found no evidence in the biblical texts of such criticism from the time contemporary with Jeroboam, perhaps that evidence has simply been lost. Admittedly, the foregoing conclusions depend heavily on an argument from silence. However, that silence does have a peculiar kind of eloquence. It has been noted that various zealously Yahwistic figures such as Ahijah, Elijah, Elisha, Jehu, and Amos from whom one might have expected opposition appear to have remained altogether silent regarding the cult sponsored by Jeroboam. Furthermore, considering DtrH's interest in impugning Jeroboam's cult, one can hardly imagine that DtrH, while selecting materials, would have passed over traditions telling of fairly powerful and dramatic opposition, if such had been available. Even so, one may still make allowance for the possibility of the existence of a longstanding, minority resistance to the cult instituted by Jeroboam. It could well be that the critical posture evidenced in the various texts examined above draws in part on such a tradition.

With DtrH, however, a severe censure of Jeroboam arose, and that gave rise to a programmatic re-construal of history. The circumstances that led to the emergence of such a vocal criticism require investigation.

---

[1] Evans, "Naram-Sin and Jeroboam," 97-125; Holder, "Presuppositions, Accusations, and Threats," 27-38.

If one could plausibly explain the roots of such censure in circumstances obtaining at a time well after Jeroboam, such an explanation would indirectly offer further confirmation for the conclusions reached above, namely, that Jeroboam pursued religious policies that corresponded with ancient and authentic Israelite practice.

A suitable place to begin such an inquiry would be in the book of Hosea because it contains the earliest attested biblical polemic against the calf iconography of the cult of the Israelite State[2] (8:1-6, 10:1-6, 13:1-3).[3] The next chapter will seek to answer why Hosea should raise so vocal an opposition to the long established cult iconography two centuries after its refurbishment by Jeroboam I.

---

[2] If one assigns Hosea's polemic to the period of the three decades prior to the ruin of Samaria in 721 BCE, then it predates even the materials critical of the calf iconography in Exod 32:7-35 which, according to the argument of section IV.c derive from a time after 721 BCE.

[3] The demarcation of forms or of original speech units in the Book of Hosea often poses almost insurmountable problems because clear reference points by which to determine where they begin or end are lacking. Furthermore, there has been considerable disagreement concerning the tradition and redaction history of the text. The position adopted here affirms the authenticity of most of the material found in the Book of Hosea along with Wolff, *Hosea*; Mays, *Hosea*, and F. I. Andersen and D. N. Freedman, *Hosea* (AB 24; Garden City: Doubleday, 1980). For another view see G. A. Yee, *Composition and Tradition in the Book of Hosea: A Redaction Critical Investigation* (SBLDS 102; Atlanta: Scholars Press, 1987).

# CHAPTER VI

# The Origins of the Deuteronomistic Criticism of the Calf Images

A possible explanation for Hosea's apparent censure of the calf iconography is that though the calf image originally served as a symbol in the cult of Yahweh it had come to be associated with Baal-Haddu or a "Baalized" Yahweh by the time of Hosea,[1] and that therefore Hosea rejected the symbol. Many scholars interpret on the basis of Hos 13:1-3 that Hosea identified the calf images as symbols for the worship of Baal-Haddu.[2] However, several considerations should be raised with respect to this interpretation.

To begin, one must ask regarding the meaning of *habba‘al* for Hosea. On the one hand, according to Hos 2:19=Eng 2:17 Hosea represents Yahweh as saying, "I will remove the names of the baals (*habbĕ‘ālîm*) from her mouth." This may indicate that Hosea objects to the cult offered to a multiplicity of deities. On the other hand, in the same context Hosea represents Yahweh as saying to Israel, "You will call me[3] *’îšî* and you will no longer call me *ba‘lî*" (Hos 2:18=Eng 2:16), indicating that in the cult Yahweh was addressed using the title *ba‘al*. Thus even the disentanglement of the relationship between *habba‘al* and Yahweh

---

[1] Mettinger, "The Veto on Images," 23.

[2] Wolff, *Hosea*, 225; Mays, *Hosea*, 172; Andersen and Freedman, *Hosea*, 243 and 631.

[3] Reconstructing *lî* with Greek, Syriac, and Vulgate.

poses a problem. Should one infer from the attribution to Yahweh of the title *baʿlî* that Yahweh was worshiped as Baal-Haddu in a syncretistic cult where the two deities were identified,[4] or did the Israelite worshipers simply ascribe this title to Yahweh with the intention of honoring Yahweh as their master or lord?

In order to determine more nearly what Hosea means by the term *baʿal*, attention must be given to its usage within the book of Hosea and also within the general context of the Hebrew Bible. In the book of Hosea the term appears six times. Consistently the term is determined, usually by a definite article but in one case, by a pronominal suffix (*baʿlî* in 2:18=Eng 2:16). It occurs three times in the plural as *habbĕʿālîm* (2:15=Eng 2:13, 2:19=Eng 2:17; 11:2) and twice in the singular as *habbaʿal* (2:10=Eng 2:8, and 13:1). The datum that the term appears only in determined form with either a pronominal suffix or with the definite article indicates that it is not being used in the sense of a proper noun.[5] Furthermore, the datum that the term appears three times in the plural prompts the query whether the term as used by Hosea had a specific deity as its referent or whether one should understand it literally as referring to a plurality of deities.[6]

It may be observed that throughout the Hebrew Bible, whenever the term *baʿal* has a deity as its referent, it consistently appears in a determined form, usually with the definite article. Evidently, then, the Hebrew Bible does not use the term as a proper name but, rather, as an honorific and generic title.[7] As a common noun used by itself the term does not *explicitly* designate a particular deity, and in fact it seldom refers (demonstrably) to a specific, single deity.[8] To the contrary, frequently the term appears in the plural in which case it has an obviously

---

4 Wolff, *Hosea*, 49.

5 By way of contrast, one may compare the use of the term *ʾĕlōhîm*, without a definite article, as a quasi-proper noun in the biblical texts.

6 A common explanation is that Hosea uses the term *habbĕʿālîm* in reference to the many local manifestations of the one Canaanite deity Baal-Haddu. So Mays, *Hosea*, 43; and Andersen and Freedman, *Hosea*, 256-57. However, others think that Hosea may refer to a plurality of distinct Canaanite deities that received this title, e.g., Baal-Berith (Judg 8:33, 9:4), Baalzebub of Ekron (2 Kgs 1:2ff), Baal Hermon (Judg 3:3), Baal Maʿon (Num 32:38), etc. So Wolff, *Hosea*, 38-39; and Smith, *The Early History of God*, 47-48.

7 So Halpern, "The Baal."

8 Its use in 1 Kgs 18:20-40 stands as an exception. In that text Elijah challenges the people to choose between Yahweh and *habbaʿal*, that is, between Yahweh and another particular deity.

generic and plural referent. Such an interpretation is required for the phrase *habbĕʿālîm wĕhāʿaštārôt* in Judg 10:6-16 because the text immediately qualifies the deities referred to by this phrase as *ʾĕlôhê ʾarām*, *ʾĕlôhê ṣîdôn*, *ʾĕlôhê môʾāb*, *ʾĕlôhê benê ʿamôn*, and *ʾĕlôhê pĕlištîm* (10:6) and later on the text identifies them simply as *habbĕʿālîm* (10:10) and as *ʾĕlôhîm ʾăhērîm* (10:13). The interchangeability of these several divine designations clearly shows that the phrase *habbĕʿālîm wĕhāʿaštārôt* must mean "gods and goddesses" (see also Judg 2:11-13, 1 Sam 12:10 and similarly 1 Sam 7:3; cf. *habbĕʿālîm wĕhāʾăšērôt* in Judg 3:7 and the Akkadian *ilāni u ištarāti*). In other biblical contexts the significance of *habbĕʿālîm* is not as transparent,[9] though nothing indicates that it should be understood differently than in the texts listed above. Its obvious use as generic and plural in these texts suggests that Hosea may also use the term in a generic sense, that his plurals are literal plurals.

B. Halpern has offered a convincing argument that in the Hebrew Bible *habbaʿal* commonly stands as a collective noun having a significance identical to that of *habbĕʿālîm*.[10] As evidence for this identification he refers to texts in which *habbaʿal* and *habbĕʿālîm* appear in collocation with no apparent distinction in their referents (Hos 2:10 and 15=Eng 2:8 and 13; Jer 2:8 considered in conjunction with 2:13 and 23; cf. 7:9 and 11:12-13 where "other gods" are equivalent to *habbaʿal*) or texts where the two terms are used interchangeably (e.g., Judg 2:11-13). Halpern argues, moreover, that *habbaʿal* as collective noun signifies the host of heaven. For this identification he cites various texts in which *habbaʿal* and the host of heaven appear interchangeably. For example, according to Jer 7:32-8:3 the cult of Topheth in the Valley of Hinnom has been offered to the sun, to the moon, and to all the host of heaven, but according to the parallel text in Jer 19:4-13 that offering has been made to other gods (v. 4), that is, to *habbaʿal* (v. 5). The text in 2 Kgs 23:5 makes such an identification even more explicitly when it refers to those who made offerings "to *habbaʿal*, that is, to the sun and to the moon and to the constellations and to all the host of heaven."[11]

The host of heaven originally signified the pantheon of gods and goddesses over which Yahweh ruled (therefore the divine name *yhwh ṣĕbāʾôt*). Such a conceptualization is presupposed in Micaiah's vision

---

9 The texts include Judg 8:33; 1 Kgs 18:18; Jer 2:23; Jer 9:13; 2 Chr 17:3, 24:7, 28:2, 33:3, and 34:4.

10 "The Baal."

11 According to the MT the nouns following *labbaʿal* stand in apposition to it.

where he sees the enthroned Yahweh surrounded by the host of heaven (1 Kgs 22:19-22; cf. Isa 6) as well as in the prologue of Job where all the sons of god present themselves before Yahweh (1:6-12). The host of heaven was symbolized by astral bodies (Judg 5:20, Ps 148:3, Isa 13:4-6, and Job 38:7). It included the deities of the nations, deities who had received each their allotted territory under the overlordship of Yahweh (Deut 32:8-9, reading with Q and comparing LXX; cf. also Ps 82). It follows that *habbě⁽ālîm* included the Canaanite deities and the gods of nations around Israel.[12] As administrators over these nations these gods could appropriately be referred to as lords (*habbě⁽ālîm*).

Yahweh, supreme in the pantheon, was *habba⁽al par excellence*. For that reason Israel in its cult could address Yahweh as *ba⁽lî* (Hos 2:18=Eng 2:16). Similarly, Jeremiah could employ the verb *b⁽l* to characterize the relationship of Yahweh as husband/master over the people of Judah (Jer 3:14; cf. 31:32).

Returning to the discussion concerning Hosea, it follows that Hosea did not accuse Israelites of having forsaken Yahweh in order to worship Baal-Haddu in place of Yahweh or alongside Yahweh in some sort of syncretistic cult. Rather, it appears probable that Hosea objected to the cult which Israelites offered to the host of heaven, that is, to the deities in Yahweh's entourage. The reasons for his objection will require further exploration below.

Regarding the motivation behind Hosea's rejection of the calf iconography, the foregoing discussion requires qualification of the explanation that Hosea objected because the calf image had become a symbol for Baal-Haddu in popular perception. Such an interpretation presupposes that Hosea accused Israel of turning to one particular *ba⁽al*, namely to Baal-Haddu, the "fertility deity" for whom the bull was emblematic. However, it has been argued that Hosea speaks generically about *habbě⁽ālîm*, not about a particular deity named Baal. Besides, it merits underscoring that Hosea never makes an explicit association between the calf image and *habbě⁽ālîm*. Though Hos 13:1-3 appears to approach such an identification, 13:2 says that Israel's guilt in fashioning images, including the calf images, constitutes an additional sin which goes beyond the guilt incurred through *habba⁽al*.

---

[12] Cf. Wolff (*Hosea*, 39): "In Hosea 'Baal' has become a collective term for Canaanite deities (=foreign gods in 3:1; cf. 13:4) . . . ." The position taken above moves beyond Wolff in that it recognizes that these "Canaanite deities" were actually deities in authentic Israelite religion, that they had a place within Yahweh's entourage as subordinates to Yahweh. So Halpern, "The Baal."

Other possible explanations for the motivations behind Hosea's objection to the calf iconography must be found. One may begin by noting that a regular and integral emphasis in Hosea's criticism of the calf images falls on their material composition and their human origin:

> With their silver and gold they made idols. (Hos 8:4b)
> An artisan made it. (8:6b)
> They made for themselves a molten image
> Idols from their silver according to their skill
> All of it the work of artisans. (13:2b-d)

Similarly, 10:6a underlines the materiality and helplessness of the calf image:

> Indeed they shall carry it off to Assyria,
> As tribute for the great king.[13]

Such reflection on the nature of the icon apparently grounds Hosea's repudiation of the image, "It is not God! (*ʾĕlōhîm*)" (8:6c; cf. 14:4b). With these words Hosea contradicts the affirmation reportedly spoken by Jeroboam over the newly established calf images, *hinnēh ʾĕlōhêkā yiśrāʾēl . . .*" (1 Kgs 12:28e).

Could the denial, "It is not God!" simply signify that Hosea repudiated Israel for having identified a material image with the god? Though this could explain Hosea's position in part, one should not suppose that the Israelites were so unsophisticated as to view the calf image as identical with the deity. Rather it appears probable that Israel shared the Mesopotamian conceptualization of the cult image according to which the deity became transubstantiated in the cult image that represented it though at the same time the deity remained transcendent in relation to it.[14] Probably Hosea did more than deny the identity of the image with the deity. Hosea will have intended much more to deny the adequacy of the image as a symbol or as a representation of the deity. The denial, "It is not God!" suggests that for Hosea the offence of the calf icon lies in that the symbol or representation has displaced what in Hosea's perspective ought to be the true object of worship.[15]

---

[13] The MT reads *melek yārēb*, possibly a mis-division of *malkî rāb* which would be an Israelite rendition of the Assyrian honorific title *šarru rabū*. Cf. also Hos 5:13. See the textual notes by Wolff, *Hosea*, 104; and Andersen and Freedman, *Hosea*, 413-14.

[14] On the significance of the image in Mesopotamia see Jacobsen, "The Graven Image," 15-32. See also the discussion in section III.A.3.a.

[15] Cf. Zimmerli, "Das Bilderverbot," 253.

In order to penetrate more deeply into the motivation behind
Hosea's rejection of the calf iconography, one should place this problem
within the much broader context of an inquiry regarding Hosea's
attitude towards the cult of the Israelite State and its symbols in general.
It is important to recognize that Hosea's objection to the calf image fits
as one part of his much more broadly articulated objection to the cult of
the Israelite State. Hosea reproaches or threatens Israel's sanctuaries,
altars, pillars, and idols (3:4; 4:12, 15, 17; 8:11; 10:1-2, 8; 12:12=Eng 12:11;
14:9=Eng 14:8). Furthermore, Hosea inveighs against Israel's cult in
general by characterizing it under the metaphor of promiscuity or of
adultery. One may reasonably expect that an accounting for such objec-
tions and criticisms of the cult may help to clarify the motivation behind
Hosea's rejection of the calf iconography.

According to Hos 10:1-2 (cf. 12:12=Eng 12:11) Hosea threatened
Israel's altars and pillars with destruction from Yahweh. Some commentators have understood that the reason for this threat was that the worship in which these altars and pillars served, though perhaps originally
Yahwistic, was now directed toward other gods or toward Baal(-
Haddu).[16] Though this may explain Hosea's attitude in some sense (to
be considered further below), it does not appear to fully capture the
grounds for Hosea's reproach against the altars and pillars.

With regard to the altars, Hos 6:6 implies that Israel used them for
sacrifice directed to Yahweh because in that text Yahweh calls for loyalty
and knowledge of God in place of the sacrifices which Israel offers
(presumably) to Yahweh. Also, the specific sanctuaries against which
Hosea directs his invectives, namely Bethel, Gilgal, and Ramah (4:15; 5:8;
9:15; 10:5, 8; 12:12=Eng 12:11), had a long tradition as holy places in
Israel's worship of Yahweh. Certainly there can be no doubt that these
sanctuaries with their altars had long held a legitimate place in the
Israelite cult to Yahweh.

Regarding the pillars, it may be concluded on the basis of texts such
as Gen 28:22; 31:13; 35:14, 20; Exod 24:4 (cf. the twelve stones at Gilgal in
Joshua 4 and the one stone at Shechem in Josh 24:26-27) that they also
originally had an acceptable place in the cult to Yahweh. One may also
note that Deut 16:21-22, by its absolute prohibition of the establishment
of pillars or asherahs beside the altar of Yahweh, indicates by implica-

---

[16] Wolff, *Hosea*, 173-74; Mays, *Hosea*, 139; Andersen and Freedman, *Hosea*, 551-
53. Wolff and Mays speak in terms of the Yahwistic cult becoming pagan or
Canaanite.

tion that the pillar at one time had a place in the cult to Yahweh. If it had been otherwise there would have been no need to issue such a prohibition. Probably the pillars as well as the altars which Hosea threatens in 10:1-2 belonged to the cult of Yahweh.

Then why would Hosea have objected to them? In order to answer that question, it may be useful to consider other aspects of Hosea's reproach regarding the cult.

Hosea's criticism of Israel's cult under the metaphor of promiscuity or adultery pervades the first nine chapters of the book. The implication of the metaphor and the explicit accusation by Hosea is that Israel has abandoned Yahweh and devoted itself to *habbĕʿālîm* (Hos 2). The specific meaning of this accusation calls for elucidation because the metaphor functions, in part, to conceal that meaning.

In order to properly interpret Hosea's use of the metaphor, it is important to recognize the primarily rhetorical dimension of his formulation. One may assume that Hosea did not intend to present an objective, disinterested portrayal of Israelite religion to which a modern historian might appeal for the reconstruction of Israel's religion. On the contrary, Hosea formulated speech by which he intended to convince and convict his audience, not so much by means of logic but by the persuasive powers of imaginative language that appeals to emotions. To this end Hosea plies with the metaphor of scandal within the most intimate and jealously guarded of human relationships. That metaphor serves as a powerful rhetorical device for Hosea to persuade Israel that it has misdirected its devotion. The interpreter, having recognized this rhetorical dimension, must resist reading from the surface of the text as if Hosea portrays things "as they really were".

An argument such as Hosea's can only succeed if the parties to the argument share necessary presuppositions upon which the argument can build. Hosea's rhetoric presupposes at least three significant points of agreement between Hosea and his audience. 1) Both Hosea and his audience must have agreed that Israel's allegiance belongs to Yahweh. 2) They must have agreed that such allegiance should find expression in the cult. 3) Probably it was obvious to both that in its cult Israel also showed deference to the subsidiaries in Yahweh's entourage, i.e., to *habbĕʿālîm*.

The point of disagreement arose over the significance of Israel's deference to *habbĕʿālîm*. The Israelite audience believed that its cultic practice did express allegiance to Yahweh, that the deference they paid to *habbĕʿalîm* had an appropriate place in the worship of Yahweh.[17] But Hosea offered a radically different assessment of Israel's practice, arguing that *habbĕʿalîm* had displaced Yahweh so that Israel had in fact abandoned Yahweh.

Then one must ask how, in Hosea's perception, Israel had abandoned Yahweh in favor of *habbĕʿalîm*. The resolution of this problem requires an examination of the various contexts in which Hosea accuses Israel under the metaphors of promiscuity and adultery.[18]

According to Hos 1:2, at the beginning of his prophetic career Hosea was commanded to marry a woman characterized by promiscuity and to have children by her. This prophetic activity would stand as a sign that "the land commits great promiscuity away from Yahweh." The text does not explicitly detail the way in which the land commits promiscuity. However, one may draw an inference from the subsequent prophetic sign. Hosea names his first child Jezreel because the Jehuite dynasty is to be punished for the blood of Jezreel. It is generally agreed that the phrase "the blood of Jezreel" refers to Jehu's *coup d'état* against the Omride royal household which began at Jezreel (2 Kgs 9-10).

Why did Hosea find fault with the Jehuite dynasty for that action? Possibly Hosea considered Jehu's massacre of the Omride household excessive. Elsewhere Hosea exhibits a sensitivity to violence and bloodshed (4:2, 6:7-9). But it is more likely that Hosea objected to the political motivation behind the *coup*. Probably Jehu and his supporters opposed the Omride participation in the Aramaean alliance against Assyria, pre-

---

[17] The logical consistency of the Israelite ideology warrants careful attention. As Halpern ("The Baal") explains, "When one sacrificed, in the distributed clan sacrificial cult of the traditional social organization of Israel, one typically invited Yhwh's subordinates, along with Yhwh, to the repast"; and again, "Attention lavished on the high god's retainers, after all, was a mere corollary of the worship of the high god." Modern readers of the book of Hosea may find Israel's devotion to *habbĕʿalîm* contradictory to its claim of allegiance to Yahweh. If so these modern readers themselves give evidence of the persuasive power of Hosea's rhetoric (which, of course, is consonant with the Deuteronomic and Deuteronomistic "Yahweh alone" rhetoric).

[18] Terms that derive from the two roots *znh* and *nʾp* provide the primary linguistic stock for these metaphors. Words that derive from *znh* appear twenty-two times—1:2 (four times); 2:4, 6, 7; 3:3; 4:10, 11, 12 (twice), 13, 14 (twice), 15, 18 (twice); 5:3, 4; 6:10, and 9:1. Words that derive from *nʾp* appear six times—2:4; 3:1; 4:2, 13, 14; and 7:4. The distribution indicates a concentration of this vocabulary in chaps. 1-4 with lesser attestation in the material up to Hosea 9.

ferring rather to cast their lot with Assyria.[19] That political issues had a significant place among Hosea's concerns finds confirmation in the fact that elsewhere Hosea ridicules and criticizes political alignment with Egypt or Assyria (7:8-16, 8:7-10).[20]

The precise explanation for Hosea's objection to Jehu's *coup* remains somewhat conjectural. However, one may assert with confidence that in Hos 1:2-4 his accusation against Israel of promiscuity has reference to Israel's politics. This conclusion warrants careful attention because within the literary unit of Hos 1:2-9 only v. 4 spells out concretely the grounds for Hosea's threatening proclamation, and as such it provides the best locus within Hosea 1 from which one may draw inferences regarding the motivation for Hosea's charge of promiscuity.

In another context Hosea derides Israel's political alignment with Assyria under the metaphor of promiscuity:

> For they have gone up to Assyria
> A wild ass going his own way
> Ephraim *has hired lovers*. (8:9)

Hosea ridicules not only alignment with Assyria but also alliance with Egypt or alliances with the nations in general (7:8, 11; 8:8, 10). In the historical setting within which Hosea worked, Israel had two feasible choices regarding alliances. Either Israel could opt for alliance with the Aramaeans together with other neighboring states and supported by Egypt, or Israel could opt for alliance with Assyria. Evidently Israel's foreign policy vacillated between these choices (7:11), and, just as evidently, Hosea opposed both options.

Why would Hosea describe Israel's alliances as promiscuous (8:9) or as a straying from Yahweh (7:13)? It is noteworthy that Hosea was not alone in opposing political alliances. Other prophets also demanded allegiance and trust in Yahweh alone (perhaps following Hosea's lead— Isa 7:1-17; 20:1-5; 30:1-5; 31:1-3; Jer 2:17-18; cf. Ezekiel 23, and 16, esp. vv.

---

[19] So M. C. Astour, "841 BC: The First Assyrian Invasion of Israel," *JAOS* 91 (1971) 383-9; H. Donner, "The Separate States of Israel and Judah," 412.

[20] For interpretation of Hosea that is sensitive to his political concerns one may refer to J. H. Hayes and J. K. Kuan, "The Final Years of Samaria (730-720 BC)," *Bib* 72 (1991) 153-81; and J. H. Hayes, "Hosea's Baals and Lovers: Religion or Politics?" a paper presented to the Israelite Prophetic Literature Section at the Society of Biblical Literature meetings in New Orleans, November 19, 1990.

23-29). Hosea must have perceived that the alliances had unacceptable ramifications for Israel's allegiance to Yahweh.[21]

If, in accordance with the theology of the Israelite State, the subsidiary deities in Yahweh's entourage had received the nations as their allotments (Deut 32:8-9, cf. Ps 82), then as a consequence of Israel's involvement in international affairs, it will have followed quite naturally that deities of foreign nations would receive devotion within Israel's cult to Yahweh. Thus, for example, when the Omride dynasty formed alliance with the Tyrians, the Tyrian Baal (Shamen?) received devotion in the Israelite State (1 Kgs 16:31-32).[22] That the worship of these deities occurred within the context of the Yahwistic cult is suggested by the fact that in the parallel cult in Judah, cultic paraphernalia pertaining to various deities had a place in the Temple of Yahweh (2 Kgs 21:4-7; 23:4, 11-12). However, when the Israelite State could no longer maintain its dominant or parity position within international alliances, that may have entailed setting deities other than Yahweh into greater prominence within the cult of the Israelite State. For Hosea alliances will have posed a theological problem regarding the status of other deities relative to Yahweh. Hosea perceived that the gods had displaced Yahweh.[23] Consequently, Israel's alliances could be described as straying from Yahweh, as promiscuous involvement with lovers.

Hosea characterizes the assassinations of kings in the Israelite court using the metaphor of adultery and a simile of devouring heat:

> They are all adulterers;
> they are like a heated oven.
> . . . . . . . . . . . . . . . . . . . . . . . . .
> . . . . . . . . . . . . . . . . . . . . . . . . .
> They are all hot like an oven,
> and they devour their rulers.
> All their kings have fallen;
> none of them calls upon me. (7:4-7)

---

[21] On possible ramifications see H. Spieckermann, *Juda unter Assur in der Sargonidenzeit* (FRLANT 129; Göttingen: Vandenhoeck & Ruprecht, 1982); M. Cogan, *Imperialism and Religion: Assyria, Judah and Israel in the Eighth and Seventh Centuries B.C.E.* (Missoula: Scholars Press, 1974); and J. McKay, *Religion in Judah under the Assyrians* (SBT, second series 26; London: SCM, 1973).

[22] Similarly during Solomonic imperial times Ashtarte of Sidon, Milcom of Ammon, and Chemosh of Moab received cult in Jerusalem (1 Kgs 11:5-8).

[23] Similarly, Halpern ("The Baal,") explains that "Hosea's main complaint is that attention to the baals entailed forgetfulness about Yhwh's being the one who really—behind the scenes—promoted welfare. That is, the baals are real enough, but Yhwh is the director of their actions."

Hosea also reproaches Israel for making kings without Yahweh's direction (8:4). In these contexts Hosea probably refers to the turbulent sequence of assassination and succession of kings in Samaria during the last three decades before Samaria's ruin. Probably the *coup d'états* should be understood in connection with Israel's vacillation between alliance with Assyria and alliance with Aram and Egypt (7:11). Jehu, having adopted a pro-Assyrian policy, overthrew the pro-Aramaean Omrides. In turn the pro-Aramaean Shallum assassinated the last Jehuite dynast only to be assassinated himself by the pro-Assyrian Menahem.[24] Pekah who obviously pursued a pro-Aramaean policy (2 Kgs 16:5, cf. Isa 7) assassinated Pekahiah, himself to be assassinated by Hoshea (2 Kgs 15:30) whom Tiglath-Pileser III had established on the throne of Israel.[25]

Why did Hosea consider this series of assassinations and royal successions adulterous? If the *coup d'états* were motivated by conflicting commitments to alliance with Assyria or to alliance with Aram and Egypt, as explained above, then probably one should explain that Hosea perceived the failure in fidelity to lie precisely in those commitments. According to 8:4a Hosea voiced the complaint that Israel carried on as if independent of Yahweh (cf. 7:7d). As in its foreign policies, so in the intrigues of its royal court Israel pursued its own political machinations that denied allegiance to and reliance on Yahweh.

The complaint about human manipulation in king-making at Hos 8:4a leads into another subject, namely, into the manufacture of idols from silver and gold (8:4b). One may wonder why the two subjects appear side by side in this context. In a similar manner Hos 14:4=Eng 14:3 makes a connection between reliance on Assyria and idolatrous devotion to the work of human hands. One should probably understand that at least in part the idols stand as religious symbols of the foreign policies to which Hosea objects. But evidently Hosea's basic complaint concerns human attempts at manipulation to secure their own well-being. This attempted manipulation occurs by way of court intrigue, foreign policy, and the institution of certain religious symbols, that is,

---

[24] 2 Kgs 15:19 confirms Menahem's pro-Assyrian position. The report by 2 Kgs 15:16 of Menahem's military activity against territory within Israel offers a clue as to the extent of civil strife surrounding the change of kings.

[25] On Hoshea see *ANET*, 284. Admittedly, this sketch of the political alignments of these Israelite kings remains somewhat conjectural. See also Miller and Hayes, *A History of Ancient Israel and Judah*, 326-334; and J. H. Hayes and P. K. Hooker, *A New Chronology for the Kings of Israel and Judah and its Implications for Biblical History and Literature* (Atlanta: John Knox, 1988) 42-43, 55, and 60-65.

idols. In Hosea's perspective, it all amounts to a failure to fulfill the requirement of allegiance to Yahweh.

Under the metaphor of Israel's promiscuity Hosea also refers to violence, robbery, and murder. It appears evident at 6:10 that the promiscuity of Ephraim has to do with the violent deeds, particularly murder, just catalogued in the preceding section (6:7-9). Unfortunately the text gives inadequate information on the basis of which to reconstruct the incidents concerned. They may well have had a connection with the political strife in the Israelite State. For example, there may be some significance to the correspondence between Hosea's reproach of Gilead as a "city of evildoers, tracked with blood" and the note in 2 Kgs 15:25 that fifty Gileadites assisted Pekah in his conspiracy against Pekahiah. Hosea's denunciation of conspiratorial violence under the metaphor of promiscuity appears most transparent at 1:4.

Hosea's most sustained accusation against Israel under the metaphor of promiscuity and adultery occurs in Hosea 2. There *habbě'ālîm* and *habba'al* are the lovers for whom Israel has forsaken Yahweh. Evidently Hosea perceives that Israel credits them for the gifts of fertile field, flock, and economic prosperity (2:10=Eng 2:8 which lists the gifts of grain, wine, oil, silver, and gold). Generally scholars have understood *habbě'ālîm* as Canaanite fertility deities, i.e., as local manifestations of Baal-Haddu; and they have understood Hosea's criticism of Israel's cult as directed especially against its licentiousness and its displacement of Yahweh in favor of the *habbě'ālîm* of the Canaanite fertility religion.[26]

Certainly Hosea's concern that Israel has forsaken Yahweh in favor of *habbě'ālîm* is altogether evident. As Hosea perceives it, the problem is that Israel has failed to recognize the true source of the sustaining gifts it receives. Hosea does not criticize the cult as a means for seeking the fruits of fertility, i.e., for its materiality.[27] Rather, he asserts that it is Yahweh rather than *habbě'ālîm* who gives these things, the gifts of grain, wine, oil, silver, and gold. Hosea even likens Yahweh to the fertilizing

---

[26] See Mays, *Hosea*, 43; Andersen and Freedman, *Hosea*, 256-57; Wolff, *Hosea*, 38-39; and Smith, *The Early History of God*, 47-48 regarding the *habbě'ālîm*; and see the commentaries, especially on 4:2-14 regarding the licentiousness of the cult. A fine critique and reassessment has been offered by Hayes, "Hosea's Baals and Lovers: Religion or Politics?"

[27] Contrast Eichrodt (*Theology of the Old Testament*, I: 117) who thinks that Hosea's concern was the "increasingly materialistic conception of God."

dew (14:6=Eng 14:5) and to the ever green, fruit-bearing cypress (=the tree of life, following the unemended MT at 14:9).[28]

Moreover, the frequently advanced interpretation that Hosea faulted the cult of the Israelite State for its licentiousness requires qualification. It is often explained that the cult to the Canaanite fertility deities included ritual prostitution or ritual intercourse in imitation of the fertilizing activity of Baal-Haddu, and that these sexual rituals were intended to secure ongoing fertility in field, flock, and human community.[29] The explanation goes on to say that these Canaanite practices had crept into the religion of the Israelite State and that Hosea inveighed against them.

Recent studies have severely undermined the foundations of this interpretation. E. J. Fisher, D. R. Hillers, and R. A. Oden, Jr. have underscored the meagerness and equivocal nature of evidence from Canaanite and Mesopotamian sources for the existence of such sexual rituals in Canaanite and Mesopotamian religion.[30] They point out that scholars have relied primarily on the Greek historian Herodotus and on other Greek, Latin, and Christian sources, most of which depend on Herodotus, for evidence to reconstruct these sexual rites. These sources have doubtful value as evidence because they derive from a time centuries removed from the historical period under consideration and from authors who, being firmly convinced of the superiority of their own cultures and religions, might have had an inclination to disdain and distort the religious practices of Canaan and Mesopotamia.

Consequently, one should judge the historical reconstruction of sexual rituals in Canaanite and Mesopotamian religion as improbable and certainly as undemonstrated. Then one can no longer confidently explain that Israel in Hosea's time adopted such cultic practices under the influence of its Canaanite environment. It must be seriously questioned whether the language of promiscuity and adultery in the book of Hosea at any point actually refers to the practice of ritual sex.

Most often in the book of Hosea the terminology for promiscuity and adultery occurs within metaphors depicting Israel's failure in

---

[28] So Wolff, *Hosea*, 237. Contrast the NRSV.

[29] Again see the commentaries, particularly regarding Hos 4:12-14.

[30] Fisher, "Cultic Prostitution in the Ancient Near East? A Reassessment," *BTB* 6 (1976) 225-36; Hillers, "Analyzing the Abominable: Our Understanding of Canaanite Religion," 253-69; and Oden, *The Bible Without Theology* (New Voices in Biblical Studies; San Francisco: Harper & Row, 1987) 131-53.

devotion to Yahweh.[31] It is true that scholars have often seen a double freight in this language, especially in chapters 1-4. For example, K. Koch says that Hosea "believes that in Israelite religion harlotry is rife—in both the literal and the transferred sense."[32] However, since the reconstruction of sexual ritual in Canaanite religion has come under such serious question, one may rightly ask whether Hosea does not use the promiscuity and adultery language in a purely metaphorical sense.[33] Only within the context of Hos 4:12-14 does it appear quite certain that the language is used both in a metaphorical and in a literal sense, and, moreover, it appears in conjunction with cultic language. However, P. Bird has convincingly explained that the fornicating and adulterous behavior of the daughters and daughters-in-law as described in 4:13b does not occur at the cultic sites as ritual activity, but rather, that Hosea perceives it to arise as a consequence of the (metaphorically speaking) promiscuous cultic behavior described in 4:12-13a.[34] Hosea underscores his point about the "promiscuous" cult further at 4:14b by charging that the men perform their worship with prostitutes (zōnôt) and hierodules (qĕdēšôt),[35] but this does not refer to sexual ritual either, certainly not in any explicit sense.

---

[31] That Hosea uses the language in a metaphorical sense is clear from the fact that it is *the land* that commits promiscuity rather than the Israelites (1:2; and similarly 2:5=Eng 2:3). Furthermore, to characterize children as promiscuous (1:2, 2:6=Eng 2:4) does not make sense literally because such terminology normally refers to a woman's activity. See P. Bird, "'To Play the Harlot': An Inquiry into an Old Testament Metaphor," in *Gender and Difference in Ancient Israel*, ed. P. L. Day (Minneapolis: Fortress, 1989) 80-81.

[32] *The Prophets*, 2 vols (Philadelphia: Fortress, 1982) I: 81.

[33] On this point see P. Bird, "'To Play the Harlot'," 75-94. She says in summary, "Despite the innuendo of chapter 2 [Hos 2], the suggestion of cultic sex remains just that. The sexual language belongs exclusively to the allegory, while the cultic activity to which it points is represented in terms elsewhere descriptive of normative Yahweh worship: pilgrim feast (ḥet), new moon, and sabbath—every appointed feast (kōl mǒʿēd) (v. 11)" (p. 83).

[34] Ibid., 86. Bird explains, "The men's worst offense is to dishonor God by their perverted worship. The women's worst offense is to dishonor their fathers and fathers-in-law by their sexual conduct. The men dishonor their Lord (metaphorical use of zānā, v. 12b); the women dishonor their lords (literal use of zānā, v. 13b)." Compare the somewhat similar conclusion regarding this text by Fisher, "Cultic Prostitution," 235.

[35] The terms qōdēš and qĕdēšâ have generally been translated as "cultic prostitute" (male and female respectively—so NRSV). However, evidence from cognate languages and from the Hebrew Bible itself does not demonstrably support such a translation. See H. M. Barstad, *The Religious Polemics of Amos* (VTSup 34; Leiden: E. J.

The foregoing discussion leads to the conclusion that when Hosea speaks of the promiscuity of the land he refers simply to the fact that Israel offers cult to *habbĕʿālîm* rather than to Yahweh alone. Hosea makes no reference to ritual sexual intercourse or ritual prostitution. Furthermore, as has been explained above, *habbĕʿālîm* does not signify multiple manifestations of the Canaanite Baal-Haddu but rather, the host of heaven of which Baal-Haddu would have been a member. According to traditional theology Yahweh stood supreme over the host of heaven. Also according to that theology, the host of heaven included deities having jurisdiction over each of the nations of the world, presumably including the gods of Canaan, of Syria, of Egypt, and of Assyria (Deut 32:8). These nations and their gods were the lovers whom Israel pursued in its political machinations and in its cultic observances, seeking from them the support and sustenance it required.

The foregoing discussion of Hosea's criticism of the cult of the Israelite State and its symbols provides a broad context within which to pursue further the more particular question of why Hosea objected to the calf iconography. Admittedly, explanations will remain somewhat speculative.

It is probable that Hosea's contemporaries continued in the traditional understanding of the calf iconography as symbolic of Yahweh's power to liberate. Undoubtedly the priests will have preserved the traditions associated with it, regularly intoning that ancient Israelite cultic formula, *hinnēh ʾĕlōhêkā yiśrāʾēl ʾăšer heʿĕlûkā mēʾereṣ miṣrāyim*, in the context of worship before the calf image. That formula will have served to recall Yahweh's ancient, constitutive, liberating actions on behalf of Israel against Egypt. Such cultic activity would have occurred all the more during times of national crisis such as the Israelite State experienced during Hosea's time. But now Hosea may have perceived that the significance of the symbol had been fundamentally compromised and contradicted by Israel's foreign policy. The policy of alliance with foreign nations implied that Israel could not rely fully and absolutely on the liberator symbolized by the calf iconography. Furthermore, possibly other divine images or idols, symbolic of the new political alignments, also appeared in Israel's sanctuaries. In these symbols Hosea will also have perceived a further compromise of the significance of the calf iconography.

---

Brill, 1984) 26-33; Fisher, "Cultic Prostitution," 231-35; Oden, *Bible Without Theology*, 149; and Bird, "'To Play the Harlot'," 86-87.

Then it is understandable that Hosea would emphasize the material composition and human manufacture of idols with the intention of ridiculing the compromised theology according to which Israel sought to manipulate the divine world to bring about a desirable outcome. To this end Israel had made kings, alliances, and idols, making calculated attempts to secure its future, but it had failed to recognize the transcendence of Yahweh, and it had failed to recognize Yahweh's direction of events from a point encompassing the human sphere.[36] According to Hosea, Yahweh as the great king demands absolute allegiance, but Hosea perceives that Israel has not met the demand.

Another possible motivation for Hosea's objection to the calf iconography warrants consideration. Above it was observed that Hosea viewed violence, robbery, and murder under the metaphor of promiscuity (Hos 6:7-10; cf. 4:2; and 11:6-7). Hosea like his contemporary Amos gives witness to social circumstances marked by violent and oppressive activity. One may expect that the crises Israel endured during the last three decades before the ruin of Samaria in 721 BCE will only have exacerbated social inequities and oppression. The tribute payments required by the Assyrians will have been secured through oppressive taxation. Conscripts for the army will have been drawn from among the peasants, thus siphoning off the laborers required to maintain viable farms. Certainly the ravages of military incursions will have had a severely negative impact on the countryside, and Israel's vacillation in foreign policy in itself resulted in considerable civil strife, in repeated violent intrigues involving the elimination of political rivals.

In these circumstances Hosea may have perceived another contradiction to the meaning of the calf iconography. The image signified Yahweh as victorious, liberating warrior, but in the Israelite State those who posed as liberating agents ruling on Yahweh's behalf in effect acted as agents of violence and oppression because of domestic and foreign policies they adopted.

Such a perspective is perhaps more evident in what Hosea says regarding altars. Hosea reproaches the altars as Ephraim's places for sinning (8:11) and as high places of iniquity (i.e., bāmôt ᵓāwen, 10:8; cf. bêt ᵓāwen as a designation for the royal sanctuary at Bethel in 4:15, 5:8, 10:5). The perceived problem becomes apparent at 6:6 where Hosea specifies

---

[36] K. Koch (The Prophets, I: 70-77, 144-156) writes in terms of Yahweh involved in *metahistory* to describe conceptualization which he finds in Amos, Hosea, and Isaiah.

that God desires covenant loyalty and knowledge of God instead of sacrifice and burnt offering. Evidently God finds these qualities, on which covenant relationship depends, lacking in Israel; Israel has fulfilled only the cultic observances. Israel's failure to keep covenant is demonstrated by the catalogue of sins presented in 6:7-9. Similarly, in 4:1-2 it is noted that instead of faithfulness, loyalty, and knowledge of God, that is, instead of commitment to the covenant there is cursing, lying, killing, stealing, committing adultery, and one deed of bloodshed upon another. Also, in 10:4, in context of a reproach against Bethel and its calf, Hosea levels an accusation that compares justice in Israel to the sprouting of poisonous weeds (cf. Amos 4:15; 8:14). For Hosea, Israel's piety as expressed at the altar deserved censure because it stood absolutely contradicted and invalidated by the impiety expressed in Israel's record for breach of covenant, that is in its acts of theft, violence and injustice.

With regard to his evaluation of the sanctuaries with their altars as places of sin, Hosea appears to agree with his contemporary, Amos (e.g., Amos 4:4-5; 5:4-5). Hosea has a message comparable to that of Amos with regard to the perversion of justice (compare especially Hos 10:4c-d and Amos 6:12c-d; 5:7) and the worthlessness of the cult when right social relationships are neglected or even obstructed. The comparison with Amos may serve to clarify Hosea's concern. In the case of Amos it is more transparent that the root of the prophetic censure against the cult did not lie in the conviction that cultic practices marked a departure from legitimate ancient traditions. Rather, Amos' censure of the cult of the Israelite State grew out of his conviction that devotion to Yahweh entailed first and foremost the maintenance of social relationships built on loyalty, justice, and righteousness, especially in favor of the disadvantaged (so especially Amos 5:21-24); and according to Amos, Israel had failed utterly in this point. Hosea, like Amos, found fault with the cult because Israel had by its injustice breached the very covenant relationship with Yahweh which Israel presumed to celebrate in its cult.

Hosea's objection to altars, pillars, sanctuaries, and calf iconography probably had little to do with the particular cultic institutions in themselves. Rather, Hosea perceived that Israel, in its religious and theological adjustments to meet the crisis of the time, had compromised its fealty to Yahweh the great king, and moreover, that Israel failed to recognize that devotion acceptable to Yahweh did not reside in the cult itself. The cult which should have had a representative function to facilitate the expression of covenant faithfulness had become religion itself. The calf image, though it had been intended to serve as a representation to point the worshiper to Yahweh, had instead become the object of devotion and of misplaced confidence. For Hosea all the symbols and icons of the cult in the Israelite State stood under the same censure. They had in effect become instruments of false worship.[37] Hosea does exhibit a very significant aniconic tendency, but the reason for the iconoclasm does not appear to lie in some philosophically grounded rejection of the symbols and icons in themselves, nor in the notion that they are illegitimate in terms of tradition or that they are un-Yahwistic, un-Israelite, and foreign.

For the purposes of understanding Hosea's contribution toward the programmatic censure of Jeroboam's cult by DtrH, it can be argued that Hosea provided a powerful impetus towards an increasingly stringent iconoclasm within the Israelite State and later in Judah.[38] This claim finds confirmation in that this stringent iconoclastic attitude is not observable in connection with earlier, staunchly Yahwistic figures such as Elijah, Elisha, or Jehu. Instead, the evidence suggests a rather broad tendency beginning with Hosea and developed by Deuteronomic and Deuteronomistic writers toward the rationalization or even rejection of icons or symbols which formerly held a secure place in the Israelite cult and (to broaden the base of the argument) in the Judahite cult. Such a claim holds true for the pillar, for the asherah, for the bronze serpent, and for the ark and cherubim.

It has been argued above that pillars originally had an accepted place in the Israelite cult of Yahweh. However, Deut 16:22 uncompromisingly prohibits their use in the cult. Several Deuteronomic and Deuteronomistic texts prescribe their destruction (Exod 23:24; 34:13; Deut 7:5; 12:3),[39] condemn their establishment (1 Kgs 14:23, 2 Kgs 17:10),

---

[37] Cf. B. Halpern, "'Brisker Pipes than Poetry:' The Development of Israelite Monotheism," in *Judaic Perspectives on Ancient Israel*, ed. J. Neusner, B. A. Levine, and E. S. Frerichs (Philadelphia: Fortress, 1987) 95.

[38] As implied by this formulation, aniconism in Israelite Yahwism predates Hosea. Probably, as C. Dohmen (*Das Bilderverbot. Seine Entstehung und seine Entwicklung im Alten Testament* [BBB 62; Bonn; Peter Hanstein, 1985]) argues, a relatively unreflective aniconism derives from the earliest Israelite heritage. This aniconism will have excluded images as direct representations of Yahweh, but it will have allowed for representation of attributes such as that provided by the cherubim throne or the calf iconography.

[39] Regarding the Deuteronomic authorship of Exod 23:24 and 34:13 see Childs, *Exodus*, 460-61 and 608. As for the designation of the altars, pillars, and asherahs as pre-Israelite and Canaanite rather than Yahwistic in these verses, probably one

or commend kings for their removal (2 Kgs 18:4, 23:14). Whereas Hosea threatens them with divine judgment, the Deuteronomic and Deuteronomistic authors appear to go even further, making a categorical prohibition of what formerly had held a legitimate place in Israelite worship. The development of a more absolute position against the pillars in the Deuteronomic and Deuteronomistic literature suggests that the direction of influence ran from Hosea to Deuteronomy.[40]

With respect to the asherah, S. M. Olyan has recently dealt with the evidence and argued to a conclusion that corresponds to that reached regarding the pillar.[41] Probably the asherah was a tree or a stylized tree.[42] From the ancestral narratives one may gather that it held a significant place in the early Yahwistic cult at Beersheba (Gen 21:33) and at Shechem (Gen 12:6-7; cf. Josh 24:26). Certainly there would have been no need for the proscriptive statement in Deut 16:21, "You shall not plant any tree as an asherah beside the altar of Yahweh your God which you shall make," if the asherah had not held a prominent place in the Yahweh cult. According to the historical texts an asherah stood in the temple of Yahweh at Jerusalem (2 Kgs 21:3, 7; 23:4, 6; cf. 18:4), and the inscriptions at Khirbet el Qôm[43] (late eighth century) and Kuntillet ʿAjrud[44] (eighth century BCE) which offer blessings by Yahweh and his asherah make evident that the asherah held a significant place in popular Israelite and Judahite piety. However, in the Deuteronomic and Deuteronomistic texts there exists a sustained polemic against the asherah (Deut 7:1-5; 12:1-3; 2 Kgs 17:9-12). This polemic associates it

---

should view this as a polemical re-categorization by the Deuteronomic authors, as will be argued subsequently.

[40] For further comment on the relationship between Hosea and Deuteronomy see M. Weinfeld, *Deuteronomy and the Deuteronomic School* (Oxford, 1972) 367; Mettinger, "The Veto on Images," 24; and Zimmerli, "Das Bilderverbot," 257.

[41] *Asherah and the Cult of Yahweh in Israel* (SBLMS 34; Atlanta: Scholars Press, 1988).

[42] This judgment is grounded in the observation that a tree may be "planted" (*ntʿ*, Deut 16:21) as an asherah, or that an asherah may be built (*bnh*, 1 Kgs 14:23) or "erected" (*nṣb* in 2 Kgs 17:10, *ʿmd* [H stem] in 2 Chr 33:19) or "cut down" (*krt*, Jdgs 6:25). See also Olyan, *Asherah*, 1-2.

[43] See the *editio princeps* by W. G. Dever, "Iron Age Epigraphic Material from the Area of Khirbet el-Kôm," *HUCA* 40/41 (1970) 139-204; also P. D. Miller, "Psalms and Inscriptions," in *Congress Volume: Vienna 1980* (VTSup, 32; Leiden: E. J. Brill, 1981) 311-32; and for further bibliography, Olyan, *Asherah*, 23-24.

[44] For the publication of several photographs of the inscriptions see Z. Meshel, "Did Yahweh Have a Consort?" *BARev* 5 (1979) 24-36; and for further bibliography see Olyan, *Asherah*, 25-37.

with *habba'al* rather than with Yahweh and rejects it as Canaanite in origin. Why an item that originally had its associations with the cult of Yahweh should now come to have associations with *habba'al* is a question which will receive consideration below, but surely Olyan has correctly recognized this criticism of the asherah as a Deuteronomic and Deuteronomistic contribution.[45]

From 2 Kgs 18:4 one may gather that a bronze serpent icon, legitimated by the tradition attributing its creation to Moses (cf. Num 21:4-9), had its place in the cult of Yahweh in Judah until the time of Hezekiah. Hezekiah, however, destroyed the icon because the people were burning incense to it. Probably this action should be considered as part of his larger iconoclastic policy towards the cult in which he removed high places, pillars, and the asherah (2 Kgs 18:4). One may venture as reasonable speculation that this policy received its inspiration from Deuteronomic groups who had immigrated as refugees from the Israelite State around 721 BCE and were already active in Jerusalem.

Even the cherubim and the ark appear to have fallen victim to iconoclasm after the period of Hosea. From early times when the cherubim and the ark stood at Shiloh and also later when they stood in the temple in Jerusalem they apparently signified the throne and footstool of Yahweh as King (1 Sam 4:4, 2 Sam 6:2, 2 Kgs 19:15). However, with the author of Deuteronomy a striking demythologization or rationalization occurred.[46] Deut 10:1-5 presents the ark as a wooden box built as a receptacle for the tablets containing the law. This conception abandons the older connection of the ark with the cherubim as a representation of Yahweh the King. The ark no longer stands as a cultic symbol marking the presence of Yahweh as King. Rather, it now functions as a receptacle for the law which in itself represents the presence of Yahweh. Evidently the older cultic symbolism of the ark had been rejected. However, due to its great venerability, the cultic apparatus itself remained, but the author of Deuteronomy attached a new and more acceptable significance and function to it.[47]

It is probably significant that in the period shortly after the ruin of Israel in 721 BCE, Hezekiah moved the Judahite cult in an iconoclastic

---

45 Olyan, *Asherah*, 22.

46 G. von Rad, *Studies in Deuteronomy* (London, 1953) 40.

47 On the changing concept of the ark see T. E. Fretheim, "The Ark in Deuteronomy" *CBQ* 30 (1968) 1-14; Zimmerli, "Das Bilderverbot," 258-60; and von Rad, "The Tent and the Ark" in *The Problem of the Hexateuch and Other Essays* (London: SCM, 1984) 106.

direction in a programmatic way. According to 2 Kgs 18:4, "he removed the high places, he shattered the pillars, he cut down the asherah, and he crushed the bronze serpent which Moses had made . . . ." The explanation lies ready at hand that Hosea, though not exactly iconoclastic himself, had provided an impetus towards iconoclasm, that Hosea's preaching had in effect received its vindication in the disaster of 721 BCE, that the Deuteronomic group took its inspiration for iconoclasm from Hosea, and that Hezekiah responded to the new doctrine by purging the Judahite cult of symbols and icons which till his time had had their legitimate place in the Yahweh cult.[48] Hezekiah's new religious policies in turn seemed to receive their vindication from the fact that Jerusalem was spared destruction in 701 BCE, and this gave impetus to the continued iconoclastic zeal of the Deuteronomists and, later, of Josiah.

If this argument holds, then the criticism of Jeroboam I for his sponsorship of the calf iconography as presented in 1 Kgs 12:26-30 and in numerous refrains within 1 and 2 Kings probably came about as a development of an impetus toward iconoclasm first attested in Hosea and then confirmed into a strict doctrine for the Deuteronomic group by the catalyst of the experience of 721 BCE. This explanation for the origins of the strict iconoclastic attitude and for the biblical criticism of Jeroboam permits greater confidence in the conclusion already stated above, that Jeroboam fostered the ancient religious traditions of Israel, that he sponsored an authentic Israelite Yahwistic cult, and that this cult was generally perceived as legitimate in its own time and probably down to the time of Hosea.

Returning now to the question of the association of the calf iconography with *habbaʿal*, the question may be considered against the context of Hosea's general reproach against the cult. Above it has been noted

that in general the symbols and icons which shared a place in the traditional Yahweh cult including pillars, bull images, altars, and even specific sanctuaries such as Bethel and Gilgal, came under censure or the
verdict of judgment by Hosea. It is noteworthy that several of these
symbols or representations that originally held a respectable place in
Yahwistic cult eventually came to be regarded as accretions from the
Canaanite religion, as originally foreign to Israelite religion. This occurs
specifically in Deuteronomic and Deuteronomistic texts with reference
to the high places, pillars, and asherahs (Exod 23:24; 34:13; Deut 7:1-5;
12:1-3; and 2 Kgs 17:9-12). Along with Halpern one may conclude that
the period towards the end of the eighth century is marked by the
systematic turning of xenophobic rhetoric inward against aspects that
were traditional in Israelite religion.[49] Cultic symbols that once held an
accepted and integral place in the cult of Yahweh now came to be
regarded as illegitimate, and if they were judged illegitimate then they
must also be un-Yahwistic and foreign, and if they were judged un-
Yahwistic and foreign they could be considered symbols belonging to
the worship of other gods, that is, to the worship of *habbĕʿālîm*.

It is most probable that neither Hosea nor the ordinary Israelite
pilgrims at the shrines of the Israelite State considered the calf iconography as representative of a deity other than Yahweh. Neither the book of
Hosea nor any other biblical text gives evidence for such a conclusion. If
Hosea's perspective somehow eventually led to the association of the
calf iconography with *habbaʿal*, one may do well to inquire whether it
was not due to Hosea's peculiar rationalization according to which
many symbols and icons from the cult of the Israelite State were repudiated on the grounds that they and the cult in which they served had
become compromised in a cult which failed as an expression of true
covenant loyalty.

---

49 "Brisker Pipes Than Poetry," 96.

# Bibliography

Aberbach, M., and Smolar, L., "Aaron, Jeroboam, and the Golden Calves." *JBL* 86 (1967) 129-40.

Ackroyd, P. "Chronicles, I and II." *IDBSup*, 156-58.

Aharoni, Y. *The Land of the Bible: A Historical Geography*. Rev. and enlarged ed., trans. and ed. A. F. Rainey. Philadelphia: Westminster, 1979.

Ahlström, G. W. *Aspects of Syncretism in Israelite Religion*. Horae Soederblomianae 5. Lund: C.W.K. Gleerup, 1963.

————. *Royal Administration and National Religion in Ancient Palestine*. Leiden: E. J. Brill, 1982.

————. "Where Did the Israelites Live?" *JNES* 41 (1982) 133-38.

Albright, W. F. "The Oracles of Balaam." *JBL* 63 (1944) 207-33.

————. "The List of Levitic Cities." *Louis Ginzberg Jubilee Volume*. New York: American Academy for Jewish Research, 1945. Pp. 49-73.

————. *From the Stone Age to Christianity*. 2d ed. Garden City: Doubleday, 1957.

————. *Archaeology and the Religion of Israel*. 5th ed. Baltimore: John Hopkins, 1968.

————. *Yahweh and the Gods of Canaan*. London: Athlone, 1968.

Albright, W. F., and Kelso, J. L. *The Excavation of Bethel (1934- 1960)*. AASOR 39. Cambridge: American Schools of Oriental Research, 1968.

Alt, A. "Bermerkungen zu einigen judäischen Ortslisten des Alten Testaments." *Kleine Schriften zur Geschichte des Volkes Israel*. 3 vols. München: C. H. Beck, 1953. 2: 289-305.

————. "Israels Gaue unter Salomo." *Kleine Schriften zur Geschichte des Volkes Israel*. 3 vols. München: C. H. Beck, 1953. 2: 76-89.

———. "The God of the Fathers." *Essays on Old Testament History and Religion*. Oxford: Basil Blackwell, 1966. Pp. 3-77.

———. "The Monarchy in the Kingdoms of Israel and Judah." *Essays on Old Testament History and Religion*. Oxford: Basil Blackwell, 1966.

Andersen, F. I. and Freedman, D. N. *Hosea*. AB 24. Garden City: Doubleday, 1980.

Astour, M. C. "841 BC: The First Assyrian Invasion of Israel." *JAOS* 91 (1971) 383-9.

Attridge, H. W. and Oden, R. A. Jr. *Philo of Byblos: The Phoenician History*. CBQMS 9. Washington, DC: The Catholic Biblical Association of America, 1981.

Avigad, N. "New Names on Hebrew Seals." *EI* 12 (1975) 66-71 (In Hebrew).

———. "The Contribution of Hebrew Seals to an Understanding of Israelite Religion and Society." *AIR*. Pp. 195-208.

———. "Hebrew Seals and Sealings and their Significance for Biblical Research." *Congress Volume: Jerusalem 1986*. VTSup 40. Ed. J. A. Emerton. Leiden: E. J. Brill, 1988. Pp. 7-16.

Bailey, L. R. "The Golden Calf." *HUCA* 42 (1971) 97-115.

Barstad, H. M. *The Religious Polemics of Amos*. VTSup 34. Leiden: E. J. Brill, 1984.

Beyerlin, W. *Origins and History of the Oldest Sinaitic Traditions*. Oxford: Basil Blackwell, 1965.

Biran, A. "Tel Dan." *BA* 37 (1974) 26-51.

———. "An Israelite Horned Altar at Dan." *BA* 37 (1974) 106-7.

———. "Tell Dan Five Years Later." *BA* 43 (1981) 168-82.

———. "Notes and News: Tel Dan, 1984." *IEJ* 35 (1985) 186-89.

———. "The Dancer from Dan, the Empty Tomb and the Altar Room." *IEJ* 36 (1986) 168-87.

———. "Twenty Years of Digging at Tel Dan." *BAR* 13 (1987) 12-25.

———. "Dan." In *Archaeology and Biblical Interpretation: Essays in Memory of D. Glenn Rose*. Ed. L. G. Perdue, L. E. Toombs, G. L. Johnson. Atlanta: John Knox, 1987. Pp. 101-111.

Bird, P. "'To Play the Harlot': An Inquiry into an Old Testament Metaphor." In *Gender and Difference in Ancient Israel*. Ed. P. L. Day. Minneapolis: Fortress, 1989. Pp. 75-94.

Boling, R. G. *Judges*. AB 6A. Garden City: Doubleday, 1975.

Boling, R. G. and Campbell, E. F. "Jeroboam and Rehoboam at Shechem." In *Archaeology and Biblical Interpretation: Essays in Memory of D. Glenn Rose*. Ed. L. G. Perdue, L. E. Toombs, G. L. Johnson. Atlanta: John Knox, 1987. Pp. 259-72.

Braun, R. *1 Chronicles*. WBC 14. Waco: Word Books, 1986.

Buccellati, G. *Cities and Nations of Ancient Syria: An Essay on Political Institutions with Special Reference to the Israelite Kingdom*. Studi Semitici 26. Rome: Istituto di Studi del Vicino Oriente, 1967.

Budde, K. *Die Büche Samuel*. KHAT 8. Tübingen: J. C. B. Mohr, 1902.

Bull, R. J; Callaway, J. A.; Campbell, E. F.; Ross, J. F.; and Wright, G. E. "The Fifth Campaign at Balâṭah (Shechem)." *BASOR* 180 (1965) 7-41.

Buren, E. D. van. *Symbols of the Gods in Mesopotamian Art.* ANOR 23. Rome: Pontificium Institutum Biblicum, 1945.

Burney, C. F. *The Book of Judges.* Library of Biblical Studies. New York: KTAV, 1970.

Campbell, E. F. "Shechem (City)." *IDBSup*, 821-22.

Carroll, R. P. *Jeremiah.* OTL. Philadelphia: Westminster, 1986.

Childs, B. S. *The Book of Exodus.* OTL. Philadelphia: Westminster, 1974.

Coats, G. W. *Rebellion in the Desert.* Nashville: Abingdon, 1968.

Cody, A. *A History of Old Testament Priesthood.* AnBibl 35. Rome: Pontifical Biblical Institute, 1969.

Cogan, M. *Imperialism and Religion: Assyria, Judah and Israel in the Eighth and Seventh Centuries B.C.E.* Missoula: Scholars Press, 1974.

Coogan, M. D. "Canaanite Origins and Lineage: Reflections on the Religion of Ancient Israel." In *AIR*. Pp. 115-24.

———. "Of Cults and Cultures: Reflections on the Interpretation of Archaeological Evidence." *PEQ* 119 (1987) 1-8.

Crenshaw, J. L. *Prophetic Conflict: Its Effect upon Israelite Religion.* New York: Walter de Gruyter, 1971.

Cross, F. M. *Canaanite Myth and Hebrew Epic: Essays in the History of the Religion of Israel.* Cambridge: Harvard University Press, 1973.

———. "'el." *TDOT*, I: 242-61.

———. "The Priestly Tabernacle in the Light of Recent Research." In *Temples and High Places in Biblical Times.* Jerusalem: Hebrew Union College/Jewish Institute of Religion, 1981. Pp. 169-80.

———. "Reuben, First-Born of Jacob." *ZAW* 100, Sup (1988) 46-65.

Cross, F. M., and Freedman, D. N. "The Blessing of Moses." *JBL* 67 (1948) 191-210.

———. *Studies in Ancient Yahwistic Poetry.* SBLDS 21. Missoula: Scholars Press, 1975.

Cundall, A. E. "Judges—An Apology for the Monarchy?" *ExpTim* 81 (1970) 178-81.

Danelius, E. "The Sins of Jeroboam Ben-Nabat." *JQR* 58 (1967-68) 95-114, 204-23.

Davenport, J. W. "A Study of the Golden Calf Tradition in Exodus 32." Ph. D. dissertation, Princeton Theological Seminary, 1973.

Davis, D. R. "Comic Literature—Tragic Theology: A Study of Judges 17-18." *WTJ* 46 (1984) 156-63.

de Moor, J. C. "El the Creator." In *The Bible World: Essays in Honor of Cyrus H. Gordon.* Ed. G. Rendsburg, R. Adler, M. Arfa, and N. H. Winter. New York: KTAV and the Institute of Hebrew Culture and Education of New York University, 1980. Pp. 171-87.

———. *The Rise of Yahwism: The Roots of Israelite Monotheism.* BETL 91. Leuven: Leuven University Press, 1990.

de Vaux, R. *Ancient Israel*. Vol 1: *Social Institutions*. New York: McGraw-Hill, 1965.

————. *The Bible and the Ancient Near East*. Garden City: Doubleday, 1971.

Debus, J. *Die Sünde Jerobeams: Studien zur Darstellung Jerobeams und der Geschichte des Nordreichs in der deuteronomistischen Geschichtsschreibung*. FRLANT 93. Göttingen: Vandenhoeck & Ruprecht, 1967.

Dever, W. G. "Iron Age Epigraphic Material from the Area of Khirbet el-Kôm." *HUCA* 40/41 (1970) 139-204.

————. "The Contribution of Archaeology to the Study of Canaanite and Early Israelite Religion." In *AIR*. Pp. 209-47.

DeVries, S. J. *1 Kings*. WBC 12. Waco, Texas: Word Books, 1985.

Dietrich, W. *Prophetie und Geschichte*. FRLANT 108. Göttingen: Vandenhoeck & Ruprecht, 1972.

Dohmen, C. *Das Bilderverbot. Seine Entstehung und seine Entwicklung im Alten Testament*. BBB 62. Bonn: Peter Hanstein, 1985.

Donner, H. "Hier sind deine Götter, Israel!" In *Wort und Geschichte: Fest. K. Elliger*. AOAT 18. Neukirchen-Vluyn, 1973. Pp. 45-50.

————. "The Separate States of Israel and Judah." In *Israelite and Judaean History*. Ed. J. H. Hayes and J. M. Miller. OTL. Philadelphia: Westminster, 1977. Pp. 381-434.

Dozeman, T. B. "The Way of the Man of God from Judah: True and False Prophecy in the Pre-Deuteronomistic Legend of I Kgs 13." *CBQ* 44 (1982) 379-93.

Eichrodt, W. *Theology of the Old Testament*. 2 vols. OTL. Philadelphia: Westminster, 1961-67.

Eissfeldt, O. "Lade und Stierbild." *ZAW* 58 (1940/41) 190-215.

————. "El and Yahweh." *JSS* 1 (1956) 25-37.

————. "Silo und Jerusalem." *Volume du Congress: Strasbourg 1956*. VTSup 4. Leiden: E. J. Brill, 1957. Pp. 138-47.

————. *Das Lied Moses Deuteronomium 32.1-43 und das Lehrgedicht Asaphs Psalm 78; samt einer Analyse der Umgebung des Mose-Liedes*. Berichte über die Behandlungen der Sächsischen Akademie der Wissenschaften zu Leipzig, philologisch-historische Klasse 104, 5. Berlin: Akademie Verlag, 1958.

————. "Jakobs Begegnung mit El und Moses Begegnung mit Jahwe." *OLZ* 58 (1963) 325-331.

Evans, C. D. "Naram-Sin and Jeroboam: The Archetypal *Unheilsherrscher* in Mesopotamian and Biblical Historiography." In *Scripture in Context II: More Essays on the Comparative Method*. Ed. W. W. Hallo, James C. Moyer, Leo G. Perdue. Winona Lake: Eisenbrauns, 1983. Pp. 97-125.

Finkelstein, I. "Shiloh Yields Some, but Not All of Its Secrets." *BARev* 12 (1986) 29-34.

————. *The Archaeology of the Israelite Settlement*. Jerusalem: Israel Exploration Society, 1988.

Finkelstein, I., Bunimovitz, S., and Lederman, Z. "Excavations at Shiloh 1981-84: Preliminary Report." *Tel Aviv* 12 (1985) 123-80.

Fisher, E. J. "Cultic Prostitution in the Ancient Near East? A Reassessment." *BTB* 6 (1976) 225-36

Fitzmeyer, J. A. "The Phoenician Inscription from Pyrgi." *JAOS* 86 (1966) 285-97.

Fohrer, G. *History of Israelite Religion*. Nashville: Abingdon, 1972.

Freedman, D. N. "Divine Names and Titles in Early Hebrew Poetry." In *Magnalia Dei: The Mighty Acts of God*. Ed. F. M. Cross, W. E. Lemke, and P. D. Miller. Garden City: Doubleday, 1976. Pp. 56-107.

Fretheim, T. E. "The Ark in Deuteronomy." *CBQ* 30 (1968) 1-14.

Frick, F. S. *The City in Ancient Israel*. SBLDS 36. Missoula: Scholars Press, 1977.

Gooding, D. W. "The Septuagint's Rival Versions of Jeroboam's Rise to Power." *VT* 17 (1967) 173-89.

————. "Problems of Text and Midrash in the Third Book of Reigns." *Textus* 7 (1969) 1-29.

Gottwald, N. K. *The Tribes of Yahweh*. Maryknoll, NY: Orbis, 1979.

Goulder, M. *The Psalms of the Sons of Korah*. JSOTSup 20. Sheffield: JSOT Press, 1982.

Gray, G. B. *A Critical and Exegetical Commentary on Numbers*. ICC. Edinburgh: T. &. T. Clark, 1903.

Gray, J. "Social Aspects of Canaanite Religion." In *Volume du Congrès: Genève 1965*. VTSup 15. Leiden: E. J. Brill, 1966. Pp. 170-92.

————. *I & II Kings*. 2d rev. ed. OTL. Philadelphia: Westminster, 1970.

————. *The Biblical Doctrine of the Reign of God*. Edinburgh: T & T Clark, 1979.

Gressmann, H. *Altorientalische Bilder zum Alten Testament*. 2d rev. ed. Berlin and Leipzig: Walter de Gruyter, 1927.

Gross, W. "Lying Prophet and Disobedient Man of God in I Kings 13: Role Analysis as an Instrument of Theological Interpretation of an Old Testament Narrative Text." *Semeia* 15 (1979) 97-135.

Habel, N. C. *Yahweh Versus Baal: A Conflict of Religious Cultures*. New York: Bookman Associates, 1964.

Hahn, J. *Das "Goldene Kalb": Die Jahwe-Verehrung bei Stierbildern in der Geschichte Israels*. Europäische Hochschulschriften 23, 154. Frankfurt am Main, Bern: Peter Lang, 1981.

Halpern, B. "Sectionalism and the Schism." *JBL* 93 (1974) 519-32.

————. "Levitic Participation in the Reform Cult of Jeroboam I." *JBL* 95 (1976) 31-42.

————. *The Emergence of Israel in Canaan*. SBLMS 29. Chico: Scholars Press, 1983.

————. "'Brisker Pipes than Poetry:' The Development of Israelite Monotheism." *Judaic Perspectives on Ancient Irael*. Ed. J. Neusner, B. A. Levine, and E. S. Frerichs. Philadelphia: Fortress, 1987. Pp. 77-115.

————. "The Baal (and the Asherah?) in Seventh-Century Judah." An unpublished essay, 1991, archived on the IOUDAIOS electronic discussion group's listserver. LISTSERV@YORKVM1.BITNET.

Handy, L. K. "Dissenting Deities or Obedient Angels: Divine Hierarchies in Ugarit and the Bible." *BR* 35 (1990) 18-35.

Haran, M. *Temples and Temple Service in Ancient Israel*. Winona Lake: Eisenbrauns, 1985.

Hauer, C. "David and the Levites." *JSOT* 23 (1982) 33-54.

Hayes, J. H. "Hosea's Baals and Lovers: Religion or Politics?" A paper presented to the Israelite Prophetic Literature section at the Society of Biblical Literature meetings in New Orleans, November 19, 1990.

Hayes, J. H. and Hooker, P. K. *A New Chronology for the Kings of Israel and Judah and its Implications for Biblical History and Literature*. Atlanta: John Knox, 1988.

Hayes, J. H. and Kuan, J. K. "The Final Years of Samaria (730-720 BC)." *Bib* 72 (1991) 153-81.

Hendel, R. S. "The Social Origins of the Aniconic Tradition in Early Israel." *CBQ* 50 (1988) 365-82.

Hertzberg, H. W. *I & II Samuel*. OTL. Philadelphia: Westminster, 1964.

Hertzberg, W. *Die Bücher Josua, Richter, Ruth*. ATD. Göttingen: Vandenhoeck & Ruprecht, 1953.

Hestrin, R. "The Cult Stand from Ta'anach and its Religious Background." *Studia Phoenicia V: Phoenicia and the East Mediterranean in the First Millennium B.C.* Ed. E. Lipinski. Orientalia Lovaniensia Analecta 22. Leuven: Uitgeverij Peeters, 1987. Pp. 61-77.

————. "Understanding Asherah: Exploring Semitic Iconography." *BARev* 17 (1991) 50-59.

Hillers, D. R. "Analyzing the Abominable: Our Understanding of Canaanite Religion." *JQR* 75 (1985) 253-69.

Holder, J. "The Presuppositions, Accusations, and Threats of 1 Kings 14.1-18." *JBL* 107 (1988) 27-38.

Hyatt, J. P. "Bethel (Deity)." In *IDB*, I: 390-91.

Ishida, T. *The Royal Dynasties in Ancient Israel: A Study on the Formation and Development of Royal-Dynastic Ideology*. BZAW 142. Berlin/New York: Walter de Gruyter, 1977.

Jacobsen, T. "The Graven Image." In *AIR*. Pp. 15-32.

Janzen, J. G. "The Character of the Calf and Its Cult in Exodus 32." *CBQ* 52 (1990) 597-607.

Jaroš, K. *Die Stellung des Elohisten zur kanaanäischen Religion*. OBO 4. Göttingen: Vandenhoeck & Ruprecht, 1974.

Jepsen, A. "Gottesmann und Prophet. Anmerkungen zum Kapitel I Könige 13." In *Probleme biblischer Theologie. Gerhard von Rad zum 70 Geburtstag*. München: Chr Kaiser, 1971. Pp. 171-82.

Kapelrud, A. "ʾabîr." *TDOT*, I: 42-44.

Keel, O. *Die Welt der altorientalischen Bildsymbolik und das Alte Testament: Am Beispiel der Psalmen*. Rev. ed. Zürich and Neukirchen-Vluyn: Benziger and Neukirchener, 1977.

————. *Jahwe-Visionen und Siegelkunst: Eine neue Deutung der Majestätsschilderungen in Jes 6, Ez 1 und 10 und Sach 4*. SBS 84/85. Stuttgart: Verlag Katholisches Bibelwerk, 1977.

Kempinski, A. "Joshua's Altar—An Iron Age I Watchtower." *BARev* 12 (1986) 42, 44-49.

Kennedy, J. M. "The Social Background of Early Israel's Rejection of Cultic Images: A Proposal." *BTB* 17 (1987) 138-44.

Koch, K. *The Prophets*. 2 vols. Philadelphia: Fortress, 1982.

Kraeling, C. H. and Adams, R. M. *City Invincible. A Symposium on Urbanization and Cultural Development in the Ancient Near East*. Chicago, 1960.

Kraus, H.-J. *Die Königsherrschaft Gottes im Alten Testament*. Tübingen: J. C. B. Mohr, 1951.

————. *Worship in Israel: A Cultic History of the Old Testament*. Oxford: Basil Blackwell, 1966.

————. *Psalms 1-59*. Minneapolis: Augsburg, 1988.

Lehming, S. "Versuch zu Ex. xxxii." *VT* 10 (1960) 16-50.

Lemke, Werner E. "The Way of Obedience: I Kings 13 and the Structure of the Deuteronomistic History." In *Magnalia Dei: The Mighty Acts of God: Essays on the Bible and Archaeology in Memory of G. Ernest Wright*. Ed. F. M. Cross, W. E. Lemke, and P. D. Miller. Garden City: Doubleday, 1976. Pp. 301-26.

L'Heureux, C. E. *Rank among the Canaanite Gods: El, Baʿal, and the Rephaʾim*. HSM 21; Missoula: Scholars Press, 1979.

————. "Searching for the Origins of God." In *Traditions in Transformation: Turning Points in Biblical Faith*. Ed. B. Halpern and J. D. Levenson. Winona Lake: Eisenbrauns, 1981. Pp. 33-44.

Loewenstamm, S. E. "The Ugaritic Fertility Myth—the Result of a Mistranslation." *IEJ* 12 (1962) 87-88.

————. "The Making and Destruction of the Golden Calf." *Bib* 48 (1967) 480-91.

Long, B. O. *I Kings with an Introduction to Historical Literature*. The Forms of the Old Testament Literature 9. Grand Rapids: Eerdmans, 1984.

Loretz, O. "Die Epitheta ʾl ʾlyj jśrʾl (Gn 33,20) und ʾl ʾlhj ʾbjk (Gn 46.3)." *UF* 7 (1975), 583.

————. "Die Herausführungsformel in Num 23.22 und 24.8." *UF* 7 (1975) 571-72.

Loza, J. "Exode XXXII et la redaction JE." *VT* 23 (1973) 31-55.

Malamat, A. "The Danite Migration." *Bib* 51 (1970) 1-16.

May, H. G. *Material Remains of the Megiddo Cult.* OIP 26. Chicago: University of Chicago Press, 1935.

Mays, J. L. *Hosea.* OTL. Philadelphia: Westminster, 1969.

Mazar, A. "The 'Bull Site'—An Iron Age I Open Cult Place." *BASOR* 247 (1982) 27-42.

———. "Bronze Bull found in Israelite 'High Place' from the Time of the Judges." *BARev* 9/5 (1983) 34-40.

———. "On Cult Places and Early Israelites: A Response to Michael Coogan." *BARev* 15/4 (1988) 45.

Mazar, B. "The Cities of the Priests and Levites." *Congress Volume.* VTSup 7. Leiden: E. J. Brill, 1960. Pp. 193-205.

———. "The Early Israelite Settlement in the Hill Country." *BASOR* 241 (1981) 75-85.

McCarter, P. K. *II Samuel.* AB 9. Garden City: Doubleday, 1984.

McKay, J. *Religion in Judah under the Assyrians.* SBT, second series 26. London: SCM, 1973.

McKenzie, S. L. *The Trouble with Kings: The Composition of the Book of Kings in the Deuteronomistic History.* VTSup 42; Leiden: E. J. Brill, 1991.

Meek, Th. J. *Hebrew Origins.* Rev. ed. New York: Harper, 1950.

Mendenhall, G. E. "The Hebrew Conquest of Palestine." *BA* 25 (1962) 66-87.

Meshel, Z. "Did Yahweh Have a Consort?" *BARev* 5 (1979) 24-36.

Mettinger, T. N. D. *King and Messiah: The Civil and Sacral Legitimation of the Israelite Kings.* ConBOT 8. Lund: C. W. K. Gleerup, 1976.

———. "The Veto on Images and the Aniconic God in Ancient Israel." *Religious Symbols and their Functions.* Ed. H. Biezas. Stockholm: Almqvist and Wiksell International, 1979. Pp. 15-29.

———. "YHWH SABAOTH—The Heavenly King on the Cherubim Throne." In *Studies in the Period of David and Solomon and Other Essays.* Ed. T. Ishida. Winona Lake: Eisenbrauns, 1982. Pp. 109-38.

———. *In Search of God: The Meaning and Message of the Everlasting Names.* Philadelphia: Fortress, 1988.

Miller, J. M., and Hayes, J. H. *A History of Ancient Israel and Judah.* Philadelphia: Westminster, 1986.

Miller, P. D. "El the Warrior." *HTR* 60 (1967) 411-31.

———. "Animal Names as Designations in Ugaritic and Hebrew." *UF* 2 (1970) 177-86.

———. "Ugaritic GZR and Hebrew ʿZR II." *UF* 2 (1970) 159-75.

———. "God and the Gods: History of Religion as an Approach and Context for Bible and Theology." *Affirmation* 1/5 (1973) 37-62.

————. *The Divine Warrior in Early Israel*. hsm 5. Cambridge: Harvard University Press, 1973.

————. "Psalms and Inscriptions." *Congress Volume: Vienna 1980*. vts up 32. Leiden: E. J. Brill, 1981. Pp. 311-32.

————. "Israelite Religion." *The Hebrew Bible and Its Modern Interpreters*. Ed. D. A. Knight and G. M. Tucker. Philadelphia: Fortress, 1985. Pp. 201-37.

Moberly, R. W. L. *At the Mountain of God: Story and Theology in Exodus 32-34*. jsots up 22. Sheffield: jsot Press, 1983.

Mohlenbrink, K. "Die levitischen Überlieferungen des Alten Testaments." *ZAW* 11 (1934) 184-231.

Montgomery, J. A. *A Critical and Exegetical Commentary on the Books of Kings*. Ed. H. S. Gehman. icc. New York: Scribners, 1951.

Moore, G. F. *A Critical and Exegetical Commentary on Judges*. icc. New York: Charles Scribner, 1895.

Morgenstern, J. *Amos Studies*. 2 vols. Sigmund Rheinstrom Memorial Publications 2. Cincinnati: Hebrew Union College Press, 1941.

————. "The Festival of Jeroboam I." *JBL* 83 (1964) 109-18.

Motzki, H. "Ein Beitrag zum Problem des Stierkultes in der Religionsgeschichte Israels." *VT* 25 (1975) 470-85.

Mowinckel, S. *The Psalms in Israel's Worship*. Oxford: Basil Blackwell, 1962.

Nelson, R. D. *The Double Redaction of the Deuteronomistic History*. jsots up 18. Sheffield, 1981.

Nicholson, E. W. *Deuteronomy and Tradition*. Oxford: Basil Blackwell, 1967.

Nielsen, E. *Shechem: A Traditio-Historical Investigation*. Copenhagen: G. E. C. Gad, 1955.

Noth, M. *Überlieferungsgeschichtliche Studien I: Die sammelnden und bearbeitenden Geschichtswerke im Alten Testament*. Schriften der Königsberger Gelehrten Gesellschaft 18, 2. Halle: Max Niemeyer, 1943.

————. *Das Buch Josua*. 2d rev. ed. hat I, 7. Tübingen: J. C. B. Mohr (Paul Siebeck), 1953.

————. *The History of Israel*. 2d ed. New York: Harper & Row, 1960.

————. *Exodus*. otl. Philadelphia: Westminster, 1962.

————. "The Background of Judges 17-18." In *Israel's Prophetic Heritage: Essays in Honor of James Muilenburg*. Ed. B. W. Anderson and W. Harrelson. New York: Harper and Row, 1962. Pp. 68-85.

————. *Die israelitischen Personennamen im Rahmen der gemeinsemitischen Namengebung*. Hildesheim: Georg Olms, 1966.

————. *Könige*. bkat IX, 1. Neukirchen-Vluyn: Neukirchener, 1968.

————. *A History of Pentateuchal Traditions*. Chico, California: Scholars Press, 1981.

————. *The Deuteronomistic History*. jsots up 15. Sheffield: jsot Press, 1981.

Obbink, H. Th. "Jahwebilder." *ZAW* 47 (1929) 264-74.

O'Brien, M. A. *The Deuteronomistic History Hypothesis: A Reassessment*. OBO 92. Göttingen: Vandenhoeck & Ruprecht, 1989.

Oded, B. "Judah and the Exile." In *Israelite and Judaean History*. Ed. J. H. Hayes and J. M. Miller. OTL. Philadelphia: Westminster, 1977. Pp. 435-88.

Oden, R. A. *The Bible Without Theology: The Theological Tradition and Alternatives to It*. New Voices in Biblical Studies. San Francisco: Harper & Row, 1987.

Olivier, J. P. J. "In Search of a Capital for the Northern Kingdom." *JNSL* 11 (1983) 117-32.

Ollenburger, B. C. *Zion, the City of the Great King*. JSOTSup 41. Sheffield: JSOT Press, 1987.

Olyan, S. M. *Asherah and the Cult of Yahweh in Israel*. SBLMS 34. Atlanta: Scholars Press, 1988.

Pfeiffer, R. H. "Chronicles, I and II." *IDB*, I: 572-80.

Plein, I. "Erwägungen zur Überlieferung von I Reg. 11:26-14:20." *ZAW* 78 (1966) 8-24.

Pope, M. H. *El in the Ugaritic Texts*. VTSup 2. Leiden: E. J. Brill, 1955.

Pritchard, J. E. *The Ancient Near East in Pictures Relating to the Old Testament*. Princeton: Princeton University Press, 1954.

Provan, I. *Hezekiah and the Book of Kings*. BZAW 172. Berlin/New York: Walter de Gruyter, 1988.

Rad, G. von. *Studies in Deuteronomy*. London, 1953.

――――. *Old Testament Theology*. 2 vols. Harper & Row, 1962-65.

――――. "The Tent and the Ark." *The Problem of the Hexateuch and Other Essays*. London: SCM, 1984. Pp. 103-24.

Rainey, A. F. "Three Additional Ostraca from Tel Arad." *Tel Aviv* 4 (1977) 97-104.

――――. "The Toponymics of Eretz-Israel." *BASOR* 231 (1978) 1-17.

Ringgren, H. *Israelite Religion*. Philadelphia: Fortress, 1966.

Roberts, J. J. M. "El." *IDBSup*. Pp. 255-58.

Robertson, D. A. *Linguistic Evidence in Dating Early Hebrew Poetry*. SBLDS 3. Missoula: Society of Biblical Literature, 1972.

Rosen, B. "Early Israelite Cultic Centres in the Hill Country." *VT* 38 (1988) 114-117.

Rouillard, H. *La pericope de Balaam (Nombres 22-24): La prose et les "oracles"*. Études Bibliques, ns 4. Paris: J. Gabalda, 1985.

Šanda, A. *Die Bücher der Könige*. EHAT 9. Münster: Aschendorffsche Verlagsbuch-handlung, 1911.

Sarna, N. "The Divine Title ʾabhîr yaʿăqôbh." In *Essays on the Occasion of the Seventieth Anniversary of the Dropsie University*. Ed. A. I. Katsch and L. Nemoy. Philadelphia: Dropsie University, 1979. Pp. 389-96.

Sasson, J. M. "The Worship of the Golden Calf." In *Orient and Occident: Essays Presented to Cyrus H. Gordon on the Occasion of his Sixty-Fifth Birthday*. Ed. H. A. Hoffner, Jr. AOAT 22. Neukirchen-Vluyn: Neukirchener Verlag, 1973. Pp. 151-59.

Schaeffer, C. F. A. "Nouveaux témoignages du culte de El et de Baal a Ras Shamra-Ugarit et ailleurs en Syrie-Palestine." *Syria* 43 (1966) 1-19.

Seebass, H. "Tradition und Interpretation bei Jehu ben Chanani und Ahia von Silo." *VT* 25 (1975) 175-90.

Seow, C. L. *Myth, Drama, and the Politics of David's Dance*. HSM 46. Atlanta: Scholars Press, 1989.

Smith, H. P. *The Books of Samuel*. ICC. Edinburgh: T & T Clark, 1899.

Smith, M. S. *The Early History of God: Yahweh and the Other Deities in Ancient Israel*. San Francisco: Harper & Row, 1990.

Soggin, J. A. *Judges*. OTL. Philadelphia: Westminster, 1981.

Spieckermann, H. *Juda unter Assur in der Sargonidenzeit*. FRLANT 129. Göttingen: Vandenhoeck & Ruprecht, 1982.

Stager, L. E. "When Canaanites and Philistines Ruled Ashkelon." *BARev* 17/2 (1991) 24-43.

Stoebe, H. J. *Das erste Buch Samuelis*. KAT 8. Gütersloher Verlagshaus Gerd Mohn, 1973.

Talmon, S. "Divergences in Calendar-Reckoning in Ephraim and Judah." *VT* 8 (1958) 48-74.

Toombs, L. E. "Shechem (City), Addendum." *IDB*, IV: 315.

Tosato, A. "The Literary Structure of the First Two Poems of Balaam [Num xxiii 7-10, 18-24]." *VT* 29 (1979) 98-106.

Vanel, A. *L'iconographie du dieu de l'orage dans le proche-orient ancien jusqu'au VII$^e$ siècle avant J.-C.* CahRB 3. Paris: J. Gabalda, 1965.

Vawter, B. "The Canaanite Background of Genesis 49." *CBQ* 17 (1955) 1-18.

Ward, W. H. *The Seal Cylinders of Western Asia*. Washington, D.C.: Carnegie Institute, 1910.

Watson, P. L. "The Death of 'Death' in the Ugaritic Texts." *JAOS* 92 (1972) 60-64.

Weinfeld, M. *Deuteronomy and the Deuteronomic School*. Oxford: Clarendon, 1972.

Weippert, M. "Gott und Stier." *ZDPV* 77 (1961) 93-117.

Weiser, A. *The Psalms*. OTL. Philadelphia: Westminster, 1962.

Wellhausen, J. *Prolegomena to the History of Ancient Israel*. Meridian Books. Cleveland: World Publishing, 1957.

Welten, P. *Geschichte und Geschichtsdarstellung in den Chronikbüchern*. WMANT 42. Neukirchen: Neukirchener Verlag, 1973.

Westermann, C. *Genesis 12-36*. Minneapolis: Augsburg, 1985.

Whitaker, R. E. *A Concordance of the Ugaritic Literature*. Cambridge, Mass. 1972.

Williamson, H. G. M. *1 and 2 Chronicles*. NCBC. Grand Rapids: Eerdmans, 1982.

Wolff, H. W. *Hosea*. Hermeneia. Philadelphia: Fortress, 1974.

Wright, G. E. *The Old Testament Against its Environment*. London: SCM, 1950.

————. *Shechem: The Biography of a Biblical City*. New York: McGraw-Hill, 1965.

Würthwein, E. "Die Erzählung vom Gottesmann aus Juda in Bethel. Zur Komposition von I Kön 13." *Wort und Geschichte: K. Elliger Festschrift*. AOAT 18. Neukirchen: Butzon & Bercker Kevelaer, 1973. Pp. 181-89.

————. *Das Erste Buch der Könige Kapitel 1-16*. ATD 11/1. Göttingen: Vandenhoeck & Ruprecht, 1977.

Yadin, Y. "The Fourth Season of Excavations at Hazor." *BA* 32 (1959).

Yee, G. A. *Composition and Tradition in the Book of Hosea: A Redaction Critical Investigation*. SBLDS 102. Atlanta: Scholars Press, 1987.

Zertal, A. "Has Joshua's Altar Been Found on Mt. Ebal?" *BARev* 11 (1985) 26-43.

————. "How Can Kempinski Be So Wrong?" *BARev* 12 (1986) 43, 49-53.

————. "An Early Iron Age Cultic Site on Mount Ebal." *TA* 13-14 (1986-87) 105-65.

Zimmerli, W. "Das Bilderverbot in der Geschichte des alten Israel. Goldenes Kalb, eherne Schlange, Mazzeben und Lade." In *Studien zur alttestamentlichen Theologie und Prophetie: Gesammelte Aufsätze II*. TBüAT 51. München: Chr. Kaiser, 1974. Pp. 247- 60.

# Index of Ancient Texts

# Index of Modern Authors